IMMIGRATION CRISIS: ISSUES, POLICIES AND CONSEQUENCES

IMMIGRATION CRISIS: ISSUES, POLICIES AND CONSEQUENCES

PAUL W. HICKMAN AND THOMAS P. CURTIS
EDITORS

Nova Science Publishers, Inc.
New York

LIBRARY OF CONGRESS CATALOGING-IN-PUBLICATION DATA

Immigration crisis : issues, policies and consequences / Paul W. Hickman and Thomas P. Curtis (editor).
    p. cm.
 ISBN 978-1-60456-096-1 (hardcover)
 1. United States--Emigration and immigration--Government policy. 2. Alien labor--United States.
3. Labor market--United States. I. Hickman, Paul W. II. Curtis, Thomas P.
 JV6483.I55425 2007
 325.73--dc22
                  2007041486

Published by Nova Science Publishers, Inc.   ✦   New York

CONTENTS

PREFACE

One of the hotest topics in America is the burning issue of immigration. On the one hand, immigration is what has kept America growing and prospering. On the other hand, the demographics are politically sensitive, the emotions high and sometimes mean-spirited, and some state government services in as bad shape as America's bridges.This new book presents important issues on this nontrivial issue.

Chapter 1 - At present, the United States has two main programs for temporarily importing low-skilled workers, sometimes referred to as guest workers. Agricultural guest workers enter through the H-2A visa program, and other guest workers enter through the H-2B visa program. Employers interested in importing workers under either program must first apply to the U.S. Department of Labor for a certification that U.S. workers capable of performing the work are not available and that the employment of alien workers will not adversely affect the wages and working conditions of similarly employed U.S. workers. Other requirements of the programs differ.

The 109th Congress revised the H-2B program in the FY2005 Emergency Supplemental Appropriations Act (P.L. 109-13). Among the changes, a temporary provision was added to the Immigration and Nationality Act (INA) to exempt certain returning H-2B workers from the H-2B annual numerical cap. The FY2007 Department of Defense authorization P.L. 109-364) extended this exemption through FY2007. Other bills before the 109th Congress proposed to make changes to the H2A program (S. 359/H.R. 884, H.R. 3857, S. 2087, Senate-passed S. 2611), the H-2B program (S. 278, H.R. 1587, S. 1438, S. 1918), and the "H" visa category generally (H.R. 3333), and to establish new temporary worker visas (S. 1033/H.R. 2330, S. 1438, S. 1918, H.R. 4065, Senate-passed S. 2611). Some of these bills also would have established mechanisms for certain foreign workers to become U.S. legal permanent residents (LPRs). None of these bills were enacted. President George W. Bush proposed a new, expanded temporary worker program in January 2004 when he announced his principles for immigration reform. In a May 2006 national address on comprehensive immigration reform, he reiterated his support for a temporary worker program.

Guest worker bills before the 110th Congress include proposals to reform the H2A program (S. 237/S. 340/H.R. 371, S. 1639, H.R. 1645) and the H-2B program (S. 1639), and to establish new temporary worker visas (S. 330, S. 1639, H.R. 1645). Some of these bills also would establish mechanisms for certain foreign workers to become LPRs.

The current discussion of guest worker programs takes place against a backdrop of historically high levels of unauthorized migration to the United States. Supporters of a large-scale temporary worker program argue that such a program would help reduce unauthorized immigration by providing a legal alternative for prospective foreign workers. Critics reject this reasoning and instead maintain that a new guest worker program would likely exacerbate the problem of illegal migration.

The consideration of any proposed guest worker program raises various issues, including how new program requirements would compare with those of the H-2A and H-2B programs, how the eligible population would be defined, and whether the program would include a mechanism for participants to obtain LPR status.

This report will be updated as legislative developments occur.

Chapter 2 - Since the September 11, 2001, terrorist attacks, the enforcement of our nation's immigration laws has received a significant amount of attention. Some observers contend that the federal government does not have adequate resources to enforce immigration law and that state and local law enforcement entities should be utilized. Several proposals introduced in the 109th Congress would enhance the role of state and local officials in the enforcement of immigration law, including H.R. 4437, S. 2612, S. 2454, H.R. 2092, H.R. 3137, S. 1362, S. 1438, H.R. 3333, H.R. 3776, H.R. 3938, S. 2611, and H.R. 1817. This proposed shift has prompted many to question what role state and local law enforcement agencies should have in the enforcement of immigration law, if any.

Congress defined our nation's immigration laws in the Immigration and Nationality Act (INA) (8 U.S.C. §§1101 *et seq.*), which contains both *criminal* and *civil* enforcement measures. Historically, the authority for state and local law enforcement officials to enforce immigration law has been construed to be limited to the *criminal* provisions of the INA; by contrast, the enforcement of the *civil* provisions, which includes apprehension and removal of deportable aliens, has strictly been viewed as a federal responsibility, with states playing an incidental supporting role. The legislative proposals that have been introduced, however, would appear to expand the role of state and local law enforcement agencies in the *civil* enforcement aspects of the INA.

Congress, through various amendments to the INA, has gradually broadened the authority for state and local law enforcement officials to enforce immigration law, and some recent statutes have begun to carve out possible state roles in the enforcement of *civil* matters. Indeed, several jurisdictions have signed agreements (INA §287(g)) with the federal government to allow their respective state and local law enforcement agencies to perform new, limited duties relating to immigration law enforcement. Still, the enforcement of immigration by state and local officials has sparked debate among many who question what the proper role of state and local law enforcement officials should be in enforcing immigration law. For example, many have expressed concern over proper training, finite resources at the local level, possible civil rights violations, and the overall impact on communities. Some localities, for example, even provide "sanctuary" for illegal aliens and will generally promote policies that ensure such aliens will not be turned over to federal authorities.

This report examines some of the policy and legal issues that may accompany the increasing role of state and local law officials in the enforcement of immigration law. This report will be updated as warranted.

Chapter 3 - When President George W. Bush announced his principles for immigration reform in January 2004, he included an increase in permanent immigration as a key component. President Bush has stated that immigration reform is a top priority of his second term and has prompted a lively debate on the issue. Of an array of bills to revise permanent admissions introduced, only one was enacted in the 109th Congress: A provision in P.L. 109-13 (H.R. 1268, the emergency FY2005 supplemental appropriation) makes up to 50,000 employment-based visas available for foreign nationals coming to work as medical professionals. There is a widely held expectation that the 110th Congress will consider immigration reform.

During the 109th Congress, the Comprehensive Immigration Reform Act (S. 2611) would have substantially increased legal immigration and would have restructured the allocation of these visas. S. 2611 would have doubled the number of family-based and employment-based immigrants admitted over the next decade, as well as expanded the categories of immigrants who may come without numerical limits. The Senate passed S. 2611 on May 25, 2006. The major House-passed immigration bill (H.R. 4437) did not revise family-based and employment-based immigration. Proposals to alter permanent admissions were included in several other immigration proposals (S. 1033/H.R. 2330, S. 1438, H.R. 3700, H.R. 3938, S. 1919). Thus far in the 110th Congress, H.R. 75, H.R. 938, H.R. 1645, and S. 1348 would revise categories for permanent admissions.

Four major principles underlie current U.S. policy on permanent immigration: the reunification of families, the admission of immigrants with needed skills, the protection of refugees, and the diversity of admissions by country of origin. These principles are embodied in the Immigration and Nationality Act (INA). The INA specifies a complex set of numerical limits and preference categories that give priorities for permanent immigration reflecting these principles. Legal permanent residents (LPRs) refer to foreign nationals who live lawfully and permanently in the United States.

During FY2005, a total of 1,122,373 aliens became LPRs in the United States. Of this total, 57.8% entered on the basis of family ties. Additional major immigrant groups in FY2005 were employment-based preference immigrants (including spouses and children) at 22.0%, and refugees and asylees adjusting to immigrant status at 12.7%. Mexico led all countries with 161,445 aliens who became LPRs in FY2005. India followed at a distant second with 84,681 LPRs. China came in third with 69,967. These three countries comprise 30% of all LPRs in FY2005.

Significant backlogs are due to the sheer volume of aliens eligible to immigrate to the United States. Citizens and LPRs first file petitions for their relatives. After the petitions are processed, these relatives then wait for a visa to become available through the numerically limited categories. The siblings of U.S. citizens are waiting 11 years. Prospective LPRs from the Philippines have the most substantial waiting times; consular officers are now considering the petitions of the brothers and sisters of U.S. citizens from the Philippines who filed more than 22 years ago.

Chapter 4 - Expedited removal, an immigration enforcement strategy originally conceived to operate at the borders and ports of entry, is being expanded, raising a set of policy, resource, and logistical questions. Expedited removal is a provision under which an alien who lacks proper documentation or has committed fraud or willful misrepresentation of facts may be removed from the United States without any further hearings or review, unless the alien indicates a fear of persecution. Congress added expedited removal to the Immigration and Nationality Act (INA) in 1996, making it mandatory for arriving aliens, and giving the Attorney General the option of applying it to aliens in the interior of the country who have not been admitted or paroled into the United States and who cannot affirmatively show that they have been physically present in the United States continuously for two years. Until recently, expedited removal was only applied to aliens at ports of entry.

In the 110th Congress, H.R. 519 would require that expedited removal be applied to all aliens eligible for expedited removal under the statute. Proponents of expanding expedited removal point to the lengthy procedural delays and costs of the alien removal process. They cite statistics that indicate that the government is much more successful at removing detained aliens (aliens in expedited removal must be detained) than those not detained. They argue that aliens who entered the country illegally should not be afforded the due process and appeals that those who entered legally are given under the law. They point to the provision added to INA in 1996 that clarified that aliens who are in the United States without inspection are deemed to be "arriving" (i.e., not considered to have entered the United States and acquired the legal protections it entails). Advocates for requiring mandatory expedited removal maintain that it is an essential policy tool to handle the estimated 12 million unauthorized aliens in the United States.

Opponents of the expansion of mandatory expedited removal to the interior argue that it poses significant logistical problems, and cite increased costs caused by mandatory detention and the travel costs of repatriation. They also express concern that apprehended aliens will not be given ample opportunity to produce evidence that they are not subject to expedited removal, and argue that expedited removal limits an alien's access to relief from deportation. Some predict diplomatic problems if the United States increases repatriations of aliens who have not been afforded a judicial hearing. The Bush Administration is taking a an incremental approach to expanding expedited removal. From April 1997 to November 2002, expedited removal only applied to arriving aliens at ports of entry. In November 2002, it was expanded to aliens arriving by sea who are not admitted or paroled. Subsequently, in August 2004, expedited removal was expanded to aliens who are present without being admitted or paroled, are encountered by an immigration officer within 100 air miles of the U.S. southwest land border, and can not establish to the satisfaction of the immigration officer that they have been physically present in the United States continuously for the 14-day period immediately preceding the date of encounter. In January 2006, expedited removal was reportedly expanded along all U.S. borders. This report will be updated.

Chapter 5 - The connections between trade and migration are as longstanding as the historic movements of goods and people. The desire for commerce may often be the principal motivation, but the need to send people to facilitate the transactions soon follows. Recognition of this phenomenon is incorporated into the Immigration and Nationality Act (INA), which includes provisions for aliens who are entering the United States solely as "treaty traders" and "treaty investors." Although the United States has not created a common market for the movement of labor with our trading partners, there are immigration provisions in existing free trade agreements (FTAs) that spell out reciprocal terms regulating the "temporary entry of business persons."

Immigration issues often raised in the context of the FTAs include whether FTAs should contain provisions that expressly expand immigration between the countries as well as whether FTAs should require that the immigrant-sending countries restrain unwanted migration (typically expressed as illegal aliens). The question of whether the movement of people — especially temporary workers — is subsumed under the broader category of "provision of services" and thus an inherent part of any free trade agreement also arises. Even in FTAs that do not have explicit immigration provisions, such as the United States-

Dominican Republic-Central America Free Trade Agreement (DR-CAFTA), there may be a debate over the effects that FTAs might have on future migration.

There are a variety of approaches to study the impact of trade agreements on migration, and this report draws on several different perspectives. The volume of trade that the United States has with its top trading partners correlates with the number of times foreign nationals from these countries enter the United States, regardless of whether there is an FTA. Research on the aftermath of the North American Free Trade Agreement (NAFTA) found upward trends in the temporary migration of business and professional workers between the United States and Canada during the years that followed the implementation of the Canada-United States FTA (later NAFTA). Another set of analyses revealed that the number of Mexican-born residents of the United States who report that they came in to the country during the years after NAFTA came into force is substantial and resembles the "migration hump" that economists predicted. Many factors other than NAFTA, however, have been instrumental in shaping this trend in Mexican migration.

This report provides background and analysis on the complex nexus of immigration and trade. It does not track legislation and will not be regularly updated.

Chapter 6 - U.S. law provides for the temporary admission of various categories of foreign nationals, who are known as nonimmigrants. Nonimmigrants are admitted for a designated period of time and a specific purpose. They include a wide range of visitors, including tourists, foreign students, diplomats, and temporary workers. There are 24 major nonimmigrant visa categories, and 72 specific types of nonimmigrant visas issued currently. These visa categories are commonly referred to by the letter and numeral that denotes their subsection in the Immigration and Nationality Act (INA), e.g., B-2 tourists, E-2 treaty investors, F-1 foreign students, H-1B temporary professional workers, J-1 cultural exchange participants, or S-4 terrorist informants.

Interest in nonimmigrant visas soared immediately following the September 11, 2001 terrorist attacks, which were conducted by foreign nationals apparently admitted to the United States on legal visas. Since that time, policy makers have raised a series of questions about aliens in the United States and the extent that the federal government monitors their admission and presence in this country. Some of the specific visa categories are the focus of legislative activity (e.g., guest workers).

The U.S. Department of State (DOS) consular officer, at the time of application for a visa, as well as the Department of Homeland Security (DHS) immigration inspectors, at the time of application for admission, must be satisfied that the alien is entitled to nonimmigrant status. The burden of proof is on the applicant to establish eligibility for nonimmigrant status and the type of nonimmigrant visa for which the application is made. Both DOS consular officers (when the alien is petitioning abroad) and DHS inspectors (when the alien is entering the United States) must confirm that the alien is not ineligible for a visa under the so-called "grounds for inadmissibility" of the INA, which include criminal, terrorist, and public health grounds for exclusion.

Nonimmigrant visas issued abroad dipped to 5.0 million in FY2004 after peaking at 7.6 million in FY2001. The FY2005 data inched back up to 5.4 million nonimmigrant visas issued. Over the past 12 years, DOS has typically issued around 6 million nonimmigrant visas annually. The growth in the late 1990s has been largely attributable to the issuances of border crossing cards to residents of Canada and Mexico and the issuances of temporary worker visas. Combined, visitors for tourism and business comprised the largest group of nonimmigrants in FY2005, about 3.42 million, down from 5.7 million in FY2000. Other notable categories were students and exchange visitors (9.4%) and temporary workers (17.9%).

The law and regulations usually set strict terms for nonimmigrant lengths of stay in the United States, typically have foreign residency requirements, and often limit what aliens are permitted to do in the United States (e.g., gain employment or enroll in school), but many observers assert that the policies are not uniformly or rigorously enforced. Achieving an optimal balance among major policy priorities, such as ensuring national security, facilitating trade and commerce, protecting public health and safety, and fostering international cooperation, remains a challenge.

Chapter 7 - The connection between farm labor and immigration policies is a longstanding one, particularly with regard to U.S. employers' use of workers from Mexico. The Congress is revisiting the issue as it continues debate over initiation of a broad-based guest worker program, increased border enforcement, and employer sanctions to curb the flow of unauthorized workers into the United States.

Two decades ago, the Congress passed the Immigration Reform and Control Act (IRCA, P.L. 99-603) to reduce illegal entry into the United States by imposing sanctions on employers who knowingly hire individuals who lack permission to work in the country. In addition to a general legalization program, IRCA included legalization programs specific to the agricultural industry that were intended to compensate for the act's expected impact on the farm labor supply and encourage the development of a legal crop workforce. These provisions of the act, however, have not operated in the offsetting manner that was intended, as substantial numbers of unauthorized aliens have continued to join legal farmworkers in performing seasonal agricultural services (SAS).

Currently, a little more than one-half of the SAS workforce is not authorized to hold U.S. jobs. Perishable crop growers contend that their sizable presence implies a shortage of native-born workers willing to undertake seasonal farm jobs. (An increasing share of IRCA-legalized farmworkers have entered the ages of diminished participation in the SAS workforce, as well.) Grower advocates argue that farmers would rather not employ unauthorized workers because doing so puts them at risk of incurring penalties. Farmworker advocates counter that crop growers prefer unauthorized workers because they are in a weak bargaining position with regard to wages and working conditions. If the supply of unauthorized workers were curtailed, it is claimed, farmers could adjust to a smaller workforce by introducing labor-efficient technologies and management practices, and by raising wages, which, in turn, would entice more U.S. workers to seek farm employment. Farmers respond that further mechanization would be difficult for some crops, and that substantially higher wages would make the U.S. industry uncompetitive in the world marketplace — without expanding the legal farm labor force. These remain untested arguments because perishable crop growers have rarely, if ever, operated without unauthorized aliens in their workforces.

Trends in the agricultural labor market generally do not suggest the existence of a nationwide shortage of domestically available farmworkers, in part because the government's databases cover authorized *and* unauthorized employment. (This finding does not preclude the possibility of spot labor shortages, however.) Farm employment did not show the same upward trend of total U.S. employment during the 1990s expansion. The length of time hired farmworkers are employed has changed little or decreased over the years. Their unemployment rate has varied little and remains well above the U.S. average, and underemployment among farmworkers also remains substantial. These agricultural employees earn about 50 cents for every dollar paid to other employees in the private sector. This report will be updated as warranted.

Chapter 8 - Immigration patterns have changed substantially since 1952, when policy makers codifying the Immigration and Nationality Act assumed that most aliens becoming legal permanent residents (LPRs) of the United States would be arriving from abroad. In 1975, more than 80% of all LPRs arrived from abroad. By 2005, however, only 34% of all aliens who became LPRs had arrived from abroad; most LPRs adjust status within the United States. This report summarizes the main avenues for foreign nationals currently in the United States — legally or illegally — to become LPRs. Alien legalization or "amnesty," as well as adjustment of status and cancellation of removal options, are briefly discussed. Designed as a primer on the issues, the report provides references to other CRS products that track pertinent legislation and analyze these issues more fully. This report will be updated as needed.

In: Immigration Crisis: Issues, Policies and Consequences   ISBN: 978-1-60456-096-1
Editors: P. W. Hickman and T. P. Curtis, pp. 1-40   © 2008 Nova Science Publishers, Inc.

Chapter 1

IMMIGRATION: POLICY CONSIDERATIONS RELATED TO GUEST WORKER PROGRAMS*

Andorra Bruno

ABSTRACT

At present, the United States has two main programs for temporarily importing low-skilled workers, sometimes referred to as guest workers. Agricultural guest workers enter through the H-2A visa program, and other guest workers enter through the H-2B visa program. Employers interested in importing workers under either program must first apply to the U.S. Department of Labor for a certification that U.S. workers capable of performing the work are not available and that the employment of alien workers will not adversely affect the wages and working conditions of similarly employed U.S. workers. Other requirements of the programs differ.

The 109th Congress revised the H-2B program in the FY2005 Emergency Supplemental Appropriations Act (P.L. 109-13). Among the changes, a temporary provision was added to the Immigration and Nationality Act (INA) to exempt certain returning H-2B workers from the H-2B annual numerical cap. The FY2007 Department of Defense authorization P.L. 109-364) extended this exemption through FY2007. Other bills before the 109th Congress proposed to make changes to the H2A program (S. 359/H.R. 884, H.R. 3857, S. 2087, Senate-passed S. 2611), the H-2B program (S. 278, H.R. 1587, S. 1438, S. 1918), and the "H" visa category generally (H.R. 3333), and to establish new temporary worker visas (S. 1033/H.R. 2330, S. 1438, S. 1918, H.R. 4065, Senate-passed S. 2611). Some of these bills also would have established mechanisms for certain foreign workers to become U.S. legal permanent residents (LPRs). None of these bills were enacted. President George W. Bush proposed a new, expanded temporary worker program in January 2004 when he announced his principles for immigration reform. In a May 2006 national address on comprehensive immigration reform, he reiterated his support for a temporary worker program.

Guest worker bills before the 110th Congress include proposals to reform the H2A program (S. 237/S. 340/H.R. 371, S. 1639, H.R. 1645) and the H-2B program (S. 1639), and to establish new temporary worker visas (S. 330, S. 1639, H.R. 1645). Some of these bills also would establish mechanisms for certain foreign workers to become LPRs.

---

* Excerpted from CRS Report RL32044, dated June 27, 2007.

The current discussion of guest worker programs takes place against a backdrop of historically high levels of unauthorized migration to the United States. Supporters of a large-scale temporary worker program argue that such a program would help reduce unauthorized immigration by providing a legal alternative for prospective foreign workers. Critics reject this reasoning and instead maintain that a new guest worker program would likely exacerbate the problem of illegal migration.

The consideration of any proposed guest worker program raises various issues, including how new program requirements would compare with those of the H-2A and H-2B programs, how the eligible population would be defined, and whether the program would include a mechanism for participants to obtain LPR status.

This report will be updated as legislative developments occur.

INTRODUCTION

In 2001, the United States and Mexico began Cabinet-level talks on migration. Although the details of these discussions were not made public, two issues — legalization and a temporary worker program — dominated media coverage. The talks lost momentum after the terrorist attacks of September 11, 2001, as the Bush Administration focused its attention on security-related matters. A temporary worker program (not limited to Mexico), however, remains of interest to some Members of Congress and Administration officials. Various bills to reform existing programs for foreign temporary workers and to create new temporary worker programs have been introduced in recent Congresses. Among them, in the 110th Congress, is S. 1639, which would provide for comprehensive immigration reform. In January 2004, the Bush Administration outlined a proposal for a new temporary worker program. The President reiterated his support for a temporary worker program in a May 2006 national address. The temporary worker programs under discussion presumably would cover largely low-skilled workers.

BACKGROUND

The term *guest worker* has typically been applied to foreign temporary low-skilled laborers, often in agriculture or other seasonal employment. In the past, guest worker programs have been established in the United States to address worker shortages during times of war. During World War I, for example, tens of thousands of Mexican workers performed mainly agricultural labor as part of a temporary worker program. The Bracero program, which began during World War II and lasted until 1964, brought several million Mexican agricultural workers into the United States. At its peak in the late 1950s, the Bracero program employed more than 400,000 Mexican workers annually.[1]

The Immigration and Nationality Act (INA) of 1952, as originally enacted,[2] authorized a temporary foreign worker program known as the H-2 program. It covered both agricultural and nonagricultural workers who were coming temporarily to the United States to perform temporary services (other than services of an exceptional nature requiring distinguished merit and ability) or labor. Aliens who are admitted to the United States for a temporary period of time and a specific purpose are known as nonimmigrants. The 1986 Immigration Reform and Control Act (IRCA)[3] amended the INA to subdivide the H-2 program into the current H-2A and H-2B programs and to detail the admissions process for H-2A workers. The H-2A and H-2B visas are subcategories of the larger "H" nonimmigrant visa category for temporary workers.[4]

CURRENT PROGRAMS

The United States currently has two main programs for importing temporary low-skilled workers. Agricultural workers enter through the H-2A program and other temporary workers enter through the H-2B program.[5] The programs take their names from the sections of the INA that established them — Section 101(a)(15)(H)(ii)(a) and Section 101(a)(15)(H)(ii)(b), respectively. Both programs are administered by the Employment and Training Administration (ETA) of the U.S. Department of Labor (DOL) and U.S. Citizenship and Immigration Services (USCIS) of the U.S. Department of Homeland Security (DHS).[6]

H-2A Program

The H-2A program allows for the temporary admission of foreign workers to the United States to perform agricultural work of a seasonal or temporary nature, provided that U.S. workers are not available. An approved H-2A visa petition is generally valid for an initial period of up to one year. An alien's total period of stay as an H-2A worker may not exceed three consecutive years.

Employers who want to import H-2A workers must first apply to DOL for a certification that (1) there are not sufficient U.S. workers who are qualified and available to perform the work; and (2) the employment of foreign workers will not adversely affect the wages and working conditions of U.S. workers who are similarly employed. As part of this labor certification process, employers must attempt to recruit U.S. workers and must cooperate with DOL-funded state employment service agencies (also known as state workforce agencies) in local, intrastate, and interstate recruitment efforts. Employers must pay their H-2A workers and similarly employed U.S. workers the highest of the federal or applicable state minimum wage, the prevailing wage rate,[7] or the adverse effect wage rate (AEWR).[8] They also must provide workers with housing, transportation, and other benefits, including workers' compensation insurance.[9] No health insurance coverage is required.[10]

Both growers and labor advocates criticize the H-2A program in its current form. Growers complain that the H-2A program is overly cumbersome and does not meet their labor needs. Labor advocates argue that the program provides too few protections for U.S. workers.

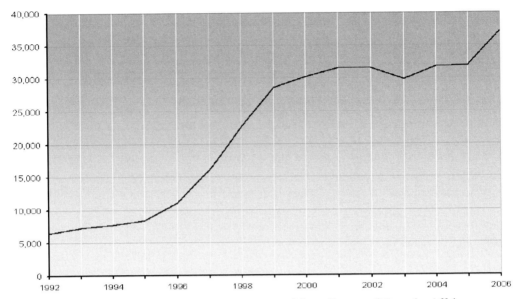

Source: CRS Presentation of data from U.S. Department of State, Bureau of Consular Affairs.

Figure 1. H-2A Visas Issued, FY1992-FY2006.

H-2A Visas Issued

The H-2A program, which is not subject to numerical limits, has grown significantly since 1992. One way to measure the program's growth is to consider changes in the number of H-2A visas issued annually by the Department of State (DOS).[11] As illustrated in figure 1, the number of H-2A visas issued increased from 6,445 in FY1992 to 30,201 in FY2000. H-2A visa issuances remained at about 30,000 annually until FY2006, when, according to preliminary data, 37,149 H-2A visas were issued. The H-2A program, however, remains quite small relative to total hired farm employment, which stood at about 1.1 million in 2005, according to the Department of Agriculture's National Agricultural Statistics Service.[12]

H-2B Program

The H-2B program provides for the temporary admission of foreign workers to the United States to perform temporary non-agricultural work, if unemployed U.S. workers cannot be found. Foreign medical graduates coming to perform medical services are explicitly excluded from the program. An approved H-2B visa petition is valid for an initial period of up to one year. An alien's total period of stay as an H-2B worker may not exceed three consecutive years.[13]

Like prospective H-2A employers, prospective H-2B employers must first apply to DOL for a certification that U.S. workers capable of performing the work are not available and that the employment of alien workers will not adversely affect the wages and working conditions of similarly employed U.S. workers. H-2Bemployers must pay their workers at least the prevailing wage rate. Unlike H-2A employers, they are not subject to the AEWR and do not have to provide housing, transportation,[14] and other benefits required under the H-2A program.

In January 2005, USCIS proposed regulations to streamline the H-2B petitioning process, which would significantly alter procedures.[15] Among other changes, the proposed rule would eliminate the requirement that prospective H-2B employers file for a labor certification from DOL in most cases. Instead, employers seeking H-2B workers in areas other than logging, the entertainment industry, and professional athletics would include certain labor attestations as part of the H-2B petition they file with USCIS. According to the proposed rule, this H-2B attestation process would be similar to the process currently used for H-1B professional specialty workers.[16]

A key limitation of the H-2B visa concerns the requirement that the work be temporary. Under the applicable immigration regulations, work is considered to be temporary if the employer's need for the duties to be performed by the worker is a one-time occurrence, seasonal need, peakload need, or intermittent need.[17] According to DOL data on H-2B labor certifications, top H-2B occupations in recent years, in terms of the number of workers certified, included landscape laborer, forestry worker, maid and housekeeping cleaner, and construction worker.

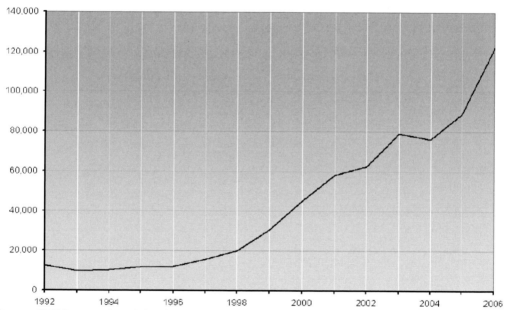

Source: CRS Presentation of data from U.S. Department of State, Bureau of Consular Affairs.

Figure 2. H-2B Visas Issued, FY1992-FY2006. 9"

H-2B Visas Issued and the Statutory Cap

Unlike the H-2A visa, the H2B visa is subject to a statutory numerical limit. Under the INA, the total number of aliens who may be issued H-2B visas or otherwise provided H-2B status during a fiscal year may not exceed 66,000.[18] This cap does not apply to all H-2B petitions. Petitions for current H-2B workers to extend their stay, change their terms of employment, or change or add employers do not count towards the cap. As shown in figure 2, the number of H-2B visas issued by DOS dipped from 12,552 in FY1992 to 9,691 in FY1993 and then began to increase steadily.[19]

In FY2003, DOS issued 78,955 H-2B visas, and in FY2004, it issued 76,169 H2B visas. While for various reasons not all visas issued during a fiscal year necessarily count against that year's cap or, in some cases, any year's cap, USCIS acknowledged that the H-2B cap was exceeded in FY2003. With respect to the FY2004 cap, USCIS announced on March 10, 2004, that it had received a sufficient number of H-2B petitions to meet that cap. On January 4, 2005, it announced that it had received a sufficient number of H-2B petitions to meet the FY2005 cap.

Following the enactment of new H-2B provisions as part of the FY2005 Emergency Supplemental Appropriations Act for Defense, the Global War on Terror, and Tsunami Relief (P.L. 109-13),[20] USCIS announced that on May 25, 2005, it would start accepting additional petitions for H-2B workers for FY2005.[21] Under P.L. 109-13, for FY2005 and FY2006, returning H-2B workers counted against the annual 66,000 cap during any one of the three prior fiscal years were not to be counted again. USCIS determined that approximately 35,000 previously approved H-2B workers for FY2005 qualified as returning workers who, under P.L. 109-13, were exempt from that year's cap, opening up 35,000 slots for other H-2B workers. Employers were able to file FY2005 petitions for new H-2B workers to fill those slots, as well as for cap-exempt returning H-2B workers. According to preliminary data, 89,135 H-2B visas were issued in FY2005 and 122,541 H-2B visas were issued in FY2006. According to DOS, 50,854 of the FY2006 H-2B visas were issued to cap-exempt returning H-2B workers. The John Warner National Defense Authorization Act for FY2007 (P.L. 109-364) extends through FY2007 the provision exempting returning H-2B workers from the H-2B annual cap.

UNAUTHORIZED IMMIGRATION

The current discussion of guest worker programs has been prompted, in part, by the continued high levels of illegal, or unauthorized, immigration to the United States and related deaths along the U.S.-Mexican border. Analyses by the Pew Hispanic Center based on data from the Current Population Survey (CPS) and other sources estimate that the unauthorized resident alien population totaled 10.3 million in March 2004, 11.1 million in March 2005, and 11.5 to 12 million in March 2006, and that since 2000, this population has grown at an average annual rate of more than 500,000 per year.[22] DHS's estimates of the unauthorized alien population and its growth are somewhat lower. Based on data from the 2004 American Community Survey and other sources, DHS estimates that there were 10.5 million unauthorized aliens residing in the United States in January 2005 and that the unauthorized resident population grew at an average annual rate of 408,000 during the 2000-2004 period.[23]

Mexico remains the largest source country for unauthorized immigration. According to the Pew Hispanic Center, the unauthorized Mexican population in the United States stood at about 6.2 million in 2005, comprising 56% of the total unauthorized population. DHS estimates that there were nearly 6 million unauthorized Mexicans residing in the United States in 2005, comprising 57% of the total unauthorized population. With respect to migrant deaths, data from the United States Border Patrol indicate that more than 300 migrants died at the U.S.-Mexican border each year from FY2000 through FY2004 and that there were 472 migrant deaths at the border in FY2005.[24]

Unauthorized Workers

Unauthorized workers are a subpopulation of the total unauthorized alien population. According to the March 2006 report by the Pew Hispanic Center, there were an estimated 7.2 million unauthorized workers in the U.S. civilian labor force in March 2005.[25] These workers represented about 4.9% of the labor force. In some occupations and industries, however, their share of the labor force was considerably higher. The report states:

> Unauthorized workers are employed in a variety of occupations throughout the labor force, although the distribution of the unauthorized workforce across occupations differs from that of native-born workers.
> Unauthorized workers are notably underrepresented in white-collar occupations.... On the other hand, unauthorized migrants are much more likely to be in major occupation groups that require little education or do not have licensing requirements.[26]

Unauthorized aliens are also overrepresented in certain industries relative to their share of the overall labor force. Table 1 presents data from the Pew Hispanic Center report on industries with high concentrations of unauthorized workers. Unauthorized aliens accounted for between 10% and 21% of workers in the industries shown.

Table 1. Estimates of Unauthorized Employment in Selected Industries, 2005

Industry Group	Unauthorized Workers (in Industry)
Private Households	21%
Food Manufacturing	14%
Agriculture	13%
Furniture Manufacturing	13%
Construction	12%
Textile, Apparel, and Leather Manufacturing	12%
Food Services	12%
Administrative and Support Services	11%
Accommodation	10%

Source: Jeffrey S. Passel, Size and Characteristics of the Unauthorized Migrant Population in the U.S., Pew Hispanic Center, March 7, 2006.

Supporters of a large-scale guest worker program contend that such a program would help reduce unauthorized immigration by providing a legal alternative for prospective foreign workers. Critics reject this reasoning and instead maintain that a guest worker program would likely exacerbate the problem of illegal immigration; they argue, for example, that many guest workers would fail to leave the country at the end of their authorized period of stay.

LEGISLATION IN THE 105TH -107TH CONGRESSES

Major guest worker legislation introduced in the 105th , 106th , and 107th Congresses was limited to the H-2A program. No major nonagricultural guest worker bills were offered.[27] In the 105th Congress, for example, a Senate-approved amendment to S. 2260, an FY1999 Departments of Commerce, Justice, and State appropriations bill, would have replaced the existing labor certification process with a new set of procedures for importing H-2A workers. It would have established a system of agricultural worker registries containing the names of eligible U.S. agricultural workers. Employers interested in importing H-2A workers would first have applied to DOL for the referral of U.S. workers through a registry search. If a sufficient number of workers were not found, the employer would have been allowed to import H-2A workers to cover the shortfall. The Senate measure also would have changed wage and other requirements. The provision was not enacted.

Provisions to establish a system of worker registries and to change existing H2A-related requirements were likewise included in two H-2A reform proposals introduced in the 106th Congress (S. 1814/H.R. 4056[28] and H.R. 4548). In addition, S. 1814/H.R. 4056 would have established a two-stage legalization program, under which farm workers satisfying specified work requirements could have obtained temporary resident status and then legal permanent resident (LPR) status. Although formal congressional consideration was limited to a Senate Immigration Subcommittee hearing, S. 1814/H.R. 4056 became the basis of a bipartisan compromise on foreign agricultural workers. That agreement, however, fell apart at the end of the 106th Congress. H.R. 4548, the other reform bill before the 106th Congress, differed from S. 1814/H.R. 4056 in that it sought to establish a pilot H-2C alien agricultural worker program to supplement, rather than replace, the H-2A program. H.R. 4548 also did not include a legalization program. H.R. 4548 was reported by the House Judiciary Committee in October 2000, but saw no further action.

Like S. 1814/H.R. 4056 in the 106th Congress, key bills before the 107th Congress coupled significant H-2A reform with legalization. S. 1161 and S. 1313/H.R. 2736 would have streamlined the process of importing H-2A workers, particularly for jobs covered by collective bargaining agreements. With respect to legalization, both proposals would have allowed foreign agricultural workers who met specified work requirements to adjust to LPR status through a two-stage process like that in S. 1814/H.R. 4056. The requirements for adjustment of status in S. 1313/H.R. 2736 differed from those in S. 1161, with the latter being more stringent. Among the other major differences between the proposals, S. 1161 would have eased existing wage requirements, while S. 1313/H.R. 2736 would have mandated a study of the wage issue. No action beyond committee referral occurred on either proposal.

LEGISLATION IN THE 108TH CONGRESS

Bills to reform the H-2A program, the H-2B program, and the "H" visa category generally, as well as bills to establish new guest worker programs, were introduced in the 108th Congress. Some of these bills would have enabled certain workers to obtain LPR status. No action beyond committee referral occurred on any of the bills.

Congressional committees held related hearings during the 108th Congress. The House Agriculture Committee held a hearing on the potential impact of recent guest worker proposals on the agricultural sector, and the House Judiciary Committee's Subcommittee on Immigration, Border Security, and Claims held a hearing on the impact of guest workers on U.S. workers. In the Senate, the Judiciary Committee's Subcommittee on Immigration, Border Security, and Citizenship held hearings on evaluating a guest worker proposal and on border security under a guest worker program.

S. 1645/H.R. 3142 and S. 2823

The Agricultural Job Opportunity, Benefits, and Security Act of 2003 (AgJOBS Act; S. 1645/H.R. 3142) would have overhauled the H-2A agricultural worker program. It was introduced, respectively, by Senator Craig for himself and a bipartisan group of cosponsors and by Representative Cannon for himself and Representative Berman. Like the major H-2A reform bills before the 107th Congress, S. 1645/H.R. 3142 would have streamlined the process of importing H-2A workers, particularly for jobs covered by collective bargaining agreements. Under S. 1645/H.R. 3142, prospective H-2A employers would have had to file applications with DOL containing certain assurances. In the case of a job covered by a collective bargaining agreement, the employer would have had to assure, among other things, that there was an applicable union contract and that the bargaining representatives of the employer's employees had been notified of the filing of the application for H-2A workers. An employer interested in filling a job not covered by a collective bargaining agreement would have been subject to a longer list of required assurances. Among these, the employer would have had to assure that he or she would take specified steps to recruit U.S. workers and would provide workers with required benefits, wages, and working conditions. Both groups of employers would have had to assure that the job was temporary or seasonal and that the employer would offer the job to any equally qualified, available U.S. worker who applied. Unless an employer's application was incomplete or obviously inaccurate, DOL would have certified within seven days of the filing date that the employer had filed the required application.

S. 1645/H.R. 3142 further proposed to make changes to the H-2A program's requirements regarding minimum benefits, wages, and working conditions. Among these proposed changes, the adverse effect wage rate (discussed above) would have remained at the January 2003 level for three years after the date of enactment, and employers would have been permitted to provide housing allowances, in lieu of housing, to their workers if the governor of the relevant state certified that adequate housing was available.

Under S. 1645/H.R. 3142, an H-2A worker's initial period of employment could not have exceeded 10 months. The worker's stay could have been extended in increments of up to 10 months each, but the worker's total continuous period of stay, including any extensions, could not have exceeded three years.

In addition to these H-2A reform provisions, S. 1645/H.R. 3142 would have established a two-stage legalization program for agricultural workers. To obtain temporary resident status, the alien worker would have had to establish that he or she performed at least 575 hours, or 100 work days, of agricultural employment in the United States during 12 consecutive months in the 18-month period ending on August 31, 2003, and meet other requirements. To be eligible to adjust to LPR status, the alien would have had to perform at least 2,060 hours, or 360 work days, of agricultural work in the United States between September 1, 2003, and August 31, 2009, and meet other requirements. Existing numerical limits under the INA would not have applied to adjustments of status under the bill.[29]

On September 21, 2004, Senator Craig introduced a modified version of S. 1645 for himself and Senator Kennedy. The revised bill, S. 2823, was very similar to S. 1645, but there were substantive differences in the two bills' legalization provisions. Among these differences, S. 2823 contained a new provision stating that aliens acquiring temporary resident status under the bill would not be eligible for certain federal public benefits until five years after they obtained permanent resident status.[30]

H.R. 3604

Like S. 1645/H.R. 3142, the Temporary Agricultural Labor Reform Act of 2003 (H.R. 3604) proposed to overhaul the H-2A agricultural worker program. It was introduced by Representative Goodlatte for himself and more than 30 co-sponsors.

H.R. 3604 would have streamlined the process of importing H-2A workers. Prospective H-2A employers would have had to file applications with DOL containing certain assurances, including that the job was temporary or seasonal; the employer would provide workers with required benefits, wages, and working conditions; the employer had made positive efforts to recruit U.S. workers; and the employer would offer the job to any equally qualified, available U.S. worker who applied. Unless an employer's application was incomplete or obviously inaccurate, DOL would have certified within seven days of the filing date that the employer had filed the required application.

H.R. 3604 would have made changes to current H-2A requirements regarding minimum benefits, wages, and working conditions. Under H.R. 3604, H-2A employers would have had to pay workers the higher of the prevailing wage rate or the applicable state minimum wage; they would not have been subject to the adverse effect wage rate (discussed above). With respect to housing, employers could have provided housing allowances, in lieu of housing, to their workers if the governor of the relevant state certified that adequate housing was available.

Under H.R. 3604, an H-2A worker's initial period of employment could not have exceeded 10 months. The worker's stay could have been extended in increments of up to 10 months each, but the worker's total continuous period of stay, including any extensions, could not have exceeded two years. H.R. 3604 would not have established a mechanism for agricultural workers to obtain LPR status.

S. 2185

Another H-2A reform bill, introduced by Senator Chambliss, was the Temporary Agricultural Work Reform Act of 2004 (S. 2185). It was similar, but not identical, to H.R. 3604. S. 2185 would have streamlined the process of importing H-2A workers. Prospective H-2A employers would have had to file applications with DOL containing certain assurances, including that the job was temporary or seasonal; the employer would provide workers with required benefits, wages, and working conditions; the employer had attempted to recruit U.S. workers using the state workforce agency; and the employer would offer the job to any equally qualified, available U.S. worker who applied. Unless an employer's application was incomplete or obviously inaccurate, DOL would have certified within 15 days of the filing date that the employer had filed the required application.

S. 2185 proposed to change current H-2A requirements concerning minimum benefits, wages, and working conditions. Under S. 2185, H-2A employers would have had to pay workers the higher of the prevailing wage rate or the applicable state minimum wage. In lieu of offering housing, they could have provided housing allowances if the governor of the relevant state certified that adequate housing was available.

S. 2185 did not contain provisions regarding the period of admission, extension of stay, or maximum period of stay of H-2A workers. It also would not have established a mechanism for agricultural workers to obtain LPR status.

S. 2010

The Immigration Reform Act of 2004: Strengthening America's National Security, Economy, and Families (S. 2010), introduced by Senator Hagel for himself and Senator Daschle, would have reformed the H-2B nonimmigrant visa. The bill would have eliminated the current restriction that H-2B workers can perform only temporary service or labor, and instead would have required that they perform "shortterm service or labor, lasting not more than 9 months." S. 2010 also proposed a new H-2C visa for temporary workers coming to perform "labor or services, other than those occupation classifications" covered under the H-2A, H-2B, or specified high-skilled visa categories, if qualified U.S. workers could not be found.

Both the H-2B and H-2C categories would have been numerically limited. In each of the five fiscal years following issuance of final implementing regulations, the H-2B program would have been capped at 100,000. The cap would have then reverted back to the current 66,000 level. The H-2C program would have been capped at 250,000 in each of the five fiscal years following issuance of final implementing regulations. After these five years, the H-2C program would have terminated.

S. 2010 would have subjected both the H-2B and H-2C programs to a broad set of requirements covering recruitment, application procedures, and worker protections, among other issues. Prior to filing an application with DOL for H-2B or H-2C workers, prospective employers would have had to take specified steps to recruit U.S. workers, including posting the job on DOL's online "America's Job Bank" and with local job banks, and would have had to offer the job to any qualified, available U.S. worker who applied. In the application to DOL, the employer would have had to attest to various items, including that he or she was offering wages to H2B or H-2C workers that were the greater of the prevailing wage rate or the actual wage paid by the employer to other similarly employed and qualified workers, and that he or she would abide by all applicable laws and regulations relating to the rights of workers to organize. DOL would have reviewed the application and required documentation for completeness and accuracy, and issued a determination not later than 21 days after the filing date.

The initial period of admission for an H-2B worker could not have exceeded nine months in a one-year period. An H-2B worker's total period of admission could not have exceeded 36 months in a four-year period. The initial period of admission for an H-2C worker could not have exceeded two years and could have been extended for an additional period of up to two years. An H-2C worker's total period of admission could not have exceeded four years.

S. 2010 would have enabled H-2B and H-2C nonimmigrants to obtain LPR status. Employment-based *immigrant* visas would have been made available to these nonimmigrants without regard to existing numerical limits under the INA. An employment-based petition could have been filed by an employer or any collective bargaining agent of the alien, or after the alien had been employed in H-2B or H-2C status for at least three years, by the alien. In addition, S. 2010 would have established a legalization program for certain unauthorized aliens in the United States.

S. 2381/H.R. 4262

The Safe, Orderly, Legal Visas and Enforcement Act of 2004 (S. 2381/H.R. 4262) was introduced, respectively, by Senator Kennedy for himself and Senators Feingold and Clinton and by Representative Gutierrez for himself and a group of cosponsors. Known as the "S.O.L.V.E. Act," the measure would have reformed the H-2B nonimmigrant visa. It would have eliminated the current restriction that H-2B workers can perform only temporary service or labor, and instead would have required that they perform "short-term service or labor, lasting not more than 9 months." S. 2381/H.R. 4262 also proposed a new H-1D visa for temporary workers coming to perform "labor or services, other than those occupation classifications" covered under the H-2A or specified high-skilled visa categories, if qualified U.S. workers could not be found.

Both the H-2B and H-1D categories would have been numerically limited. The H-2B program would have been capped at 100,000 annually, an increase from the current annual limit of 66,000. The H-1D program would have been capped at 250,000 annually.

S. 2381/H.R. 4262 would have subjected both the H-2B and H-1D programs to a broad set of requirements covering recruitment, application procedures, and worker protections, among other issues. Prior to filing an application with DOL for H-2B or H-1D workers, prospective employers would have had to take specified steps to recruit U.S. workers, including posting the job on DOL's America's Job Bank and with local job banks, and would have had to offer the job to any qualified, available U.S. worker who applied. In the application to DOL, the employer would have had to attest to various items. Among these were that the employer was offering to H-2B or H-1D workers the prevailing wage, to be determined as specified in the bill. The employer also would have had to abide by all applicable laws and regulations relating to the rights of workers to organize. DOL would have reviewed the application and required documentation for completeness and accuracy, and issued a determination not later than 10 working days after the filing date.

The initial period of admission for an H-2B worker could not have exceeded nine months in a one-year period. An H-2B worker's total period of admission could not have exceeded 40 months in the aggregate. The initial period of admission for an H-1D worker could not have exceeded two years and could have been extended for two additional periods of up to two years each. An H-1D worker's total period of admission could not have exceeded six years.

S. 2381/H.R. 4262 would have enabled H-2B and H-1D nonimmigrants to obtain LPR status. Employment-based *immigrant* visas would have been made available to these nonimmigrants without numerical limitation. An employment-based petition could have been filed by an employer, or after the alien had been employed in H-2B or H-1D status for at least two years, by the alien. In addition, S. 2381/H.R. 4262 would have established a legalization program for certain unauthorized aliens in the United States.

H.R. 3534

The Border Enforcement and Revolving Employment to Assist Laborers Act of 2003 (H.R. 3534), introduced by Representative Tancredo for himself and several cosponsors, proposed to amend the INA's "H" visa category generally. It would have eliminated the current subcategories, including the H-2A and H-2B visas, and replaced them with a single category covering aliens coming temporarily to the United States to perform skilled or unskilled work if qualified U.S. workers were not available.

An employer interested in importing "H" workers would have filed an application with DOL. Prior to doing so, the employer would have been required to post a job announcement on an Internet-based job bank that the bill would have directed DOL to create. Among other requirements of the program, the employer would have had to offer wages at least equal to the prevailing wage rate and would have had to provide "H" workers with health insurance.

H nonimmigrants could only have been admitted from abroad. They would have applied to be added to a database of workers and would have had to remain in their home countries until an approved employer wanted to hire them. Their period of authorized admission could not have exceeded 365 days in a two-year period. After the two-year period, H nonimmigrant visas could have been renewed. H nonimmigrants would not have been permitted to change or adjust to any other nonimmigrant or immigrant status.

Under H.R. 3534, however, the proposed guest worker program would not have been implemented until the Secretary of Homeland Security, in consultation with the Attorney General and the Secretary of State, had made certain certifications to Congress. The Secretary of Homeland Security would have had to certify, among other items, that all noncitizens legally in the United States and all aliens authorized to enter the country had been issued biometric, machine-readable travel or entry documents, and that the number of aliens who overstayed nonimmigrant visas, but were not removed from the United States, was less than 5,000.

S. 1387

The Border Security and Immigration Reform Act of 2003 (S. 1387), introduced by Senator Cornyn, would have authorized new temporary worker programs under the INA for seasonal and nonseasonal workers. S. 1387 would have established a new "W" nonimmigrant visa category for these workers, which would not have been subject to numerical limits. The W-1 visa would have covered seasonal workers, and the W-2 visa would have covered nonseasonal workers. Under the proposal, the Secretary of Homeland Security and the Secretary of State would have jointly established and administered guest worker programs with foreign countries that entered into agreements with the United States. The bill would have directed the Secretary of Homeland Security, in cooperation with the Secretary of State and the participating foreign governments, to establish a database to monitor guest workers' entry into and exit from the United States and to track employer compliance.

In order to import workers through the new programs, employers would have had to file an application with DOL. As part of the application, the employer would have had to request an attestation from DOL that there were not sufficient U.S. workers who were qualified and available to perform the work, and that the hiring of alien workers would not adversely affect the wages and working conditions of similarly employed U.S. workers. The employer also would have needed to provide various assurances in the application, including that the employer would offer the job to any equally qualified, available U.S. worker who applied; would advertise the job opening in a local publication; and would pay workers at least the higher of the federal or applicable state minimum wage. Unless an employer's application was incomplete or obviously inaccurate, DOL would have certified within 14 days of the filing date that the application had been filed. Beginning 12 months after enactment, employers would have been subject to increased penalties for knowingly employing unauthorized aliens.

The authorized period of stay for a W-1 seasonal worker could not have exceeded 270 days per year. Such a worker could have reapplied for admission to the United States each year. The initial authorized period of stay for a W-2 nonseasonal worker could not have exceeded one year, but could have been extended in increments of up to one year each; a W-2 worker's total period of stay could not have exceeded three consecutive years. Unauthorized workers in the United States would have had 12 months from enactment to apply for the program.

Among the other provisions, the bill would have created investment accounts for the guest workers, into which the Social Security taxes paid by them and by their employers on their behalf would have been deposited. The investment accounts would have been the sole property of the guest workers. In most cases, however, distributions of account funds could have been made only after the workers had permanently left the guest worker program and returned to their home countries.

Under S. 1387, guest workers could have applied for U.S. legal permanent residency only after they had returned to their home countries. Their applications would have been evaluated based on a point system to be established by the Secretary of Homeland Security. The bill did not propose a legalization mechanism for guest workers outside of existing channels, and according to Senator Cornyn's office, guest workers would have had to meet all the relevant requirements under current law.[31]

S. 1461/H.R. 2899

The Border Security and Immigration Improvement Act (S. 1461/H.R. 2899), introduced, respectively, by Senator McCain and by Representative Kolbe for himself and Representative Flake, would have established two new temporary worker visas under the INA — the H-4A and H-4B visas. S. 1461/H.R. 2899 would have placed no numerical limit on the H-4A or H-4B visas.

The H-4A visa would have covered aliens coming to the United States to perform temporary full-time employment. An employer interested in importing H4A workers would have had to file a petition with DHS. DHS could only have approved the petition once it determined that the employer had satisfied recruitment requirements, including advertising the job opportunity to U.S. workers on an electronic job registry established by DOL and offering the job to any equally qualified U.S. worker who applied through the registry. The employer also would have had to attest in the petition that he or she: would use the employment eligibility confirmation system established by the bill to verify the alien workers' identity and employment authorization; would provide the alien workers with the same benefits, wages, and working conditions as other similarly employed workers; and did not and would not displace U.S. workers during a specified 180-day period. Aliens granted H-4A status would have been issued machine-readable, tamper-resistant visas and other documents containing biometric identifiers.

An H-4A worker's initial authorized period of staywould have been three years, and could have been extended for an additional three years. S. 1461/H.R. 2899 also would have enabled H-4A nonimmigrants to adjust to LPR status. Petitions for employment-based *immigrant* visas could have been filed by an H-4A worker's employer, or by the H-4A worker, if he or she had maintained H-4A status for at least three years. Employment-based *immigrant* visas would have been made available to H-4A workers adjusting status without numerical limitation.

The H-4B visa established by the bill would have covered aliens unlawfully present and employed in the United States since before August 1, 2003. An H-4B alien's authorized period of stay would have been three years. The alien could have applied to change to H-4A status or another nonimmigrant or immigrant category, but such a change of status could not have taken place until the end of the three years. H-4B employers would have been required to use the employment eligibility confirmation system mentioned above and to comply with specified requirements applicable to H-4A employers, including providing benefits, wages, and working conditions to H-4B workers equal to those provided to other similarly employed workers.

H.R. 3651

The Alien Accountability Act (H.R. 3651), introduced by Representative Issa, would have authorized a new "W" nonimmigrant visa category under the INA for unauthorized aliens. The category would have covered aliens unlawfully present in the United States on December 8, 2003, as well as aliens residing in foreign contiguous territory who had been habitually unlawfully present in the United States during the six-month period ending on December 8, 2003. In order to be eligible for W status, the alien would first have had to register with DHS. Employment would not have been a strict requirement for W status, but the alien would have had to demonstrate an adequate means of financial support. The new category would have sunset six years after the first alien was granted W status.

The initial period of authorized admission of a W nonimmigrant would have been one year and could have been renewed up to five times in one-year increments.

H.R. 3651 would not have established a special mechanism for W nonimmigrants to adjust to LPR status. It, however, would not have precluded them from doing so if they satisfied the applicable requirements under current law.

LEGISLATION IN THE 109TH CONGRESS

As in the 108th Congress, bills were introduced in the 109th Congress to reform the H-2A and H-2B programs, to reform the "H" visa category, and to establish new temporary worker visas. An amendment based on one of the H-2B bills (S. 352/H.R. 793) was enacted as part of the FY2005 Emergency Supplemental Appropriations Act for Defense, the Global War on Terror, and Tsunami Relief (P.L. 109-13). Subsequently, the John Warner National Defense Authorization Act for FY2007 (P.L. 109-364) extended one of the temporary H-2B provisions in P.L. 109-13.

As discussed below, the Comprehensive Immigration Reform Act of 2006 (S. 2611), as passed by the Senate, would have reformed the H-2A program and established a new guest worker program for nonagricultural workers. During consideration of the Border Protection, Antiterrorism, and Illegal Immigration Control Act of 2005 (H.R. 4437) by the House Judiciary Committee and on the House floor, efforts were made to add guest worker programs and language expressing support for a guest worker program, but they were unsuccessful. H.R. 4437, as passed by the House, did not contain any guest worker provisions.

The 109th Congress also held a number of hearings on immigration issues relevant to a guest worker program. The House Judiciary Committee's Subcommittee on Immigration, Border Security, and Claims held hearings on employment eligibility verification and work site enforcement. The Senate Judiciary Committee's Subcommittee on Immigration, Border Security, and Citizenship held hearings on immigration reform issues, including the establishment of a new guest worker program. The full Senate Judiciary Committee held hearings on comprehensive immigration reform, at which two major reform proposals (S. 1033/H.R. 2330 and S. 1438) were discussed.

S. 352/H.R. 793 and Related H-2b Legislation

The Save Our Small and Seasonal Businesses Act (S. 352/H.R. 793),[32] introduced respectively by Senator Mikulski and Representative Gilchrest for themselves and bipartisan groups of cosponsors, proposed to revise the H-2B program. During Senate consideration of the FY2005 Emergency Supplemental Appropriations bill (H.R. 1268) in April 2005, Senator Mikulski offered a floor amendment based on S. 352/H.R. 793. On April 19, 2005, the Senate adopted the Mikulski Amendment, as modified, by a vote of 94 to 6, and the amendment was included in the enacted measure (P.L. 109-13) as Division B, Title IV.

The H-2B title of P.L. 109-13 caps at 33,000 the number of H-2B slots available during the first six months of a fiscal year. It also requires DHS to submit specified information to Congress on the H-2B program on a regular basis, imposes a new fraud-prevention and detection fee on H-2B employers, and authorizes DHS to impose additional penalties on H-2B employers in certain circumstances. In addition, the H-2B title of P.L. 109-13 contains a temporary provision, initially scheduled to expire at the end of FY2006, that keeps aliens who have been counted toward the H2B cap in any of the past three years from being counted again. The John Warner National Defense Authorization Act for FY2007 (P.L. 109-364; §1074) extends this returning H-2B worker exemption through FY2007. Thus, aliens who have been counted toward the H-2B cap in FY2004, FY2005, or FY2006 are not to be counted toward the FY2007 cap.

S. 2611

In March 2006, the Senate Judiciary Committee considered an immigration measure by Chairman Specter, known as the Chairman's mark. Among its many provisions, this measure, as amended and approved by the Committee, proposed to reform the H-2A program and establish a new guest worker program for nonagricultural workers. The Committee-approved measure evolved into the Comprehensive Immigration Act of 2006 (S. 2611), which the Senate passed, as amended, on May 25, 2006 on a vote of 62 to 36.

Title VI, Subtitle B of S. 2611 contained provisions on agricultural workers. These provisions were similar to those in the Agricultural Job Opportunities, Benefits, and Security Act of 2005 (AgJOBS Act; S. 359/H.R. 884), discussed below. Like S. 359/H.R. 884, Title VI, Subtitle B of S. 2611 would have streamlined the process of importing H-2A workers, particularly for jobs covered by collective bargaining agreements. Prospective H-2A employers would have had to file applications with DOL containing certain assurances. In the case of a job covered by a collective bargaining agreement, the employer would have had to assure, among other things, that there was an applicable union contract and that the bargaining representatives of the employer's employees had been notified of the filing of the application for H-2A workers. An employer interested in filling a job not covered by a collective bargaining agreement would have been subject to a longer list of required assurances. Among these, the employer would have had to assure that he or she would take specified steps to recruit U.S. workers and would provide workers with required benefits, wages, and working conditions. Both groups of employers would have had to assure that the job was temporary or seasonal and that the employer would offer the job to any equally qualified, available U.S. worker who applied. Unless an employer's application was incomplete or obviously inaccurate, DOL would have certified within seven days of the filing date that the employer had filed the required application.

Title VI, Subtitle B of S. 2611 would have made changes to the H-2A program's requirements regarding minimum benefits, wages, and working conditions. Among these proposed changes, the adverse effect wage rate (discussed above) would have remained at the January 2003 level for three years after the date of enactment, and employers would have been permitted to provide housing allowances, in lieu of housing, to their workers if the governor of the relevant state certified that adequate housing was available. An H-2A worker's initial period of employment could not have exceeded 10 months. The worker's stay could have been extended in increments of up to 10 months each, but the worker's total continuous period of stay, including any extensions, could not have exceeded three years.

Title VI, Subtitle B of S. 2611 also proposed a legalization program for agricultural workers. This program followed the basic design of the legalization program in S. 359/H.R. 884, but included different work and other requirements and used different terminology.

Under the program in S. 2611, the Secretary of DHS would have conferred "blue card status" (akin to S. 359/H.R. 884's temporary resident status)[33] on an alien worker who had performed at least 863 hours, or 150 work days, of agricultural employment in the United States during the 24-month period ending on December 31, 2005, and met other requirements. No more than 1.5 million blue cards could have been issued during the five-year period beginning on the date of enactment. To be eligible to adjust to LPR status, the alien in blue card status would have had to, among other requirements, perform either at least 575 hours of U.S. agricultural work per year for the five years after enactment, or at least 863 hours of U.S. agricultural work per year for three of the five years after enactment. Existing numerical limits under the INA would not have applied to adjustments of status under the bill.[34]

Title IV, Subtitle A of S. 2611 proposed to establish a new H-2C nonagricultural guest worker visa, which, as amended on the Senate floor, would have been capped at 200,000 annually. The H-2C visa would have covered aliens coming temporarily to the United States to perform temporary labor or services other than the labor or services covered under the H-2A visa or other specified visa categories. A prospective H-2C employer would have had to file a petition with DHS. In the petition the employer would have had to attest to various items, including that the employer was offering wages to H-2C workers that were the greater of the prevailing wage rate for the occupational classification in the area of employment or the actual wage paid by the employer to other similarly employed and qualified workers; and that there were not sufficient qualified and available U.S. workers to perform the work. Prior to filing the petition, the prospective employer also would have been required to make efforts to recruit U.S. workers in accordance with DOL regulations. To be eligible for H-2C status, the alien would have needed to have evidence of employment and meet other requirements.

An H-2C worker's initial authorized period of stay would have been three years, and could have been extended for an additional three years. H-2C aliens could not have changed to another nonimmigrant visa category. As in S. 1438 (discussed below), an H-2C alien who failed to depart the United States when required to do so would have been ineligible for any immigration relief or benefit, except for specified forms of humanitarian relief. At the same time, H-2C nonimmigrants in the United States could have applied to adjust to LPR status. Petitions for employment-based *immigrant* visas could have been filed by an H-2C worker's employer or, if the H-2C worker had maintained H-2C status for a total of four years, by the worker.

S. 359/H.R. 884

The Agricultural Job Opportunities, Benefits, and Security Act of 2005 (AgJOBS Act; S. 359/H.R. 884) proposed to overhaul the H-2A agricultural worker program. The bills were introduced, respectively, by Senator Craig and Representative Cannon for themselves and bipartisan groups of cosponsors. S. 359/H.R. 884 was very similar to the AgJOBs bills before the 108th Congress (S. 1645/H.R. 3142, S. 2823). Like these bills, S. 359/H.R. 884 would have streamlined the process of importing H-2A workers, particularly for jobs covered by collective bargaining agreements. Prospective H-2A employers would have had to file applications with DOL containing certain assurances. In the case of a job covered by a collective bargaining agreement, the employer would have had to assure, among other things, that there was an applicable union contract and that the bargaining representatives of the employer's employees had been notified of the filing of the application for H-2A workers. An employer interested in filling a job not covered by a collective bargaining agreement would have been subject to a longer list of required assurances. Among these, the employer would have had to assure that he or she would take specified steps to recruit U.S. workers and would provide workers with required benefits, wages, and working conditions. Both groups of employers would have had to assure that the job was temporary or seasonal and that the employer would offer the job to any equally qualified, available U.S. worker who applied. Unless an employer's application was incomplete or obviously inaccurate, DOL would have certified within seven days of the filing date that the employer had filed the required application.

S. 359/H.R. 884 would have made changes to the H-2A program's requirements regarding minimum benefits, wages, and working conditions. Among these proposed changes, the adverse effect wage rate (discussed above) would have remained at the January 2003 level for three years after the date of enactment, and employers would have been permitted to provide housing allowances, in lieu of housing, to their workers if the governor of the relevant state certified that adequate housing was available.

Under S. 359/H.R. 884, an H-2A worker would have been admitted for an initial period of employment not to exceed 10 months. The worker's stay could have been extended in increments of up to 10 months each, but the worker's total continuous period of stay, including any extensions, could not have exceeded three years.[35]

In addition to these H-2A reform provisions, S. 359/H.R. 884 would have established a two-stage legalization program for agricultural workers. To obtain temporary resident status, the alien worker would have had to establish that he or she had performed at least 575 hours, or 100 work days, of agricultural employment in the United States during 12 consecutive months in the 18-month period ending on December 31, 2004, and meet other requirements. To be eligible to adjust to LPR status, the alien would have had to perform at least 2,060 hours, or 360 work days, of agricultural work in the United States during the six years following the date of enactment, and meet other requirements. Existing numerical limits under the INA would not have applied to adjustments of status under the bills.[36]

H.R. 3857

The Temporary Agricultural Labor Reform Act of 2005 (H.R. 3857), an H-2A reform bill introduced by Representative Goodlatte on behalf of himself and a group of cosponsors, was a revision of a bill of the same name that he had introduced in the 108th Congress. H.R. 3857 would have streamlined the process of importing H-2A workers. Prospective H-2A employers would have had to file petitions with DHS containing certain attestations; they would not have filed applications with DOL as they currently do. Employers would have had to attest that the job was temporary or seasonal; that they would provide workers with required benefits, wages, and working conditions; that they had made efforts to recruit U.S. workers; and that they would offer the job to any equally qualified, available U.S. worker who applied. Unless an employer's application was incomplete or obviously inaccurate, DHS would have adjudicated the petition within seven days of the filing date.

H.R. 3857 would have changed current H-2A requirements regarding minimum benefits, wages, and working conditions. Under the bill, H-2A employers would have had to pay workers the higher of the prevailing wage rate or the applicable state minimum wage; employers would not have been subject to the adverse effect wage rate (discussed above). With respect to housing, employers could have provided allowances, in lieu of housing, to their workers if the governor of the relevant state certified that adequate housing was available.[37]

Under H.R. 3857, an H-2A worker would have been admitted for an initial period of employment not to exceed 10 months. The worker's stay could have been extended in increments of up to 10 months each, but the worker's total continuous period of stay, including any extensions, could not have exceeded 20 months.

S. 2087

The Agricultural Employment and Workforce Protection Act of 2005 (S. 2087), introduced by Senator Chambliss, would have reformed the H-2A program. It would have eliminated the current limitation that H-2A nonimmigrants can perform only temporary or seasonal work and would have broadened the definition of agricultural labor or services for purposes of the H-2A visa to cover labor or services relating to such activities as dairy, forestry, landscaping, and meat processing. Like S. 359/H.R. 884 and H.R. 3857, S. 2087 proposed to streamline the process of importing H-2A workers. As under H.R. 3857, a prospective H-2A employer would have filed a petition with DHS containing certain attestations. Among them, the employer would have had to attest that he or she: would provide workers with required benefits, wages, and working conditions; had made efforts to recruit U.S. workers; and would offer the job to any equally qualified, available U.S. worker who applied. Unless the petition was incomplete or obviously inaccurate, DHS would have approved or denied it not later than seven days after the filing date.

Also like S. 359/H.R. 884 and H.R. 3857, S. 2087 would have changed current H-2A requirements regarding minimum benefits, wages, and working conditions. Under S. 2087, H-2A employers would have had to pay workers the higher of the prevailing wage rate or the applicable state minimum wage; employers would not have been subject to the adverse effect wage rate (discussed above). As under both S. 359/H.R. 884 and H.R. 3857, employers could have provided housing allowances, in lieu of housing, to their workers if the governor of the relevant state certified that adequate housing was available. Under S. 2087, an H-2A worker would have been admitted for an initial period of employment of 11 months. The worker's stay could have been extended for up to two consecutive contract periods.

Unlike S. 359/H.R. 884 and H.R. 3857, S. 2087 would have established subcategories of H-2A nonimmigrants. It would have defined a "Level II H-2A worker" as a nonimmigrant who had been employed as an H-2A worker for at least three years and worked in a supervisory capacity. The bill would have made provision for an employer of a Level II H-2A worker, who had been employed in such status for not less than five years, to file an application for an employment-based adjustment of status for that worker. Such a Level II H-2A worker could have continued working in such status until his or her application was adjudicated. Under the bill, an "H-2AA worker" would have been defined as an H-2A worker who participated in the cross-border worker program the bill would have established. These H-2AA workers would have been allowed to enter and exit the United States each work day in accordance with DHS regulations.

In addition, the bill would have established a blue card program through which the Secretary of DHS could have conferred "blue card status" upon an alien, including an unauthorized alien, who had performed at least 1,600 hours of agricultural employment for an employer in the United States in 2005 and met other requirements. An alien could have been granted blue card status for a period of up to two years, at the end of which the alien would have had to return to his or her home country. Aliens in blue card status would not have been eligible to change to a nonimmigrant status or adjust to LPR status.

S. 278

The Summer Operations and Seasonal Equity Act of 2005 (S. 278), introduced by Senator Collins, would have made changes to the numerical limits under the H-2B program. It would have required that at least 12,000 of the total number of H-2B slots available annually (currently, 66,000) be made available in each quarter of each fiscal year. It would have exempted an alien who had been counted toward the annual H-2B numerical limit within the past three years from being counted again. Both of these provisions would have expired at the end of FY2007. S. 278 also would have required DHS to submit specified information to Congress on the H-2B program on a regular basis.

H.R. 1587

H.R. 1587, introduced by Representative Tancredo for himself and several cosponsors, would have raised the H-2B cap and placed new requirements on the H2B program. It would have increased to 131,000 the number of aliens who could be issued H-2B visas or otherwise provided H-2B status annually. Not more than half of these slots, or 65,500, would have been available during the first six months of a fiscal year. H.R. 1587 would have added new recruitment-related requirements for prospective H-2B employers, and would have mandated H-2B employer participation in the Basic Pilot program, an electronic employment eligibility verification system.

H.R. 1587 also would have imposed new requirements on H-2B nonimmigrants. Among them, these aliens could no longer have been accompanied by family members.

S. 1918

The Strengthening America's Workforce Act of 2005 (S. 1918), introduced by Senator Hagel, contained guest worker provisions similar to those in the bill he introduced in the 108th Congress. S. 1918 would have revised the H-2B visa and eliminated the current restriction that H-2B workers can perform only temporary service or labor. Instead, the bill would have required workers to perform "shortterm service or labor, lasting not more than nine months." S. 1918 also would have established a new H-2C visa for temporary workers coming to perform "labor or services, other than those occupation classifications" covered under the H-

2A, H-2B, or specified high-skilled visa categories. The H-2B visa would have been capped at 100,000 annually, and the H-2C visa would have been capped at 250,000 annually.

S. 1918 would have subjected the H-2B and H-2C programs to a broad set of requirements concerning recruitment, application procedures, and worker protections, among other issues. Prior to filing an application with DOL for H-2B or H-2C workers, prospective employers would have had to take specified steps to recruit U.S. workers, including authorizing DOL to post the job on the online America's Job Bank and on local job banks. Employers also would have had to offer the job to any qualified, available U.S. worker who applied. In the application to DOL, the employer would have had to attest to various items. Among these were that the employer would offer wages to H-2B or H-2C workers that were the greater of the prevailing wage rate or the actual wage paid by the employer to other similarly employed and qualified workers, and that the employer would abide by all applicable laws and regulations relating to the rights of workers to organize. DOL would have reviewed the application for completeness and accuracy and issued a determination not later than 21 days after the filing date.

The initial period of admission for an H-2B worker could not have exceeded nine months in a one-year period. An H-2B worker's total period of admission could not have exceeded 36 months in a four-year period. The initial period of admission for an H-2C worker could not have exceeded two years and could have been extended for an additional period of up to two years. An H-2C worker's total period of admission could not have exceeded four years.

S. 1918 would have enabled H-2B and H-2C nonimmigrants to obtain LPR status. Employment-based *immigrant* visas would have been made available to these nonimmigrants without regard to existing numerical limits under the INA. An employment-based petition could have been filed by an alien's employer or collective bargaining agent or, after the alien had been employed in H-2B or H-2C status for at least three years, by the alien.

H.R. 3333

The Rewarding Employers that Abide by the Law and Guaranteeing Uniform Enforcement to Stop Terrorism Act of 2005 (H.R. 3333), introduced by Representative Tancredo, contained temporary worker provisions similar to those in the bill he had introduced in the 108th Congress. H.R. 3333 would have eliminated all the current "H" visa subcategories, including the H-2A and H-2B visas, and replaced them with a single "H" visa covering aliens coming temporarily to the United States to perform skilled or unskilled work. There would have been no cap on the H visa.

An employer interested in employing H nonimmigrants would have had to recruit U.S. workers by posting the job opportunity on America's Job Bank and would have had to offer the job to any equally qualified U.S. worker who applied. The employer would have had to file an application with DOL containing certain assurances, including that he or she had complied with the recruitment requirements.

Prospective H nonimmigrants, who could only have been admitted from abroad, would have had to apply to be included in a database of workers, which DOL would have been tasked with establishing and maintaining. Once an employer's application had been approved, DOL would have provided the employer with a list of possible job candidates from the database. Aliens admitted on H visas could not have changed to another nonimmigrant status or been adjusted to LPR status in the United States.

Under H.R. 3333, the new H visa program could not have been implemented until the Secretary of Homeland Security made certain certifications to Congress, including that a congressionally mandated automated entry-exit system was fully operational[38] and that at least 80% of aliens who overstayed their nonimmigrants visas were removed within one year of overstaying.

S. 1033/H.R. 2330

The Secure America and Orderly Immigration Act (S. 1033/H.R. 2330) was introduced, respectively, by Senator McCain and Representative Kolbe for themselves and bipartisan groups of cosponsors. It was discussed at the Senate Judiciary Committee hearings on comprehensive immigration reform held in July 2005 and October 2005. Its guest worker and legalization provisions were similar in some respects to provisions in bills from the 108th Congress, including S. 1461/H.R. 2899, S. 2010, and S. 2381/H.R. 4262. S. 1033/H.R. 2330 would have established two new temporary worker visas under the INA — the H-5A and H-5B visas. It would have capped the H-5A visa initially at 400,000, and established a process for adjusting the cap in subsequent fiscal years based on demand for the visas. It would have placed no cap on the H-5B visa.

The H-5A visa would have covered aliens coming temporarily to the United States *initially* to perform labor or services "other than those occupational classifications" covered under the H-2A or specified high-skilled visa categories. Prospective H-5A nonimmigrants would have filed visa applications on their own behalf. Employers would not have filed petitions with DHS for them, as they currently do to employ other nonimmigrant workers. Under S. 1033/H.R. 2330, the Secretary of State could have granted an H-5A visa to an alien who demonstrated an intent to perform work covered by the visa. To be eligible for H-5A status, an alien would have needed to have evidence of employment and to meet other requirements. Before hiring a prospective H-5A worker, an employer would have had to post the job opportunity on a DOL electronic job registry to recruit U.S. workers. H-5A employers also would have been required to comply with all applicable federal, state, and local laws, and to use an employment eligibility confirmation system, to be established by the Social Security Administration, to verify the employment eligibility of newly hired H-5A workers.

An H-5A worker's initial authorized period of stay would have been three years, and could have been extended for an additional three years. Under S. 1033/H.R. 2330, H-5A nonimmigrants in the United States could have adjusted to LPR status. Petitions for employment-based *immigrant* visas could have been filed by an H-5A worker's employer or, if the H-5A worker had maintained H-5A status for a total of four years, by the worker.

The H-5B visa established by the bill would have covered aliens present and employed in the United States since before May 12, 2005. Aliens lawfully present in the United States as nonimmigrants on that date would not have been eligible for H-5B status. An H-5B alien's authorized period of stay would have been six years. At the end of that six-year period, the alien could have applied to adjust to LPR status, subject to various requirements. Such adjustments of status would not have been subject to numerical limitations.

S. 1438

The Comprehensive Enforcement and Immigration Reform Act of 2005 (S. 1438) was introduced by Senator Cornyn for himself and Senator Kyl. Like S. 1033/H.R. 2330, it was discussed at the Senate Judiciary Committee hearings on comprehensive immigration reform held in July 2005 and October 2005. It would have established a new "W" temporary worker visa under the INA. S. 1438 would not have placed a cap on the W visa, but would have authorized DOL to do so in the future based on the recommendations of a task force the bill would have established. In addition, S. 1438 would have amended the INA to authorize DHS to grant a new status — Deferred Mandatory Departure (DMD) status — to certain unauthorized aliens in the United States. It would have placed no limit on the number of aliens who could have received that status.

The W visa would have covered aliens coming temporarily to the United States to perform temporary labor or service other than that covered under the H-2A or specified high-skilled visa categories. S. 1438 would have repealed the H-2B visa category. Prospective W nonimmigrants would have filed applications on their own behalf. Employers would not have filed petitions with DHS on behalf of W workers, as they currently do to employ other nonimmigrant workers. Under S. 1438, the Secretary of State could have granted a W visa to an alien who demonstrated an intent to perform eligible work. To be eligible for W status, the alien would have needed to have evidence of employment, among other requirements. An employer interested in hiring a W nonimmigrant would have had to apply for authorization to do so through an Alien Employment Management System to be established by DHS. Before an employer could have been granted such authorization, he or she would have had to post the position on a DOL electronic job registry and offer the position to any equally qualified U.S. worker who applied. S. 1438 would have made it mandatory for all employers, including W employers, to verify the employment eligibility of new hires through an electronic system. Current electronic employment eligibility verification is conducted through the largely voluntary Basic Pilot program.

A W nonimmigrant's authorized period of stay would have been two years, and could *not* have been extended. After residing in his or her home country for one year, however, an alien could have been readmitted to the United States in W status. An alien's total period of admission as a W nonimmigrant could not have exceeded six years. These stay limitations would not have applied to aliens who spent less than six months a year in W status, or who commuted to the United States to work in W status but resided outside the country. S. 1438 would have made W nonimmigrants ineligible to change to another nonimmigrant status and would not have provided them with any special mechanism to obtain LPR status. Furthermore, a W nonimmigrant who did not depart the United States when required to do so would have been ineligible for any immigration benefit or relief, except for specified forms of humanitarian relief.

Aliens present in the United States since July 20, 2004, and employed since before July 20, 2005, could have applied to DHS for Deferred Mandatory Departure (DMD) status. Aliens lawfully present in the United States as nonimmigrants would not have been eligible. DHS could have granted an alien DMD status for a period of up to five years. Employers interested in employing aliens granted DMD status would have had to apply for authorization through the Alien Employment Management System mentioned above. Aliens in DMD status could not have applied to change to a nonimmigrant status or, unless otherwise eligible under

INA §245(i), to adjust to LPR status.[39] Aliens who complied with the terms of DMD status and departed prior to its expiration date would not have been subject to the INA provision that bars previously unlawfully present aliens from being admitted to the United States for 3 or 10 years, depending on the length of their unlawful stay.[40] If otherwise eligible, these aliens could immediately have sought admission as nonimmigrants or immigrants. However, they would not have received any special consideration for admission. Aliens granted DMD status who failed to depart prior to the expiration of that status would have been ineligible for any immigration benefit or relief, except for specified forms of humanitarian relief, for 10 years.

H.R. 4065

The Temporary Worker Registration and Visa Act of 2005 (H.R. 4065), introduced by Representative Osborne, would have established a process for registering aliens who had been continuouslyunlawfully present and employed in the United States since January 1, 2005. Eligible aliens would have applied for this registration, which would have been valid for six months. Registered aliens would have been given work authorization and would have been eligible for a new "W" temporary worker visa established by the bill. To obtain a W visa, a registered alien would have had to apply at a consular office in his or her home country not later than six months after his or her registration was approved. H.R. 4065 would have placed no numerical limit on the W visa.

The initial period of authorized admission for a W nonimmigrant would have been three years and could have been extended in three year increments without limit.

H.R. 4065 would have required that W nonimmigrants be continuously employed but would have placed no restriction on the type of work they could perform. W nonimmigrants would not have been prohibited from changing to another nonimmigrant classification or adjusting to LPR status. H.R. 4065, however, would have made no special provision for them to do so.

LEGISLATION IN THE 110TH CONGRESS

Bills have been introduced in the 110th Congress to reform the H-2A program and the H-2B program and to establish new temporary worker visas. The House Judiciary Committee's Subcommittee on Immigration, Citizenship, Refugees, Border Security, and International Law also has held hearings related to guest worker programs.

S. 237/S. 340/H.R. 371

The Agricultural Job Opportunities, Benefits, and Security Act of 2007 (AgJOBS Act; S. 237/S. 340/H.R. 371) proposes to overhaul the H-2A agricultural worker program. The Senate bills were introduced by Senator Feinstein and have a bipartisan group of cosponsors. The House companion was introduced by Representative Berman and also has bipartisan cosponsorship. The provisions of the AgJOBS Act of 2007 are similar to those included in S. 2611, as passed by the Senate in the 109th Congress (discussed above).

The AgJOBS Act of 2007 would streamline the process of importing H-2A workers, particularly for jobs covered by collective bargaining agreements. Prospective H-2A employers would have to file applications with DOL containing certain assurances. In the case of a job covered by a collective bargaining agreement, the employer would have to assure, among other things, that there is an applicable union contract and that the bargaining representatives of the employer's employees have been notified of the filing of the application for H-2A workers. An employer interested in filling a job not covered by a collective bargaining agreement would be subject to a longer list of required assurances. Among these, the employer would have to assure that he or she will take specified steps to recruit U.S. workers and will provide workers with required benefits, wages, and working conditions. Both groups of employers would have to assure that the job is temporary or seasonal and that the employer will offer the job to any equally qualified, available U.S. worker who applies. Unless an employer's application is incomplete or obviously inaccurate, DOL would have to certify within seven days of the filing date that the employer had filed the required application. The employer could then file a petition with DHS for H-2A workers.

The AgJOBS Act of 2007 would likewise make changes to the H-2A program's requirements regarding minimum benefits, wages, and working conditions. Among these proposed changes, the adverse effect wage rate (discussed above) would remain at the January 2003 level for three years after the date of enactment, and employers would be permitted to provide housing allowances, in lieu of housing, to their workers if the governor of the relevant state certifies that adequate housing is available. An H-2A worker's initial period of employment could not exceed 10 months. The worker's stay could be extended in increments of up to 10 months each, but the worker's total continuous period of stay, including any extensions, could not exceed three years.

The AgJOBS Act of 2007 also proposes a legalization program for agricultural workers similar to that included in S. 2611, as passed by the Senate in the 109th Congress. Under the program, the Secretary of DHS would grant "blue card status" to an alien worker who had performed at least 863 hours, or 150 work days, of agricultural employment in the United States during the 24-month period ending on December 31, 2006, and meets other requirements. No more than 1.5 million blue cards could be issued during the five-year period beginning on the date of enactment. To be eligible to adjust to LPR status, the alien in blue card status would have to, among other requirements, perform either at least 100 workdays of U.S. agricultural work per year for the five years after enactment, or at least 150 workdays of U.S. agricultural work per year for the three years after enactment.[41] Existing numerical limits under the INA would not apply to adjustments of status under the bill.[42]

H.R. 1645

The Security Through Regularized Immigration and a Vibrant Economy Act of 2007 (STRIVE Act; H.R. 1645), introduced by Representative Gutierrez for himself and a bipartisan group of cosponsors, includes the AgJOBS Act of 2007 (described above) as Title VI, Subtitle C. In addition, Title IV of H.R. 1645 proposes to establish a new H-2C temporary worker program. The new H-2C visa would cover aliens coming temporarily to the United

States to initially perform temporary labor or services other than the labor or services covered under the H-2A visa or other specified visa categories. A prospective H-2C employer would have to file a petition with DOL. In the petition the employer would have to attest to various items, including that the employer is offering wages to H-2C workers that are the greater of the prevailing wage rate for the occupational classification in the area of employment or the actual wage paid by the employer to other similarly employed and qualified workers; and that there are not sufficient qualified and available U.S. workers to perform the work. In most cases, prior to filing the petition, the prospective employer also would have to make efforts to recruit U.S. workers, as specified in the bill. To be eligible for H-2C status, the alien would need to have evidence of employment and meet other requirements.

An H-2C worker's initial authorized period of stay would be three years, and could be extended for an additional three years. H-2C nonimmigrants in the United States could apply to adjust to LPR status. Petitions for employment-based *immigrant* visas could be filed by an H-2C worker's employer or, if the alien had been employed as an H-2C worker for a total of five years, by the worker.

S. 330

The Border Security and Immigration Reform Act of 2007 (S. 330), introduced by Senator Isakson, would establish a new W temporary worker program for agricultural or nonagricultural workers. The guest worker provisions are in Title III, §302 of the bill. An employer interested in importing W workers would first apply to DOL for labor certification. After receiving certification, the employer would file an application with DHS, as required by DHS. Aliens who have been unlawfully employed in the United States since January 1, 2007, could participate in the new program if they apply for registration and meet other requirements, as set forth in §301 of the bill. W visas would be issued for an initial period of up to two years and could be renewed for an unlimited number of two-year terms. The guest worker and registration provisions in S. 330 would not take effect, however, until after the Secretary of DHS certifies that specified border security and enforcement-related measures authorized under other titles of the bill are fully operational.

S. 1639

S. 1639, introduced by Senator Kennedy, is based on S.Amdt. 1150, as amended on the Senate floor in late May and early June 2007.[43] Among its many provisions, S. 1639 would repeal the H-2B program, reform the H-2A program, and establish new guest worker programs. The Senate began consideration of S. 1639 in late June 2007.

Agricultural Workers
The H-2A reform provisions are in Title IV, Subtitle B of S. 1639. These provisions are similar to those in S. 237/S. 340/H.R. 371 before the 110th Congress, and in S. 2611, as passed by the Senate in the 109th Congress (these proposals are discussed above). Section 404 of S. 1639 would streamline the process of importing H-2A workers, particularly for jobs covered by collective bargaining agreements. Prospective H-2A employers would have to file

applications with DOL containing certain assurances. In the case of a job covered by a collective bargaining agreement, the employer would have to ensure, among other things, that there is an applicable union contract and that the bargaining representatives of the employer's employees have been notified of the filing of the application for H-2A workers. An employer interested in filling a job not covered by a collective bargaining agreement would be subject to a longer list of required assurances.

Among these, the employer would have to ensure that he or she will take specified steps to recruit U.S. workers and will provide workers with required benefits, wages, and working conditions. Both groups of employers would have to ensure that the job is temporary or seasonal and that the employer will offer the job to any equally qualified, available U.S. worker who applies. Unless an employer's application is incomplete or obviously inaccurate, DOL would have to certify within seven days of the filing date that the employer had filed the required application. The employer could then file a petition with DHS for H-2A workers.

Section 404 of S. 1639 would likewise make changes to the H-2A program's requirements regarding minimum benefits, wages, and working conditions. Among these proposed changes, the adverse effect wage rate (discussed above) would remain at the January 2003 level for three years after the date of enactment, and employers would be permitted to provide housing allowances, in lieu of housing, to their workers if the governor of the relevant state certifies that adequate housing is available. Unlike in S. 237/S. 340/H.R. 371 in the 110th Congress and in S. 2611, as passed by the Senate in the 109th Congress, an H-2A worker's maximum continuous period of authorized status would be 10 months. The worker could not again apply for admission to the United States as an H-2A worker until he or she had been outside the country for a period of time, as specified.

In addition to these H-2A reform provisions, S. 1639 proposes a legalization process for agricultural workers in Title VI, Subtitle C. Under Section 622, the Secretary of DHS would grant a Z-A nonimmigrant visa to an alien worker who had performed at least 863 hours, or 150 work days, of agricultural employment in the United States during the 24-month period ending on December 31, 2006, and meets other requirements, including payment of a $100 fine. No more than 1.5 million Z-A visas could be issued. Spouses or minor children of Z-A nonimmigrants would be eligible for Z-A dependent visas, which would not be subject to a numerical limit. Not later than eight years after enactment, Z-A nonimmigrants would have to either renew the alien's Z visa status or apply to adjust to LPR status. With respect to the latter option, the Secretary of DHS would adjust the status of a Z-A alien to that of an LPR if specified requirements are met. The alien would have to perform either at least 100 workdays of U.S. agricultural work per year for the five years after enactment, or at least 150 workdays of U.S. agricultural work per year for the three years after enactment.[44] The other requirements would include payment of a $400 fine and payment of applicable federal taxes. The Z-A nonimmigrant would have to file the application for adjustment of status in person with a U.S. consulate abroad. Existing numerical limits under the INA would not apply to adjustments of status of Z-A or Z-A dependent aliens under the bill.[45]

Y Nonimmigrants

Title IV, Subtitle A of S. 1639 proposes to establish a new Y temporary worker visa category. The Y-1 visa would cover aliens coming temporarily to the United States to perform temporary labor or services other than the labor or services covered under specified nonimmigrant visas for high-skilled workers and others. The Y-1 visa program would sunset after five years. The Y-2 visa would cover aliens coming temporarily to the United States to perform seasonal nonagricultural labor or services.[46] The Y-3 visa would cover the spouses or children of Y-1 or Y-2 aliens. A prospective employer of Y nonimmigrants would have to file an application for labor certification with DOL that includes attestations regarding U.S. worker protections, wages, and other items. The employer would have to make efforts to recruit U.S. workers prior to filing the labor certification application. After receiving certification from DOL, the employer would file a petition with DHS to import Y workers.

Y-1 nonimmigrants would be granted a period of admission of two years. This period could be extended for two additional two-year periods.[47] Between each two-year period of admission, however, the alien would have to be physically present outside the United States for 12 months. Y-2B nonimmigrants[48] would be granted a period of admission of 10 months. Following this period, they would need to be physically present outside the United States for two months before they could be readmitted to the country in Y status. There would be no limit on the number of times a Y-2B nonimmigrant could be so readmitted.

Section 409 of S. 1639 proposes annual numerical limits on the Y visas. The annual cap on the Y-1 visa would be 200,000. The Y-3 visa would be capped at 20% of the Y-1 visa annual limit The Y-2 visa would be capped at 100,000 for the first fiscal year. In subsequent years, the cap would increase or decrease based on demand for the visas, subject to a maximum cap of 200,000. In addition, §409 would establish an exemption from the Y-2B cap for workers who have been present in the United States as Y-2B aliens in any one of the three fiscal years preceding the start date of the new petition.

Z Nonimmigrants

S. 1639 also would establish another new nonimmigrant category (the Z category) for certain alien workers in the United States. Although the Z category would not be a traditional nonimmigrant worker category and would provide a mechanism for certain unauthorized aliens to legalize their status,[49] aliens granted Z status would have work authorization (and some Z aliens would be required to be employed full-time) and may perform the same type of lower-skilled work as guest workers. Under Section 601 of S. 1639, the Secretary of DHS could permit Z aliens to remain lawfully in the United States under specified conditions.

The Z-1 classification would cover aliens who have been continuously physically present in the United States since January 1, 2007, and are employed. The Z-2 and Z-3 classification would cover specified family members of Z-1 aliens, where the family members have been continuously physically present in the United States since January 1, 2007. An alien making an initial application for Z-1 status would have to pay a $1,000 penalty, as well as a $500 penalty for each alien seeking Z-2 or Z-3 status as the Z-1 applicant's derivative. Section 601 of S. 1639 would provide for certain applicants for Z status to receive probationary benefits in the form of employment authorization pending final adjudication of their applications. The period of admission for a Z nonimmigrant would be four years. Provided that the Z nonimmigrant continued to be eligible for nonimmigrant status and met additional specified requirements, the alien could seek an unlimited number of four-year extensions of the period of admission. There would be no limitation on the number of aliens who could be granted Z-1, Z-2, or Z-3 status.

The Secretary of DHS could adjust the status of a Z nonimmigrant to LPR status if specified requirements are met. Among the requirements for a Z-1 nonimmigrant to adjust status, the alien would need to have an approved immigrant petition; file an adjustment of status application in person at a U.S. consulate abroad; and, if the alien is a head of household, pay a $4,000 penalty at the time of submission of the immigrant petition.

BUSH ADMINISTRATION PROPOSAL

On January 7, 2004, President Bush outlined an immigration reform proposal, at the center of which was a new temporary worker program.[50] The President featured this proposal in his 2004, 2005, and 2006 State of the Union addresses. According to a 2004 White House fact sheet on the proposal, the temporary worker program would "match willing foreign workers with willing U.S. employers when no Americans can be found to fill the jobs." The program, which would grant participants legal temporary status, would initially be open to both foreign workers abroad and unauthorized aliens within the United States. At some future date, however, it would be restricted to aliens outside the country. The temporary workers' authorized period of stay would be three years and would be renewable for an unspecified period of time. Temporary workers would be able to travel back and forth between their home countries and the United States, and, as stated in the background briefing for reporters, would "enjoy the same protections that American workers have with respect to wages and employment rights." The proposal also called for increased workplace enforcement of immigration laws.

The proposal would not establish a special mechanism for participants in the temporary worker program to obtain LPR status. According to the fact sheet, the program "should not permit undocumented workers to gain an advantage over those who have followed the rules." Temporary workers would be expected to return to their home countries at the end of their authorized period of stay, and the Administration favored providing them with economic incentives to do so. As stated in the fact sheet:

> The U.S. will work with other countries to allow aliens working in the U.S. to receive credit in their nations' retirement systems and will support the creation of tax-preferred savings accounts they can collect when they return to their native countries.

Although it does not include a permanent legalization mechanism, the program would not prohibit temporary workers from applying for legal permanent residency under existing immigration law.

According to the Administration, the proposed temporary worker program should support efforts to improve homeland security by controlling the U.S. borders. The fact sheet states that "the program should link to efforts to control our border through agreements with countries whose nationals participate in the program," but does not elaborate further on this issue.

At the October 2005 Senate Judiciary Committee hearing on comprehensive immigration reform, Labor Secretary Elaine Chao reiterated the Administration's support for the immigration reform ideas that President Bush outlined in January 2004.[51] She did not offer a detailed legislative proposal and did not take a position on any of the pending immigration reform bills. Secretary Chao described the Administration's plan as having three components — border security, interior enforcement, and a temporary worker program — and not allowing "amnesty." She maintained that "an improved temporary worker program will enhance border security and interior enforcement by providing a workable and enforceable process for hiring foreign workers."

Both in her written testimony and in responses to Senators' questions, Secretary Chao made some general statements about the type of temporary worker program the Administration favors. She made reference to "streamlining the process so that willing workers can efficiently be matched with employers ... [when] there are no willing U.S. workers." Although she did not describe this streamlined process, she did state that private for-profit or nonprofit organizations could play a role in matching employers and workers. She also explained that under the President's temporary worker program, prospective employers would be subject to labor certification, as they currently are under the H-2A and H-2B programs. In describing how the President's program would overcome problems in existing guest worker programs, Secretary Chao referred generally to "a technologically advanced new system" through which "workers will have visa documentation that clearly establishes their eligibility to work" and "employers will have access to a verification system that enables them to quickly check the eligibility and verify the identity of potential employees."

On May 15, 2006, during Senate consideration of immigration reform legislation,[52] President Bush gave a national address on immigration reform. He voiced support for comprehensive immigration reform that accomplished five objectives, including creation of a temporary worker program. The President maintained that a temporary worker program was needed to secure U.S. borders, another of his five objectives. The President outlined the type of program he favors, as follows:

> I support a temporary worker program that would create a legal path for foreign workers to enter our country in an orderly way, for a limited period of time. This program would match willing foreign workers with willing American employers for jobs Americans are not doing. Every worker who applies for the program would be required to pass criminal background checks. And temporary workers must return to their home country at the conclusion of their stay.

POLICY CONSIDERATIONS

Issues raised in connection with temporary worker programs — such as U.S. economic development, Mexican economic development, law enforcement, and worker protections — coupled with the U.S. experience with the H-2A and H-2B programs, suggest policy issues likely to arise in the evaluation of guest worker proposals.

Comparison of Program Requirements

A new guest worker program could include agricultural workers or nonagricultural workers or both. It could replace or supplement one or both of the existing H-2A and H-2B programs. The assessment of any proposed program would likely include a comparison of the requirements of the proposed and existing programs, especially in the case of a new program covering both agricultural and nonagricultural workers since current H-2A and H-2B requirements vary considerably.

The area of wages provides an example. Under the H-2B program, employers must pay their workers at least the prevailing wage rate. Employers importing agricultural workers through the H-2A program are subject to potentially higher wage requirements. As explained above, they must pay their workers the highest of the minimum wage, the prevailing wage rate, or the AEWR. Therefore, a new guest worker program that covered both agricultural and nonagricultural workers and included a unified wage requirement would represent a change in existing wage requirements for employers.

Eligible Population

A guest worker program could be limited to aliens within the country (many of whom presumably would be unauthorized aliens) or to aliens outside the country or could include both groups. The possible participation of illegal aliens in a guest worker program is controversial. Some parties would likely see their inclusion as rewarding lawbreakers and encouraging future unauthorized immigration, especially if the program enabled some participants to obtain LPR status. The option of excluding unauthorized aliens has raised another set of concerns. Some observers maintain that a large guest worker program limited to new workers could leave unauthorized aliens in the United States particularly vulnerable to exploitation by unscrupulous employers. More generally, many who view a guest worker program as a means of addressing the unauthorized alien problem see the inclusion of unauthorized aliens as integral to any proposal.

Another eligibility question is whether the program would be limited to nationals of certain countries. The Bush Administration began discussion of a guest worker program with Mexico in 2001 as part of binational migration talks, and some immigration experts maintain that "there are very good reasons for crafting a special immigration relationship with Mexico, given its propinquity, its historical ties and NAFTA."[53] Some immigrant advocacy groups, however, have argued that it would be unfair to single out Mexicans for special treatment, especially if legalization were part of the agreement.[54]

Legalization of Program Participants

The issue of whether to include a legalization or *earned adjustment* program as part of a guest worker proposal is controversial. *Earned adjustment* is the term used to describe legalization programs that require prospective beneficiaries to "earn" LPR status through work and/or other contributions. Some see permanent legalization as an essential element of a guest worker proposal,[55] while others oppose the inclusion of any type of LPR adjustment program. In the current debate, reference is often made to two legalization programs established by the Immigration Reform and Control Act (IRCA) of 1986: (1) a general program for unauthorized aliens who had been continually resident in the United States since before January 1, 1982; and (2) a special agricultural worker (SAW) program for aliens who had worked at least 90 days in seasonal agriculture during a designated year-long period.[56] Approximately 2.7 million individuals have adjusted to LPR status under these programs.[57]

Recent H-2A reform bills suggest a willingness on the part of some policymakers to establish an earned adjustment program, at least for agricultural workers. A key set of questions about any legalization mechanism proposed as part of a guest worker program would concern the proposed legalization process and associated requirements. Major H-2A reform proposals introduced in the 107th Congress (S. 1313/H.R. 2736 and S. 1161), for example, would have established similarly structured earned adjustment programs for agricultural workers. Under both proposals, workers who had performed a requisite amount of agricultural work could have applied for temporary resident status. After satisfying additional work requirements in subsequent years, they could have applied for LPR status. The applicable requirements in the proposals, however, differed significantly. For temporary resident status, S. 1313/H.R. 2736 would have required the alien to have performed at least 540 hours, or 90 work days, of agricultural work during a 12month period. S. 1161 would have required at least 900 hours, or 150 work days, of agricultural work during a similar period. To qualify for adjustment to LPR status, S. 1313/H.R. 2736 would have required at least 540 hours, or 90 work days, of agricultural work in each of three years during a four-year period. S. 1161 would have required at least 900 hours, or 150 work days, of agricultural work in each of four years during a specified six-year period.

Various issues and concerns raised in connection with such earned adjustment proposals for agricultural workers may be relevant in assessing other guest worker legalization programs. Among these issues is the feasibility of program participants' meeting the applicable requirements to obtain legal status. S. 1161, for example, was criticized for incorporating work requirements for legalization that, some observers said, many agricultural workers could not satisfy. It also has been argued that multiyear work requirements could lead to exploitation, if workers were loathe to complain about work-related matters for fear of being fired before they had worked the requisite number of years. A possible countervailing set of considerations involves the continued availability of workers for low-skilled industries, such as agriculture, meat packing, and services industries. Some parties have expressed a general concern that a quick legalization process with light work requirements could soon deprive employers of needed workers, if some newly legalized workers were to leave certain industries to pursue more desirable job opportunities.

Treatment of Family Members

The treatment of family members under a guest worker proposal is likely to be an issue. Currently, the INA allows for the admission of the spouses and minor children of alien workers on H-2A, H-2B and other "H" visas who are accompanying the worker or following to join the worker in the United States. In considering any new program, one question would be whether guest workers coming from abroad could be accompanied by their spouses and children.

If the guest worker program in question were open to unauthorized aliens in the United States, the issue of family members would become much more complicated. Relevant questions would include the following: Would the unauthorized spouse and/or minor children of the prospective guest worker be granted some type of legal temporary resident status under the program? If not, would they be expected to leave, or be removed from, the country? If the program had a legalization component, would the spouse and children be eligible for LPR status as derivatives of the guest worker?

The treatment of family members became a significant issue in the 1986 legalization programs described above. As enacted, IRCA required all aliens to qualify for legalization on their own behalf; it made no provision for granting derivative LPR status to spouses and children. Legalized aliens, thus, needed to file immigrant visa petitions on behalf of their family members. These filings were primarily in the family preference category covering spouses and children of LPRs (category 2A) and had the effect of lengthening waiting times in this category.[58] To partially address the increased demand for visa numbers, the Immigration Act of 1990[59] made a limited number of additional visa numbers available for spouses and children of IRCA-legalized aliens for FY1992 through FY1994. It also provided for temporary stays of deportation and work authorization for certain spouses and children of IRCA-legalized aliens in the United States.

As suggested by the experience of the IRCA programs, the treatment of family members in any guest worker program with a legalization component could have broad implications for the U.S. immigration system. Even in the absence of a legalization component, however, the treatment of family members in a guest worker program could have important ramifications. With respect to the program itself, for example, it could affect the willingness of aliens to apply to participate.

Labor Market Test

A key question about any guest worker program is the type of labor market conditions that would have to exist, if any, in order for an employer to import alien workers.[60] Under both the H-2A and H-2B programs, employers interested in hiring foreign workers must first go through the process of labor certification. Intended to protect job opportunities for U.S. workers, labor certification entails a determination of whether qualified U.S. workers are available to perform the needed work and whether the hiring of foreign workers will adversely affect the wages and working conditions of similarly employed U.S. workers. As described above, recruitment is the primary method used to determine U.S. worker availability. While there is widespread agreement on the goals of labor certification, the process itself has been criticized for being cumbersome, slow, and ineffective in protecting U.S. workers.[61]

A proposed guest worker program could retain some form of labor certification or could establish a different process for determining if employers could bring in foreign workers. As described above, past legislative proposals to reform the H-2A program sought to overhaul current labor certification requirements by, for example, establishing a system of worker registries. Another option suggested by some in H2A reform debates is to adopt the more streamlined labor market test used in the temporary worker program for professional specialty workers (H-1B program). That test, known as labor attestation, requires employers to attest to various conditions. Some argue that labor attestation is inadequate for unskilled jobs without educational requirements. Assuming that protecting U.S. workers remained a policy priority, the labor market test incorporated in any guest worker program would need to be evaluated to determine whether it would likely serve this purpose.

Numerical Limits

Related to the issues of labor market tests and U.S. worker protections is the question of numerical limitations on a guest worker program. A numerical cap provides a means, separate from the labor market test, of limiting the number of foreign workers. Currently, as explained above, the H-2A program is not numerically limited, while the H-2B program is capped at 66,000 annually. Like the H-2B program, other capped temporary worker programs have fixed statutory numerical limits. By contrast, a guest worker program that was outlined by former Senator Phil Gramm during the 107th Congress, but never introduced as legislation, included a different type of numerical cap — one that would have varied annually based on regional unemployment rates. According to the program prospectus released by Senator Gramm:

> Except for seasonal work, the number of guest workers permitted to enroll would be adjusted annually in response to changes in U.S. economic conditions, specifically unemployment rates, on a region-by-region basis.

Numerical limitations also are relevant in the context of unauthorized immigration. Some view a temporary worker program as a way to begin reducing the size of the current unauthorized alien population and/or future inflows. In light of the estimated current size and annual growth rate of the unauthorized population, it could be argued that a guest worker program would need to be sizeable to have any significant impact. On the other hand, critics contend that a guest worker program, especially a large one, would be a counterproductive means of controlling unauthorized immigration. In their view, temporary worker programs serve to increase, not reduce, the size of the unauthorized population.

Enforcement

Another important consideration is how the terms of a guest worker program would be enforced. Relevant questions include what types of mechanisms would be used to ensure that employers complied with program requirements. With respect to the H-2A program, for example, the INA authorizes the Labor Secretary to —

> take such actions, including imposing appropriate penalties and seeking appropriate injunctive relief and specific performance of contractual obligations, as may be necessary to assure employer compliance with terms and conditions of employment ...[62]

A related question is whether the enforcement system would be complaint-driven or whether the appropriate entity could take action in the absence of a specific complaint.

Another enforcement-related question is what type of mechanism, if any, would be used to ensure that guest workers departed the country at the end of their authorized period of stay. Historically, the removal of aliens who have overstayed their visas and thereby lapsed into unauthorized status, but have not committed crimes, has not been a priority of the U.S. immigration system. Some have suggested that a large scale guest worker program could help address the problem of visa overstaying and unauthorized immigration generally by severely limiting job opportunities for unauthorized aliens. Others doubt, however, that large numbers of unauthorized residents would voluntarily leave the country; as explained above, they argue instead that a new guest worker program would likely increase the size of the unauthorized alien population as many guest workers opted to overstay their visas.

Other ideas have been put forth to facilitate the departure of temporary workers at the end of their authorized period of stay. One suggestion is to involve the workers' home countries in the guest worker program. Another option is to create an incentive for foreign workers to leave the United States by, for example, withholding or otherwise setting aside a sum of money for each worker that would only become available once the worker returned home. In evaluating any such financially based incentive system, it may be useful to consider, among other questions, how much money would be available to a typical worker and whether such an amount would likely provide an adequate incentive to return home.

Homeland Security

A final consideration relates to border and homeland security, matters of heightened concern since the terrorist attacks of September 11, 2001. Supporters of new temporary worker programs argue that such programs would make the United States more secure. They cite security-related benefits of knowing the identities of currently unknown individuals in the country and of legalizing the inflow of alien workers and thereby freeing border personnel to concentrate on potential criminal and terrorist threats. Opponents reject the idea that guest worker programs improve homeland security and generally focus on the dangers of rewarding immigration law violators with temporary or permanent legal status. Security concerns may affect various aspects of a temporary worker program. Possible security-related provisions that may be considered as part of a new guest worker program include special screening of participants, monitoring while in the United States, and issuance of fraud-resistant documents.

CONCLUSION

The question of a new guest worker program is controversial. A key reason for this is the interrelationship between the recent discussion of guest worker programs and the issue of unauthorized immigration. The size of the current resident unauthorized alien population in the United States, along with continued unauthorized immigration and related deaths at the U.S.-Mexico border, are major factors cited in support of a new temporary worker program. At the same time, the importance of enforcing immigration law and not rewarding illegal aliens with any type of legalized status are primary reasons cited in opposition to such a program. It would seem that some bridging of this gap on the unauthorized alien question — perhaps in some of the areas analyzed above — would be a prerequisite to gaining broad support for a guest worker proposal.

REFERENCES

[1]   For additional information on these historical programs, see U.S. Congress, Senate Committee on the Judiciary, *Temporary Worker Programs: Background and Issues*, committee print, 96th Cong., 2nd sess., February 1980.

[2]   Act of June 27, 1952, ch. 477, codified at 8 U.S.C.§1101 *et seq.* The INA is the basis of current immigration law.

[3]   P.L. 99-603, November 6, 1986.

[4]   For an overview of the INA's nonimmigrant visa categories, see CRS Report RL31381, *U.S. Immigration Policy on Temporary Admissions*, by Ruth Ellen Wasem, and Chad C. Haddal.

[5]   While H-2B workers are, for the most part, low skilled, the H-2B program is not limited to workers of a particular skill level and has been used to import a variety of workers, including entertainers and athletes.

[6]   Prior to March 1, 2003, the H-2A and H-2B programs were administered by ETA and the Immigration and Naturalization Service (INS) of the Department of Justice. The Homeland Security Act of 2002 (P.L. 107-296, November 25, 2002) abolished INS and transferred most of its functions to DHS as of March 1.

[7]   The prevailing wage rate is the average wage paid to similarly employed workers in the occupation in the area of intended employment. Additional information about prevailing wages is available at [http://www.foreignlaborcert.doleta.gov/wages.cfm].

[8]   The AEWR is an hourly wage rate set by DOL for each state or region, based upon data gathered by the Department of Agriculture in quarterly wage surveys. For 2006, the AEWR ranges from $7.58 for Arkansas, Louisiana, and Mississippi to $9.99 for Hawaii. See CRS Report RL32861, *Farm Labor: The Adverse Effect Wage Rate (AEWR)*, by William G. Whittaker.

[9]   Required wages and benefits under the H-2A program are set forth in 20 C.F.R. §655.102.

[10]   H-2A workers, like nonimmigrants generally, are not eligible for federally funded public assistance, with the exception of Medicaid emergency services. For further information on alien eligibility for federal benefits, see CRS Report RL31114, *Noncitizen Eligibility for Major Federal Public Assistance Programs: Policies and Legislation*, by Ruth Ellen Wasem (Hereafter cited as CRS Report RL31114); and CRS Report RL31630, *Federal Funding for Unauthorized Aliens' Emergency Medical Expenses*, by Alison M. Siskin.

[11]   There is no precise measure available of the number of the aliens granted H-2A status in any given year. While visa data provide an approximation, these data are subject to limitations, among them that not all H-2A workers are necessarily issued visas and not all aliens who are issued visas necessarily use them to enter the United States.

[12]   For additional discussion, see CRS Report RL30395, *Farm Labor Shortages and Immigration Policy*, by Linda Levine.

[13]   Included in this three-year period is any time an H-2B alien spent in the United States under the "H" (temporary worker) or "L" (temporary intracompany transferee) visa categories.

[14] While not subject to the broader transportation requirements of the H-2A program, H-2B employers are required by law to pay the reasonable costs of return transportation abroad for an H-2B worker who is dismissed prior to the end of his or her authorized period of stay.

[15] The proposed USCIS rule is available at [http://a257.g.akamaitech.net/7/257/2422/01jan20051800/edocket.access.gpo.gov/2005/05-1240.htm]. DOL has published a companion proposal, which is available at [http://a257.g.akamaitech.net/7/257/2422/01jan20051800/edocket.access.gpo.gov/2005/05-1222.htm].

[16] For information on the H-1B nonimmigrant classification, see CRS Report RL30498, *Immigration: Legislative Issues on Nonimmigrant Professional Specialty (H-1B) Workers*, by Ruth Ellen Wasem.

[17] For definitions of these types of need, see 8 C.F.R. §214.2(h)(6)(ii).

[18] See INA §214(g)(1)(B).

[19] There is no precise measure available of the number of the aliens granted H-2B status in any given year. While visa data provide an approximation, these data are subject to limitations, among them that not all H-2A workers are necessarily issued visas and not all aliens who are issued visas necessarily use them to enter the United States.

[20] See discussion below of S. 352/H.R. 793 in the 109th Congress.

[21] U.S. Department of Homeland Security, U.S. Citizenship and Immigration Services, "USCIS to Accept Additional H-2B Filings for FY2005 and FY2006," public notice, May 23, 2005.

[22] Jeffrey S. Passel, *Estimates of the Size and Characteristics of the Undocumented Population*, Pew Hispanic Center, March 21, 2005; Jeffrey S. Passel, *Size and Characteristics of the Unauthorized Migrant Population in the U.S.; Estimates Based on the March 2005 Current Population Survey*, Pew Hispanic Center, March 7, 2006 (hereafter cited as Passel, *Size and Characteristics of the Unauthorized Migrant Population in the U.S.*, March 7, 2006). These reports are available at [http://pewhispanic.org/topics/index.php?TopicID=16].

[23] U.S. Department of Homeland Security, Office of Immigration Statistics, *Estimates of the Unauthorized Immigrant Population Residing in the United States: January 2005*, by Michael Hoefer, Nancy Rytina, and Christopher Campbell, August 2006.

[24] For further information on migrant deaths, see CRS Report RL32562, *Border Security: The Role of the U.S. Border Patrol*, by Blas Nuñez-Neto.

[25] Passel, *Size and Characteristics of the Unauthorized Migrant Population in the U.S.*, March 7, 2006, at [http://pewhispanic.org/reports/report.php?ReportID=61].

[26] Ibid., pp. 10-11.

[27] During the 107th Congress, former Senator Phil Gramm released a preliminary proposal for a new U.S.-Mexico guest worker program that would have covered both agricultural and nonagricultural workers, but he did not introduce legislation.

[28] Although S. 1814 and H.R. 4056 are not identical, they are treated as companion bills for the purposes of this discussion because they are highly similar.

[29] For a discussion of the U.S. system of permanent admissions, including numerical limits, see CRS Report RL32235, *U.S. Immigration Policy on Permanent Admissions*, by Ruth Ellen Wasem. (Hereafter cited as CRS Report RL32235.)

[30] For information on noncitizen eligibility for federal public benefits, see CRS Report RL31114.

[31] This description of S. 1387 is based on both the bill text and clarifications provided by Sen. Cornyn's office by telephone on July 22, 2003. Some clarifying language may need to be added to the bill.

[32] Although S. 352 and H.R. 793 are not identical, they are treated as companion bills here because they are nearly identical and none of their differences are substantive. The full short title of S. 352 is Save Our Small and Seasonal Businesses of 2005.

[33] The blue card status proposed under this bill is different than the blue card status proposed in S. 2087 (discussed below).

[34] For information on numerical limits, see CRS Report RL32235.

[35] Separate provisions in S. 359/H.R. 884 would have established a two-stage legalization program for agricultural workers.

[36] For information on numerical limits, see CRS Report RL32235.

[37] H.R. 3857 would not have established a mechanism for agricultural workers to obtain LPR status.

[38] For information on the entry-exit system issue, see CRS Report RL32234, *U.S. Visitor and Immigrant Status Indicator Technology (US-VISIT) Program*, by Lisa M. Seghetti and Stephen R. Viña.

[39] For an explanation of INA §245(i), see CRS Report RL31373, *Immigration: Adjustment to Permanent Resident Status Under Section 245(i)*, by Andorra Bruno.

[40] INA §212(a)(9)(B). This ground of inadmissibility, known as the "3 and 10 year bars," applies to aliens who have been unlawfully present in the United States for more than 180 days and who then depart or are removed.

[41] A "work day" is defined in the legislation as a day in which the individual is employed for at least 5.75 hours in agricultural employment.

[42] For information on numerical limits, see CRS Report RL32235.

[43] S.Amdt. 1150, the bipartisan compromise proposal for immigration reform, was proposed by Senator Kennedy as an amendment in the nature of a substitute to S. 1348. (The text of S.Amdt. 1150 appears in "Text of Amendment Submitted Monday, May 21, 2007," *Congressional Record*, daily edition, vol.153 (May 24, 2007), pp. S6625-S6687.) S. 1348, the Comprehensive Immigration Reform Act of 2007, was introduced by Senate Majority Leader Reid as the marker for Senate debate on comprehensive immigration reform; it is based on S. 2611, as passed by the Senate in the 109th Congress (discussed above).

[44] A "work day" is defined in the legislation as a day in which the individual is employed for at least 5.75 hours in agricultural employment.

[45] For information on numerical limits, see CRS Report RL32235.

[46] S. 1639 § 403(a) would define an alien admitted to the United States under the new Y-2 nonimmigrant classification as a "Y-2B nonimmigrant" or "Y-2B worker."

[47] Y-1 nonimmigrants who are accompanied by family members in Y-3 status would be limited to one additional two-year period.

[48] S. 1639 § 403(a) would define an alien admitted to the United States under the new Y-2 nonimmigrant classification as a "Y-2B nonimmigrant" or "Y-2B worker."

[49] While Z status would be available to otherwise eligible unauthorized aliens in the United States, unlawful status would not be an explicit requirement for Z status. Instead, to be eligible for Z status under §601, an alien could *not* have been lawfully present in the United States on January 1, 2007, or on the date of application for Z

status under any nonimmigrant classification or any other immigration status made available under a treaty or other multinational agreement ratified by the Senate.

[50] The Administration did *not* offer a detailed legislative proposal. Some materials on the Administration proposal, however, are available on the White House website. The President's January 7, 2004, remarks on the proposal are available at [http://www.whitehouse.gov/news/releases/2004/01/print/20040107-3.html]. A fact sheet on the proposal, entitled *Fair and Secure Immigration Reform* is available at [http://www.whitehouse.gov/news/releases/2004/01/print/20040107-3.html]. The transcript of a January 6, 2004 background briefing for reporters is available at [http://www.whitehouse.gov/news/releases/2004/01/print/20040106-3.html].

[51] Secretary Chao's written testimony is available at [http://judiciary.senate.gov/hearing .cfm?id=1634].

[52] See above discussion of S. 2611 in the 109th Congress.

[53] Comment of T. Alexander Aleinikoff, Migration Policy Institute. Quoted in Eric Schmitt, "The Nation: Separate and Unequal; You Can Come In. You Stay Out," *New York Times*, July 29, 2001, Section 4, p. 5.

[54] President Bush was asked in July 2001 whether an immigration proposal under consideration at the time to legalize the status of some unauthorized Mexicans would be expanded to cover immigrants from other countries. The President responded, "We'll consider all folks here," but did not provide further details. See Edwin Chen and Jonathan Peterson, "Bush Hints at Broader Amnesty," *Los Angeles Times*, July 27, 2001, Part A, part 1, p. 1.

[55] For example, in an August 2001 letter to President Bush and Mexican President Vicente Fox setting forth the Democrats' immigration principles, then-Senate Majority Leader Thomas Daschle and then-House Minority Leader Richard Gephardt stated that "no migration proposal can be complete without an earned adjustment program."

[56] P.L. 99-603, November 6, 1986. The general legalization program is at INA §245A, and the SAW program is at INA §210.

[57] Certain individuals who had not legalized under the general program and were participants in specified class action lawsuits were given a new time-limited opportunity to adjust to LPR status by the Legal Immigration Family Equity Act (LIFE; P.L. 106-553, Appendix B, Title XI, December 21, 2000) and the LIFE Act Amendments (P.L. 106-554, Appendix D, Title XV, December 21, 2000).

[58] See CRS Report RL32235.

[59] P.L. 101-649, November 29, 1990.

[60] Questions about the existence of industry-wide labor shortages are outside the scope of this report. For a discussion of the shortage issue with respect to agriculture, see CRS Report RL30395, *Farm Labor Shortages and Immigration Policy*, by Linda Levine. Also see CRS Report 95-712, *The Effects on U.S. Farm Workers of an Agricultural Guest Worker Program*, by Linda Levine.

[61] See U.S. Department of Labor, Office of Inspector General, *Consolidation of Labor's Enforcement Responsibilities for the H-2A Program Could Better Protect U.S. Agricultural Workers*, Report Number 04-98-004-03-321, March 31, 1998.

[62] INA §218(g)(2).

In: Immigration Crisis: Issues, Policies and Consequences   ISBN: 978-1-60456-096-1
Editors: P. W. Hickman and T. P. Curtis, pp. 41-72   © 2008 Nova Science Publishers, Inc.

Chapter 2

ENFORCING IMMIGRATION LAW: THE ROLE OF STATE AND LOCAL LAW ENFORCEMENT*

Lisa M. Seghetti, Stephen R. Vina and Karma Ester[3]

ABSTRACT

Since the September 11, 2001, terrorist attacks, the enforcement of our nation's immigration laws has received a significant amount of attention. Some observers contend that the federal government does not have adequate resources to enforce immigration law and that state and local law enforcement entities should be utilized. Several proposals introduced in the 109th Congress would enhance the role of state and local officials in the enforcement of immigration law, including H.R. 4437, S. 2612, S. 2454, H.R. 2092, H.R. 3137, S. 1362, S. 1438, H.R. 3333, H.R. 3776, H.R. 3938, S. 2611, and H.R. 1817. This proposed shift has prompted many to question what role state and local law enforcement agencies should have in the enforcement of immigration law, if any.

Congress defined our nation's immigration laws in the Immigration and Nationality Act (INA) (8 U.S.C. §§1101 *et seq.*), which contains both *criminal* and *civil* enforcement measures. Historically, the authority for state and local law enforcement officials to enforce immigration law has been construed to be limited to the *criminal* provisions of the INA; by contrast, the enforcement of the *civil* provisions, which includes apprehension and removal of deportable aliens, has strictly been viewed as a federal responsibility, with states playing an incidental supporting role. The legislative proposals that have been introduced, however, would appear to expand the role of state and local law enforcement agencies in the *civil* enforcement aspects of the INA.

Congress, through various amendments to the INA, has gradually broadened the authority for state and local law enforcement officials to enforce immigration law, and some recent statutes have begun to carve out possible state roles in the enforcement of *civil* matters. Indeed, several jurisdictions have signed agreements (INA §287(g)) with the federal government to allow their respective state and local law enforcement agencies to perform new, limited duties relating to immigration law enforcement. Still, the enforcement of immigration by state and local officials has sparked debate among many who question what the proper role of state and local law enforcement officials should be

---

* Excerpted from CRS Report RL32270, dated August 14, 2006.

in enforcing immigration law. For example, many have expressed concern over proper training, finite resources at the local level, possible civil rights violations, and the overall impact on communities. Some localities, for example, even provide "sanctuary" for illegal aliens and will generally promote policies that ensure such aliens will not be turned over to federal authorities.

This report examines some of the policy and legal issues that may accompany the increasing role of state and local law officials in the enforcement of immigration law. This report will be updated as warranted.

INTRODUCTION

Since the September 11, 2001, terrorist attacks, the enforcement of our nation's immigration laws has received a significant amount of attention. Some observers contend that the federal government has scarce resources to enforce immigration law and that state and local law enforcement entities should be utilized. To this end, several proposals have been introduced in the 109th Congress that would enhance the role of state and local law officials in the enforcement of immigration law. Still, many continue to question what role state and local law enforcement agencies should have in light of limited state and local resources and immigration expertise.

States and localities bear the primary responsibility for defining and prosecuting crimes. But beyond enforcing the laws or ordinances of their state or locality, state and local officials may also have the authority to enforce some federal laws, especially criminal laws. Immigration law provides for both *criminal* punishments (e.g., alien smuggling, which is prosecuted in the courts) and *civil* violations (e.g., lack of legal status, which may lead to removal through a separate administrative system). The states and localities have traditionally only been permitted to directly enforce the *criminal* provisions, whereas the enforcement of the *civil* provisions has been viewed as a federal responsibility with states playing an incidental supporting role.

The Immigration and Nationality Act (INA) (8 U.S.C. §§1101 *et seq.*) currently provides limited avenues for state enforcement of both its *civil* and *criminal* provisions. The legislative proposals that have been introduced, however, would appear to expand the role of state and local law enforcement agencies in the *civil* regulatory aspects of immigration law (i.e., identifying and detaining deportable aliens for purposes of removal). Adding the enforcement of *civil* immigration law to the role of state and local law enforcement could, in essence, involve the agencies in a seemingly unfamiliar mission. This potential expansion has prompted many to examine the legal authority by which state and local law enforcement agencies may enforce immigration law, particularly the civil enforcement measures.

This report examines the role of state and local law enforcement in enforcing immigration law. The discussion is limited to the role of state and local law enforcement in the investigation, arrest, and detention of all immigration violators. The report does not discuss the prosecution, adjudication, or removal of aliens who violate the law. The report opens with a brief discussion of the types of immigration interior enforcement activities that the former Immigration and Naturalization Service (INS) pursued and the current immigration activities that are now the focus of the Department of Homeland Security (DHS). A discussion of the legal authority that permits state and local law enforcement to enforce immigration law under certain circumstances follows. Current administrative efforts to involve state and local law enforcement in enforcing immigration law as well as selected issues are discussed. The report concludes with a discussion of the pros and cons of such a policy and an analysis of policy options for Congress.

BACKGROUND

The enforcement of immigration laws in the interior of the United States has been controversial. Traditionally, the debate posed concern over large numbers of "lawbreakers" (i.e., illegal aliens) depressing wages against perceptions that foreign labor benefits the economy and promotes relations with "source" countries. Nonetheless, after the attacks of September 11, attention refocused on the adequacy of interior immigration enforcement, especially the perceived lack of federal resources. Prior to the September 11, 2001 terrorist attacks, the INS had fewer than 2,000 immigration agents to enforce immigration laws within the United States. Although that number has not changed since the terrorist attacks, the merger of the interior enforcement function of the former INS with the investigative arm of the U.S. Customs Service (Customs) into the Bureau of Immigration and Customs Enforcement (ICE), which is located in DHS, has doubled the number of interior agents potentially available to enforce immigration laws.[1]

In spite of the increase in interior enforcement agents, many continue to believe that the number is still insufficient. Moreover, although the consolidation increased the number of interior enforcement agents, they now have multiple missions, which include enforcing immigration law in the interior of the United States, stemming the flow of illicit drugs, and deterring money laundering, among other things.

The enforcement of immigration law within the interior of the United States includes investigating aliens who violate the INA and other related laws. Prior to September 11, 2001, immigration interior enforcement focused on investigating: (1) aliens committing crimes; (2) suspected fraudulent activities (i.e., possessing or manufacturing fraudulent immigration documents); (3) suspected smuggling and trafficking of aliens; and (4) suspected work site violations, frequently involving aliens who work without legal permission and employers who knowingly hire illegal aliens. Since the terrorist attacks, however, the majority of ICE's resources have been directed at stemming terrorist-related activities and activities that have a national security interest.

Currently, there are express provisions in federal law that provide state and local law enforcement the authority to assist federal officers with the enforcement of immigration law under certain circumstances. Such authorities were enacted into law in 1996 in §439 of the Antiterrorism and Effective Death Penalty Act (AEDPA; P.L. 104-132) and §133 and §372 of the Illegal Immigration Reform and Immigrant Responsibility Act of 1996 (IIRIRA; P.L. 104-206).[2] In addition to the provisions enacted in AEDPA and IIRIRA, the DHS has several initiatives with state and local law enforcement agencies to facilitate the investigation, arrest and apprehension of foreign nationals who have violated the law, as discussed below.

Alien Criminal Apprehension Program

The Alien Criminal Apprehension Program (ACAP) was established in 1991 by the former INS. Through ACAP, criminal aliens are identified by immigration officials after they have been notified by state and local law enforcement officials. Upon an encounter with an immigrant whose immigration status may be in question, state and local law enforcement officials notify immigration officials, who determine the immigrant's status and, if applicable, take the immigrant into federal custody.

Quick Response Teams

Congress first authorized the former INS to establish Quick Response Teams (QRTs) in the Omnibus Consolidated and Emergency Supplemental Appropriations Act, FY1999 (P.L. 105-277). QRTs apprehend illegal aliens and deport them back to their country by working directly with state and local law enforcement officers. QRTs respond to requests from state and local law enforcement authorities who believe they have an illegal immigrant in custody. QRTs are established in areas that have experienced an increase in illegal immigration and are comprised of federal, state and local law enforcement officials. The federal law enforcement officials on a QRT usually include special agents, immigration officers and detention and removal officers. As of September 30, 2002, there were 45 QRTs in 11 different states. Congress appropriated funding for QRTs in FY1999 and FY2001.[3]

Absconder Apprehension Initiative

The Absconder Apprehension Initiative was initially created to clear up the backlog of cases of aliens who had an unexecuted final order of removal. Absconders are unauthorized or criminal aliens or nonimmigrants who violated immigration law and have been ordered deported by an immigration court. Although the identification and removal of criminal aliens had been a focus of the former INS, the terrorist attacks brought renewed interest in their removal. In 2001, the former INS Commissioner, James Ziglar, in cooperation with the Federal Bureau of Investigation (FBI), decided to list the names of absconders in the FBI's National Criminal Information Center (NCIC).[4]

CURRENT PRACTICES

Although there is quite a bit of debate with respect to state and local law enforcement officers' authority to enforce immigration law (see discussion below), as a matter of practice, it is permissible for state and local law enforcement officers to inquire into the status of an immigrant during the course of their normal duties in enforcing state and local law. This practice allows state and local law enforcement officers to play an indirect role that is incidental to their general criminal enforcement authority.

For example, when state or local officers question the immigration status of someone they have detained for a state or local violation, they may contact an ICE agent at the Law Enforcement Support Center (LESC).[5] The federal agent may then place a detainer on the suspect, requesting the state official to keep the suspect in custody until a determination can be made as to the suspect's immigration status. However, the continued detention of such a suspect beyond the needs of local law enforcement designed to aid in the enforcement of federal immigration laws may be unlawful.[6]

Indirect state participation by means of immigration detainers is not without controversy. Many have alleged such abuses as state detentions premised on immigrant status alone and custodial arrests for traffic violations or similar offenses as pretexts for verifying an individual's status with immigration authorities. Past allegations of abuse at times have led to states and localities entering into consent decrees that strictly limit their role in the enforcement of immigration law. On the other hand, some localities have been concerned that an active role in enforcing immigration law may stretch resources and hinder community cooperation in curbing criminal activity. (See discussion on Sanctuary States and Cities.)

AUTHORITIES TO ENFORCE IMMIGRATION LAW

The power to prescribe rules as to which aliens may enter the United States and which aliens may be removed solely resides with the federal government,[7] particularly with the Congress. To implement its plenary power, Congress has enacted and amended the INA — a comprehensive set of rules for legal immigration, naturalization, deportation, and enforcement. Concomitant to its exclusive power to determine which aliens may enter and which may stay, the federal government also has power to proscribe activities that subvert these rules (e.g., alien smuggling) and to set criminal or civil penalties for those who undertake these activities.

In examining the INA, it is crucial to distinguish the civil from criminal violations. Mere illegal presence in the U.S. is a *civil*, not criminal, violation of the INA, and subsequent deportation and associated administrative processes are civil proceedings.[8] For instance, a lawfully admitted non-immigrant alien may become deportable if his visitor's visa expires or if his student status changes. Criminal violations of the INA, on the other hand, include felonies and misdemeanors and are prosecuted in the federal courts. These types of violations include, for example, 8 U.S.C. §1324, which addresses the bringing in and harboring of certain undocumented aliens; §1325(a), which addresses the illegal entry of aliens; and §1326, which penalizes the reentry of aliens previously excluded or deported.[9]

Congress also has exclusive authority to prescribe procedures for determining who may enter or stay and the right of aliens in these proceedings, subject to the individual rights all aliens in the United States enjoy under the Constitution. However, exclusive authority to prescribe the rules on immigration[10] does not necessarily imply exclusive authority to enforce those rules. While enforcement standards and procedures may differ between the criminal and civil aspects of immigration law, Congress may authorize the states to assist in enforcing both, and state officers may exercise this authority to the degree permitted under federal and state law. There is a notion, however — one being more frequently articulated by the federal courts and the Executive branch — that states have "inherent" authority to enforce at least the federal *criminal* law related to immigration. This inherent authority position is now apparently beginning to be expressed with regard to the enforcement of the *civil* aspects of immigration law as well. State enforcement, nonetheless, must always be consistent with federal authority.

Even assuming states have some inherent authority to enforce immigration law, federal law preempts inconsistent state law where concurrent jurisdiction exists. Congress' power to preempt state law arises from the Supremacy Clause of the Constitution, which provides that "the Laws of the United States ... shall be the supreme Law of the Land ... any Thing in the Constitution or Laws of any State to the Contrary notwithstanding."[11] Congressional intent is paramount in preemption analysis; accordingly, a court must determine whether Congress expressly or implicitly intended to preempt state or local action.[12] Generally, a court will determine that Congress intended to preempt a state regulation or enforcement when (1) Congress expresses preemptive intent in "explicit statutory language," (2) when a state entity regulates "in a field that Congress intended the Federal Government to occupy exclusively," or (3) when a state entity's activity "actually conflicts with federal law."[13]

STATE INVOLVEMENT IN THE ENFORCEMENT
OF IMMIGRATION LAW

Setting the rules on the entry and removal of aliens is unquestionably an exclusive federal power and some would argue that uniformity in enforcing those rules is critical to the exercise of sovereign authority (i.e., it should *not* be enforced by states).[14] Accordingly, it has been suggested that state involvement in immigration law should be strictly limited to express congressional indication for such participation.[15] On the other hand, Congress can not compel the states to enforce federal immigration law and to do so in a particular way.[16]

From the states' point of view, the federal government's exclusive power over immigration does not preempt every state activity affecting aliens.[17] And it generally has been assumed that state and local officers may enforce the *criminal* provisions of the INA if state law permits them to do so but are precluded from directly enforcing the INA's *civil* provisions[18] This view may be changing, however.

State enforcement of the criminal provisions of the INA is seen as being consistent with the state's police power to make arrests for criminal acts and the expectation that states are expected to cooperate in the enforcement of federal criminal laws.[19] Civil immigration law enforcement, on the other hand, has generally been viewed as strictly a federal responsibility: The civil provisions of the INA have been assumed to constitute a pervasive and preemptive regulatory scheme — leaving no room for a direct state or local role.[20] The distinction between civil and criminal violations in the INA has been seen to suggest a bifurcated role for states and localities. For example, state and local law enforcement officers cannot arrest someone solely for illegal presence for the purpose of deporting them because it is a civil violation, but they can arrest someone for the criminal offense of entering the country illegally.[21] To the degree that it is not preempted, the authority of state and local law enforcement officers to investigate and arrest for violations of federal law is determined by reference to state law.[22] This may be done through express authorization in state law. However, this may not be necessary according to some recent decisions from the Tenth

Circuit that appear to suggest that state and local law enforcement officers may possess "inherent authority" within their respective jurisdictions to investigate and make arrests for criminal immigration matters.

The following sections briefly examine Department of Justice, Office of Legal Counsel (OLC) opinions that have examined immigration enforcement authority, analyze the major cases on the issue, and describe current provisions in law that authorize state and local involvement in the enforcement of immigration law.

Office of Legal Counsel Opinions

Several Administrations have spoken on the scope of state and local involvement. For example, a 1978 press release during the Carter Administration stressed the need for cooperation and joint federal/state law enforcement operations, but placed much emphasis on the exclusive federal role to enforce *civil* immigration law and the special training required to do so.[23] A 1983 statement issued by the Reagan Justice Department emphasized similar cooperative measures, but still made clear that *only* INS could make arrests for *civil* immigration violations and that state and local cooperation consisted primarily of notifying INS about, and detaining, suspected illegal aliens taken into police custody for state/local violations.[24] In 1989, the Department of Justice, OLC opined that local police could enforce the criminal violations of the INA, but stated that it was "unclear"under current law whether local police could enforce non-criminal federal statutes.[25] More recently, a 1996 OLC opinion concluded that state and local police *did* possess the authority to arrest aliens for *criminal* violations of the INA, but lacked recognized legal authority to enforce the *civil* provisions of immigration law.[26]

A shift in policy towards increasing the role and authority of local law enforcement officers in the field of immigration enforcement came following the terrorist attacks in September 2001. In December 2001 the INS reportedly began sending the names of thousands of noncitizens to the NCIC databases as part of the Absconder Apprehension Initiative. At a 2002 press conference, Attorney General Ashcroft confirmed the existence of a new OLC opinion that, among other things, expressed the department's view that state and local officials have "inherent authority" to enforce federal immigration law, including the *civil* enforcement provisions. According to the Attorney General:

> When federal, state and local law enforcement officers encounter an alien of national security concern who has been listed on the NCIC for violating immigration law, federal law permits them to arrest that person and transfer him to the custody of the INS. The Justice Department's Office of Legal Counsel has concluded that this narrow, limited mission that we are asking state and local police to undertake voluntarily — arresting aliens who have violated criminal provisions of the Immigration and Nationality Act or *civil provisions* that render an alien deportable, and who are listed on the NCIC — is within the *inherent authority* of states.[27] (*emphasis* added)

Initially, the Department of Justice did not release or publish the 2002 OLC opinion. Accordingly, several immigrant and public interest groups sought disclosure under the Freedom of Information Act (FOIA). The department, however, claimed that the memorandum was exempt from disclosure under FOIA based on the deliberative process and attorney-client privileges. A lawsuit seeking the release of the 2002 OLC opinion was subsequently filed by the groups against the Department of Justice. In May of 2005, the Second Circuit granted the interest groups' FOIA request and mandated that the department release the 2002 OLC opinion.[28] The department released the opinion in July of 2005 but was allowed to redact certain sections.[29]

The 2002 OLC opinion concludes that (1) states have inherent power, subject to federal preemption, to make arrests for violations of federal law; (2) the advice provided in the 1996 OLC opinion that federal law precludes state police from arresting aliens on the basis of civil deportability was mistaken; and (3) 8 U.S.C. §1252c did not preempt state authority to arrest for federal violations. As to the first conclusion, the opinion focuses on the authority of states, as *sovereign entities,* to retain certain police powers under the Constitution, namely, the inherent authority to make arrests for a violation of federal law. With respect to the second conclusion, the 2002 opinion discredits much of the authority cited in the 1996 and 1989 opinions, takes into account case law not previously considered, and frames the preemption issue differently (from the earlier opinions).[30] The analysis under the third conclusion examines the legislative history of §1252c and a Tenth Circuit case to find a strong presumption against preemption.

Critics have described the newly released opinion as "deeply flawed" and unsupported by legislative history or judicial precedent.[31] It has been stated, for example, that (1) immigration has long been recognized as a distinctly federal concern; (2) federal law authorizes state and local enforcement of the immigration laws only in specific circumstances, not broadly; (3) the opinion does not address the significant distinction between criminal and non-criminal enforcement; and (4) the opinion could have implications far beyond the immigration context.[32] It should also be recognized that although the 2002 OLC opinion describes a position in contrast to previous policy, it cannot compel state action nor does it carry the same weight as an act of Congress. Generally, interpretations contained in opinion letters are not controlling and should be followed only insofar as they have the "power to persuade."[33]

Case Law

The issue of whether state and local law enforcement agencies are precluded from enforcing provisions of the INA was analyzed in the Ninth Circuit case of *Gonzalez* v. *City of Peoria.*[34] In *Gonzalez,* the Ninth Circuit examined the City of Peoria's policies that authorized local officers to arrest illegal immigrants for violating the *criminal* entry provision of the INA (8 U.S.C. §1325).[35] The arrestees claimed that the INA represented a full federal occupation of the field, which would in turn preempt state action. The court turned to the legislative history of §1324(c)[36] and determined that when Congress specifically removed language limiting the enforcement of §1324 to federal officers and inserted specific language authorizing local enforcement, that "it implicitly made the local enforcement authority as to all three criminal statutes (i.e., §§1324, 1325, 1326) identical."[37] Accordingly, the Ninth Circuit declared that local police officers may, subject to state law, constitutionally stop or detain individuals when there is reasonable suspicion or, in the case of arrests, probable cause that such persons have violated, or are violating, the *criminal* provisions of the INA.[38]

With regards to preemption, the *Gonzalez* court determined that the criminal immigration provisions were "few in number," "relatively simple in their terms," constituted a "narrow and distinct element" of the INA, and did not require a "complex administrative structure" consistent with exclusive federal control.[39] The court, therefore, concluded that the criminal provisions did not support the inference that the federal government occupied the field of *criminal* immigration enforcement.

With respect to *civil* immigration enforcement, *Gonzalez* has been construed to support the argument that states do not possess the authority, "inherent" or otherwise, (unless specifically granted by Congress) to enforce the *civil* enforcement measures of the INA.[40] In conducting a preemption analysis for certain criminal provisions of the INA, the Ninth Circuit in *Gonzalez* made a distinction between the civil and criminal provisions of the INA, and assumed that the former constituted a pervasive and preemptive regulatory scheme, whereas the latter did not. The court stated:

> We assume that the civil provisions of the Act regulating authorized entry, length of stay, residence status, and deportation, constitute such a pervasive regulatory scheme, as would be consistent with the exclusive federal power over immigration. However, this case [*Gonzalez*] does not concern that broad scheme, but only a narrow and distinct element of it — the regulation of criminal immigration activity by aliens.[41]

Accordingly, the court concluded that the authority of state officials to enforce the provisions of the INA "is limited to criminal provisions."[42] The preemption analysis in *Gonzalez* has been criticized by some for parsing the INA when statutory construction and preemption principles generally require consideration of the whole statutory scheme in evaluating a specific provision.[43] While *Gonzalez* appears to stand for the proposition that states do not possess the authority to enforce *civil* immigration laws, it has been argued that the preemption analysis in *Gonzalez* was based merely on an assumption and was outside the holding of the case, and thus does not constitute binding precedent.[44] Whether this conclusion is completely accurate has yet to be tested in the courts in a definitive manner, although some decisions from the Tenth Circuit regarding criminal investigations may be seen by some as strengthening the role of state and local law enforcement agencies in immigration enforcement.

In the Tenth Circuit case of *United States* v. *Salinas-Calderon,*[45] a state trooper pulled over the defendant for driving erratically but soon found six individuals in the back of the defendant's truck. Because the defendant, who was eventually charged with the crime of illegally transporting aliens did not speak English, the state trooper questioned the passenger (the defendant's wife) and learned that the driver and the other six individuals were in the country illegally. From this line of questioning, the court determined that the trooper had probable cause to detain and arrest all the individuals.

In addition to the probable cause conclusion, the Tenth Circuit determined that a "state trooper has general investigatory authority to inquire into possible immigration violations."[46] It has been argued that since there was no reason to believe that the alien passengers had committed any criminal violations (i.e, they were only in the country illegally

— a civil violation), the court's statement appears to apply fully to civil as well as criminal violations.[47] The *Salinas-Calderon* court, however, did not differentiate between civil and criminal INA violations nor did it address the charges or judicial proceedings for the six alien individuals found in the back of the truck. Instead, the focus of the *Salinas-Calderon* decision was on the probable cause and potential suppression of the statements made by the six alien passengers.

In *United States v. Vasquez-Alvarez*, an Oklahoma police officer arrested a Hispanic male suspected of drug dealing because he was an "illegal alien."[48] A specific provision in the INA (8 U.S.C. §1252c) authorizes state officers to pick up and hold for deportation a previously deported alien who had been convicted of a crime in the United States and reentered illegally. Section 1225c requires state officers to obtain confirmation from the INS before making such an arrest. At the time of the arrest in *Vasquez-Alvarez*, however, the state officer did not have actual knowledge of the defendant's immigration status or past criminal behavior; it was only later discovered that the alien had a history of prior criminal convictions and deportations.

The defendant argued that the state police could only arrest him in accordance with the restrictions detailed in 8 U.S.C. §1252c and since his arrest did not meet the requirements of that provision, it was unauthorized. The Tenth Circuit, however, ultimately concluded that §1252c "does not limit or displace the preexisting general authority of state or local police officers to investigate and make arrests for violations of federal law, including immigration law. Instead, §1252c merely creates an additional vehicle for the enforcement of federal immigration law."[49]

The court also recognized that it had previously determined in *Salinas-Calderon* that state law enforcement officers have the general authority to investigate and make arrests for violations of federal immigration laws.[50] The court concluded that the "legislative history (of §1252c) does not contain the slightest indication that Congress intended to displace any preexisting enforcement power already in the hands of state and local officers."[51] While *Vasquez-Alvarez* may be interpreted to suggest that state and local police officers do in fact possess the "inherent authority" to enforce all aspects of immigration law, it should be noted that the case arose in the context of a criminal investigation and was premised on Oklahoma law, which allows local law enforcement officials to make arrests for violations of federal law, including immigration laws.[52]

Expanding on *Vasquez-Alvarez*, the Tenth Circuit, in *United States v. Santana-Garcia*,[53] again addressed the role of local law enforcement in immigration. In *Santana-Garcia*, a Utah police officer stopped a vehicle for a traffic violation. The driver of the car did not speak English and did not possess a driver's license. The passenger of the car spoke limited English and explained that they were traveling from Mexico to Colorado, which prompted the officer to ask if they were "legal." The passenger and the driver appeared to understand the question and answered "no." From these facts, the court held that the officer had probable cause to arrest both defendants for suspected violation of federal immigration law.

In recognizing that state and local police officers had "implicit authority" within their respective jurisdictions to investigate and make arrests for violations of immigration law, the court seemingly dismissed the suggestion that state law must explicitly grant local authorities the power to arrest for a federal immigration law violation.[54] To come to this conclusion, the court relied upon a number of inferences from earlier decisions that recognized the "implicit authority" or "general investigatory authority" of state officers to inquire into possible immigration violations.[55] The court also seemed to rely upon a broad understanding of a Utah state law that empowers officers to make warrantless arrests for any public offense committed in the officers presence to include violations of federal law.[56]

Although the defendants in *Santana-Garcia* were apparently in violation of a *civil* provision of the INA (i.e., illegal presence), the *Santana-Garcia* court made no distinction between the civil and criminal violations of the INA, and the authorities the court cited generally involved arrests for criminal matters. Moreover, it remains unclear how the court, pursuant to its broad understanding of the Utah state law it relied upon, would have ruled absent the initial reason for the stop — the traffic violation. Accordingly, it can be argued that this case still seems to leave unresolved the extent to which state and local police officers may enforce the civil provisions of the INA as such.

The aforementioned cases ultimately arose in the context of enforcing *criminal* matters or violations of state law. This would seem to weaken the argument for an independent role in enforcing *civil* immigration matters. Nonetheless, as the cases from the Tenth Circuit illustrate, there appears to be a general movement towards expanding the role of state and local law enforcement officers in the field of immigration law, including some aspects of civil immigration enforcement.

Express Authorization for State and Local Law Enforcement Officers to Enforce Immigration Law

Clearly preemption does not bar state and local immigration enforcement where Congress has evidenced intent to authorize such enforcement.[57] In exercising its power to regulate immigration, Congress is free to delegate to the states, among other things, the activities of arresting, holding, and transporting aliens. Indeed, Congress already has created avenues for the participation of state and local officers in the enforcement of the federal immigration laws.

8 U.S.C. §1357(g)

One of the broadest grants of authority for state and local immigration enforcement activity stems from §133 of the Illegal Immigration Reform and Immigrant Responsibility Act of 1996, which amended INA §287 (8 U.S.C. §1357(g)). This provision authorizes the AG (now the Secretary of Homeland Security) to

> enter into a written agreement with a State, or any political subdivision of a State, pursuant to which an officer or employee of the State or subdivision, who is determined by the Attorney General to be qualified to perform a function of an immigration officer in relation to the investigation, apprehension, or detention of aliens in the United States (including the transportation of such aliens across State lines to detention centers), may carry out such function at the expense of the State or political subdivision and to the extent consistent with State and local law.

Section 1357(g) allows for significant flexibility. It permits state and local entities to tailor an agreement with the AG to meet local needs, contemplates the authorization of multiple officers, and does not require the designated officers to stop performing their local duties.[58] In performing a function under §1357(g), the written agreement must articulate the specific powers and duties that may be, or are required to be, performed by the state officer, the duration of the authority, and the position of the agent of the AG who is required to supervise and direct the individual.[59]

8 U.S.C. §1357(g)(2) requires that state officers "have knowledge of and adhere to" federal law governing immigration officers in addition to requiring adequate training regarding the enforcement of immigration laws. Section 1357(g)(3) mandates that the AG direct and supervise state officers who are performing immigration functions pursuant to §1357(g). Under §1357(g)(6), the AG, in carrying out §1357(g), can not accept a service if the service will displace any federal employee. Officers designated by the AG are not federal employees except for certain tort claims and compensation matters, but they do enjoy federal immunity.[60] Section 1357(g)(9) establishes that a state is not required to enter into an agreement with the AG under §1357(g); furthermore, under §1357(g)(10) no agreement is required for a state officer to communicate with the AG regarding the immigration status of any individual or to cooperate with the AG in the identification, apprehension, detention, or removal of aliens unlawfully present in the United States.

8 U.S.C. §1103(a)(8)

Section 372 of IIRIRA amended INA §103(a) to allow the AG to call upon state and local police in an immigration emergency (8 U.S.C. §1103(a)). 8 U.S.C. §1103(a)(8) provides:

> In the event that the Attorney General determines that an actual or imminent mass influx of aliens arriving off the coast of the United States or near a land border presents urgent circumstances requiring an immediate Federal response, the Attorney General may authorize any State or local law enforcement officer, with the consent of the head of the department, agency or establishment under whose jurisdiction the individual is serving, to perform or exercise any of the power, privileges or duties conferred or imposed by the Act or regulations issued thereunder upon officers or employees of the service.

Thus, under 8 U.S.C. §1103(a)(8), state and local officers may exercise the civil or criminal arrest powers of federal immigration officers (1) when expressly authorized by the AG; (2) when given consent by the head of the state or local law enforcement agency; and (3) upon the AG's determination of an emergency due to a mass influx of aliens. Any authority given by the AG to state law enforcement officers under this provision can only be exercised during the emergency situation.

On July 24, 2002, the DOJ issued a final rule that implemented §1103(a)(8) and described the cooperative process by which state or local governments could agree to place authorized state and local law enforcement officers under the direction of the INS in exercising federal immigration enforcement authority.[61] In February of 2003, the DOJ found it necessary to amend the previous regulations, however, because it determined that the AG did not have the flexibility to address unanticipated situations that might occur during a mass influx of aliens. The new rules also allow the AG to abbreviate or waive the otherwise normally required training requirements when such an action is necessary to protect public safety, public health, or national security.[62]

8 U.S.C. §1252c

Section 1252c originated in the House of Representatives as a floor amendment to the Antiterrorism and Effective Death Penalty Act of 1996 (AEDPA §439).[63] Section 1252c authorizes the arrest of aliens by state and local officers who have presumably violated §276 of the INA (Reentry of Removed Alien). Section 1252c(a) states in part:

> [T]o the extent permitted by relevant State and local law, State and local law enforcement officials are authorized to arrest and detain an individual who —
>
> (1) is an alien illegally present in the United States; and
> (2) has previously been convicted of a felony in the United States and deported or left the United States after such conviction, but only after the State or local law enforcement officials obtain appropriate confirmation from the Immigration and Naturalization Service of the status of such individual and only for such period of time as may be required for the Service to take the individual into Federal custody for purposes of deporting or removing the alien from the United States.

The purpose of §1252c was to overcome a perceived federal limitation on the ability of state and local officers to arrest an alien known by them to be dangerous because of past crimes committed in their jurisdiction.[64] The court in *United States* v. *Vasquez-Alvarez*, however, found that neither the defendant, the government, or the court could identify any pre-§1252c limitations on the powers of state and local officers to enforce federal law.[65] Section 1252c(b) also mandates cooperation between the AG and the states to assure that information in the control of the AG, including information in the NCIC, that would assist state and local law enforcement officials in carrying out the duties of §1252c is made available to the states.

8 U.S.C. 1324(c)

Congress appears to have delegated arrest authority to local law enforcement officers in 8 U.S.C. §1324 (INA §274), which establishes a number of criminal penalties for the smuggling, transporting, concealing, and harboring of illegal aliens. Subsection (c) of §1324, entitled "Authority to Arrest" states that:

> [n]o officer or person shall have authority to make any arrest for a violation of any provision of this section except officers and employees of the Service designated by the Attorney General, either individually or as a member of a class, and *all other officers whose duty it is to enforce criminal laws.* (emphasis added)

The plain language in this subsection seems to indicate that local law enforcement officers — that is, officers authorized to enforce criminal laws — are empowered to make arrests for the smuggling, transporting, and harboring offenses described in §1324. The legislative history of §1324 confirms this understanding. The Senate-passed version of this provision stated that arrests for violations only could be made by INS agents and "other officers *of the United States* whose duty it is to enforce criminal laws."[66] The House, however, struck the words "of the United States," so that local officials could enforce this specific provision.[67] The elimination of the limiting phrase "of the United States," appears to make Congress's intent clear that all criminal law enforcement officers, federal or otherwise, are authorized to enforce §1324.[68]

CURRENT EFFORTS

As mentioned above, IIRIRA amended the INA by authorizing the AG to enter into written agreements with states or political subdivisions of a state so that qualified officers could perform specified immigration-related duties. This authority was given new urgency following the terrorist attacks in September 2001. In 2002, the AG proposed an initiative to enter into such agreements in an effort to carry out the country's anti-terrorism mission. Under the agreement, state and local law enforcement officers could be deputized to assist the federal government with enforcing certain aspects of immigration law.[69] To date Alabama, Arizona, Florida and the Los Angeles County Sheriff's Department have entered into such an agreement.[70] For FY2006, Congress appropriated $5 million for states and localities who enter into such agreements with DHS.[71]

Florida's Memorandum of Understanding

Background

In September 2002, the state of Florida Department of Law Enforcement (FDLE) and DOJ entered into a one-year memorandum of understanding (MOU).[72] The MOU was designed as a pilot program that authorized 35 state and local law enforcement officers to work on Florida's Regional Domestic Security Task Forces (RDSTF). The task forces performed immigration enforcement functions that pertain to domestic security and counter-terrorism needs of the nation and the state of Florida.

Under Florida's renewed MOU with DHS, selected officers are authorized to enforce immigration laws and policies upon successful completion of mandatory training provided by DHS instructors.[73] Officers assigned to the RDSTF are nominated by the co-directors of each RDSTF and are presented to the FDLE for consideration. Each nominee has to be a U.S. citizen, have been a sworn officer for a minimum of three years, and have, at minimum, an Associate Degree. Candidates also must be able to qualify for federal security clearances. Once selected, each candidate's employer has to indicate that it will allow the officer to work a significant portion of his work responsibilities within the RDSTF for a minimum of one year.

Training

Training for the officers is provided by ICE at a mutually designated site in Florida. The program uses ICE curriculum and competency testing, which includes information on the following: (1) the scope of the officer's authority; (2) cross-cultural issues; (3) the proper use of force; (4) civil rights law; and (5) liability issues. Officers also receive specific training on their obligations under federal law and the Vienna Convention on Consular Relations on making proper notification upon the arrest of foreign nationals.[74] All training materials are provided by DHS, while the employing agency is responsible for the salaries and benefits of the officers in training. The FDLE covers the costs of housing and meals during training.

Upon successful completion of the training, DHS provides a signed document setting forth the officer's authorization to perform specified immigration enforcement functions for an initial period of one year. The officer's performance is evaluated by the District Director and the FDLE commissioner on a quarterly basis to assure compliance with the MOU requirements. Authorization of the officer's powers could be revoked at any time by DHS, FDLE or the employing agency.

Immigration-related activities performed by the officers are supervised by DHS. Participating officers cannot perform any immigration officer functions except when fulfilling their assigned RDSTF duties and under the direct supervision of a DHS officer. The DHS officer coordinates the involvement of the officers in DHS-related operations in consultation with the RDSTF supervisor to assure appropriate utilization of personnel. Under the MOU, officers cannot be utilized in routine DHS operations unless it relates to the RDSTF's domestic security and counter-terrorism functions. All arrest made under this authority must be reported to ICE within 24 hours.

Complaint Procedures

Florida's MOU requires complaint procedures to be disseminated throughout the state in English and any other appropriate languages. Under the MOU, complaints can be accepted from any source and submitted to federal or state authorities. All complaints received by the federal government, FDLE or the officer's employing agency have to be reported to ICE's Office of Internal Audit. Under the MOU, complaints reported directly to ICE must be shared with FDLE, at which time both agencies would determine the appropriate jurisdiction for the complaint to be resolved. Under the MOU, complainants must receive notification of the receipt of the complaint, and officers involved could be removed from participation in activities covered under the MOU pending resolution of the complaint.

Program Evaluation

Under the MOU, the Secretary of DHS and the commissioner of FDLE are require to establish a steering committee to periodically review and assess the effectiveness of the operations conducted by the task forces. The reviews are intended to assure that the efforts remain focused on the investigation of domestic security and counter-terrorism related matters. According to the MOU, within nine months of certification an evaluation of the program should be conducted by DHS with cooperation from other involved entities.[75]

Alabama's Memorandum of Understanding

Background and Training

On September 10, 2003, the state of Alabama and DHS entered into an MOU that is similar to Florida's MOU. Officers are nominated by the Director of the state's Department of Public Safety (DPS) and forwarded to ICE. As with Florida's MOU, all nominees must be U.S. citizens, have at least three years of experience as a sworn law enforcement officer, and be able to qualify for federal security clearances. Unlike Florida's MOU, however, there is no minimal education requirement. Training is provided by ICE, and the curriculum is the same as provided in Florida's MOU. DPS is responsible for all expenses incurred during training and updated training will be provided to the officers at the end of their initial year of appointment.[76]

Immigration enforcement activities of the officers will be supervised and directed by ICE special agents, who are located in Huntsville, Birmingham and Montgomery, Alabama. Such activities can only be performed under direct supervision of ICE special agents. Arrests made under the authority must be reported to ICE within 24 hours, and will be reviewed by the ICE special agent on an ongoing basis to ensure compliance with immigration laws and procedures.

Los Angeles County Sheriff's Department MOU

In February 2005, the Los Angeles County Sheriff's Department (LASD) entered into an MOU with the Department of Homeland Security. The terms of the MOU are similar to those of Florida and Alabama with several exceptions. Under the MOU, LASD personnel in county jails are authorized to (1) complete required criminal alien processing; (2) prepare immigration detainers; (3) prepare affidavits and take sworn statements (4) prepare Notice to Appear (NTA) applications; and (5) interrogate in order to determine probable cause for an immigration violation.[77] The MOU explicitly states that both parties understand that the LASD will not continue to detain an alien after the alien becomes eligible for release from LASD custody in accordance to applicable law and policy, except for a period of 48 hours excluding weekends and holidays. The MOU also specifies that the LASD has sole discretion to terminate the MOU should the State Criminal Alien Assistance Program (SCAAP)[78] funding fall below an acceptable level or is terminated in its entirety.

Arizona's MOU

In September 2005, the *Arizona Department of Corrections* (ADOC) entered into an MOU with the Department of Homeland Security in an effort to enhance Arizona's capacity to deal with immigration violators in Arizona.[79] The director of the Arizona Department of Corrections nominated eight correction officer candidates and two supervisory correctional officers for initial training and certification. All candidates were required to have a minimum of two years with ADOC and be bilingual in English and Spanish. Other criteria included not being married to a person illegally present in the United States, or knowingly having family associations that could adversely impact their ability to perform ICE functions under the MOU. The selected officers' principal assignments are in Phoenix and Perryville. There is no termination date for Arizona's MOU, however, it does contain the stipulation that it can be temporarily suspended should resource constraints or competing priorities necessitate.

Complaint Procedures

Complaint procedures under the MOUs are the same as those described in the Florida MOU. Community and media relations in all MOUs are stressed. DHS will engage in community outreach with any organization or individuals expressing interest in the MOUs. All information released to the media must be coordinated between DHS and state law enforcement entities.

Commonalities in the MOUs

In all MOUs, officers are treated as federal employees for the purpose of the Federal Tort Claims Act[80] and worker's compensation claims when performing duties authorized under the MOUs. They also have the same immunities and defenses of ICE officers from personal liability from tort suits.[81] Under the MOUs, officers named as defendants in litigation arising from activities carried out under the MOU may request representation by the DOJ. The MOUs of the participants stipulate that any party can terminate the MOU at anytime. Currently, none of the MOUs discussed have termination dates.

LEGISLATION IN THE 109TH CONGRESS[82]

Since the attacks of September 11, 2001, many have called on state and local law enforcement agencies to play a larger role in the enforcement of federal immigration laws. Some question, however, whether state and local law enforcement officers possess adequate authority to enforce all immigration laws — that is, both the *civil* violations and *criminal* punishments. Several bills in Congress would address these authority issues and enhance the role of state and local law enforcement agencies in the enforcement of immigration law.

The Border Protection, Antiterrorism, and Illegal Immigration Control Act of 2005 (H.R. 4437), as passed by the House, would "reaffirm the existing inherent authority of States," as sovereign entities (including their law enforcement personnel), to investigate, identify, apprehend, arrest, detain, or transfer into federal custody aliens in the United States in the course of carrying out routine duties. Similar to H.R. 4437, the Department of Homeland Security Authorization Act for FY2006 (H.R. 1817), as passed by the House, would authorize state and local law enforcement personnel to apprehend, detain, or remove aliens in the United States in the course of carrying out routine duties. Likewise, it would reaffirm the existing general authority for state and local law enforcement personnel to carry out the above mentioned activities.[83] S. 2612, the Comprehensive Immigration Reform Act of 2006, and S. 2454, the Securing America's Borders Act would also reaffirm a state's inherent authority to investigate, identify, apprehend, arrest, detain, or transfer into federal custody aliens in the United States, but would limit such practices to the enforcement of the *criminal* provisions of the INA.

Several provisions in H.R. 4437, S. 2612, and S. 2611 would provide funding to state and local law enforcement agencies that are addressing immigration enforcement issues. H.R. 4437, for example, would authorize the Secretary of DHS to make grants to state and local police agencies for the procurement of equipment, technology, facilities, and other products that are directly related to the enforcement of immigration law; however, S. 2612 and S. 2611 would require DHS to reimburse state and local law enforcement agencies the cost of purchasing such equipment.

H.R. 4437 would allow a state to reimburse itself with certain DHS grants for activities that relate to the enforcement of federal laws aimed at preventing the unlawful entry of persons or things into the United States that are carried out under agreement with the federal government. H.R. 4437 would also require designated sheriffs within 25 miles of the southern international border of the United States to be reimbursed or provided an advance for costs associated with the transfer of aliens detained or in the custody of the sheriff. S. 2612 and S. 2611 would create a border relief grant program for eligible law enforcement agencies to address criminal activity that occurs near the border. Under the program, the Secretary of DHS would be authorized to provide grants to law enforcement agencies located within 100 miles of the northern or southern border or to agencies outside 100 miles that are located in areas certified as "high impact areas" by the Secretary. S. 2612 and S. 2611 would also authorize DHS to reimburse state and local authorities for certain training, transportation, and equipment costs related to immigration enforcement, and certain costs associated with processing criminal illegal aliens through the criminal justice system.

Several other pieces of legislation have been introduced in the 109th Congress that would enhance the role of state and local law enforcement officials in the enforcement of immigration law (see for example, the Clear Law Enforcement for Criminal Alien Removal Act of 2005, H.R. 3137; the Homeland Security Enhancement Act of 2005, S. 1362; the Comprehensive Enforcement and Immigration Reform Act of 2005, S. 1438; the Rewarding Employers that Abide by the Law and Guaranteeing Uniform Enforcement to Stop Terrorism Act of 2005, H.R. 3333; and the Enforcement First Immigration Reform Act of 2005, H.R. 3938). However, none of these bills have seen legislative action. These bills, along with H.R. 4437 (which passed the House on December 16, 2005), H.R. 1817, S. 2612, S. 2611 (which passed the Senate on May 25, 2006), and S. 2454 would in part:

- prohibit federal funding to states and localities if they have in effect a law, policy or practice that prohibits law enforcement officers from assisting or cooperating with federal immigration law enforcement in the course of carrying out official law enforcement duties (H.R. 3137, S. 1438, H.R. 3333, and H.R. 3938); require such funding to be reallocated to states that comply with federal immigration law enforcement (H.R. 3137 and H.R. 3938);
- make it a violation of 8 U.S.C. 1373(a) and 1644 for a state or locality to have in effect a law, policy or practice that prohibits law enforcement officers from assisting or cooperating with federal immigration law enforcement in the course of carrying out official law enforcement duties *or* from providing information to the federal government with respect to the immigration status of individuals who are believed to be illegally present in the United States (S. 1362);
- require DHS to reimburse state and localities for all reasonable expenses incurred as a result of providing information on possible illegal aliens apprehended in their jurisdictions (S. 1362, S. 1438, H.R. 3333, and H.R. 3938);
- impose a fine and/or increase the criminal penalty for aliens in violation of immigration laws by sentencing them to "not less than one year" (H.R. 3137), while S. 1362 would increase the penalty by up to one year; also, the bills would increase the criminal penalty for aliens in violation of immigration laws from six months to one year and subject their assets to forfeiture (H.R. 3137, S. 1362, H.R. 3333, and H.R. 3938);

- make illegal presence in the United States a felony (H.R. 4437, H.R. 3137, and H.R. 3333), while S. 1362 would make illegal presence in the United States a misdemeanor.
- allow as an *affirmative defense* with respect to illegal presence due to the alien overstaying the terms of his visa due to an "exceptional and extremely unusual hardship or physical illness" that prevented the alien's departure from the United States (S. 1362, H.R. 3333 and H.R. 3938);
- increase the civil penalties for aliens who fail to depart the country (H.R. 3137 and H.R. 3938), and subject their assets to forfeiture, under certain circumstances (H.R. 3137, S. 1362, H.R. 3333, and H.R. 3938);
- require DHS to provide specified information to the NCIC on aliens who(se): (1) have been issued a final order of removal (H.R. 4472, S. 2454, S. 2612, S. 2611, H.R. 3137, S. 1362, S. 1438, H.R. 3333, and H.R. 3938); (2) signed a voluntary departure agreement (H.R. 4472, S. 2454, S. 2612, S. 2611, H.R. 3137, and H.R. 3333); (3) is subject to a voluntary departure agreement (S. 2454, S. 2612, S. 2611, S. 1362, S. 1438, and H.R. 3333); (4) overstayed their authorized period of stay (H.R. 4472, S. 2454, S. 2612, S. 2611, H.R. 3137, S. 1362, H.R. 3333, and H.R. 3938); and (5) visa has been revoked (H.R. 3137, S. 1362, S. 1438, and H.R. 3938).[84]
- require states and localities to have a policy that provides DHS with identifying information on aliens arrested in their jurisdiction in violation of immigration laws to be included in the NCIC (H.R. 3137, S. 1362, H.R. 3333, and H.R. 3938); require states and localities to provide information to federal authorities of aliens for inclusion into the NCIC (H.R. 3137, H.R. 3333, and H.R. 3938);
- encourage states and localities to provide information on aliens arrested in their jurisdictions to DHS (H.R. 3137 and 3938);
- require DHS to make grants to states and political subdivisions that would provide for compensation for incarcerating illegal aliens (H.R. 3137);
- require DHS to verify the immigration status of aliens apprehended or arrested by state and local law enforcement agencies (S. 2612, S. 2611, and S. 2454);
- require DHS to take possession of illegal aliens within 48 hours (H.R. 3137, H.R. 3333, and H.R. 3938) or 72 hours (S. 1362, S. 1438, S. 2454, S. 2612, and S. 2611) after the state or local law enforcement agency has completed its charging process or within 48 hours (H.R. 3137, H.R. 3333, and H.R. 3938) or 72 hours (S. 1362, S. 1438, S. 2454, S. 2612, and S. 2611) after the illegal alien has been apprehended if no charges are filed; require the Secretary of DHS to establish a mechanism to collect illegal aliens from state and local law enforcement authorities (H.R. 3137, S. 1362, H.R. 3333, H.R. 3938, and S. 2454);
- require DHS to designate at least one federal, state or local prison, jail, private contracted prison or detention facility within each state as the central facility for that state to transfer custody of aliens to DHS (S. 2612, S. 2611, and S. 2454);
- require DHS to reimburse state and local law enforcement agencies for the cost incurred to incarcerate and transport illegal aliens in their custody, and authorize appropriations for the detention and transportation of illegal aliens to federal custody (S. 2612, S. 2611, S. 2454, H.R. 3137, S. 1362, S. 1438, H.R. 3333, and H.R. 3938);

- require DHS to provide transportation and officers to take illegal aliens who are apprehended by state and local law enforcement officers into DHS custody (S. 2454, S. 2612, and S. 2611);
- require DHS to reimburse states and localities for the cost to train state and local law enforcement officers in immigration enforcement if such training was provided by the state or locality (S. 2454, S. 2612, S. 2611, and S. 1817);
- require DHS to establish a training manual and pocket guide for state and local law enforcement personnel with respect to enforcing immigration law; require DHS to make the training available to state and local law enforcement officers through as many means as possible; require DHS to be responsible for the cost incurred in establishing the training manual and pocket guide (H.R. 4437, H.R. 3137, S. 1362, and H.R. 3938);
- require Cameron University (Lawton, OK) to establish and implement a demonstration project to assure the feasibility of establishing a basic immigration law enforcement nationwide e-learning training course; require the demonstration project to be carried out in selected states and sets forth the criteria (H.R. 3333);
- provide immunity to the same extent as a federal law enforcement officer for state and local law enforcement officers with respect to personal liability that may arise as a result of the officer performing his official duties (H.R. 3137, S. 1362, S. 1438, and H.R. 3938); and
- provide immunity for federal, state or local law enforcement agencies with respect to claims of money damages that may arise as a result of an officer from the agency enforcing immigration law, except to the extent a law enforcement officer committed a violation of federal, state, or local criminal law in the course of enforcing such immigration law (H.R. 3137, S. 1362, S. 1438, and H.R. 3938).

Contrary to the aforementioned bills, the Save America Comprehensive Immigration Act of 2005 (H.R. 2092) would eliminate the ban on state and local governments from prohibiting communications with DHS. The bill would also eliminate the authority in current law that permits state personnel to enforce immigration law.

SELECTED ISSUES

In addition to the legal complexities that may arise with respect to utilizing state and local law enforcement to enforce immigration law, several additional issues have been noted.

Sanctuary States and Cities

Current day "sanctuary cities" or "non-cooperation policies" have their roots in the 1980s religious sanctuary movement by American churches. These churches provided sanctuary to thousands of unauthorized Central American migrants fleeing civil war in their homelands. Most cities that are considered sanctuary cities have adopted a "don't ask-don't tell" policy where they don't require their employees, including law enforcement officers, to report to federal officials aliens who may be illegally present in the country.

Localities, and in some cases individual police departments, in such areas that are considered "sanctuary cities," have utilized various mechanisms to ensure that unauthorized aliens who may be present in their jurisdiction illegally are not turned in to federal authorities.[85] Some municipalities address the issue through resolutions, executive orders or city ordinances, while many police departments address the issues through special orders, departmental policy and general orders. To date, there are two statewide policies regarding providing sanctuary for unauthorized aliens. In May 2003, Alaska's state legislature passed a joint resolution prohibiting state agencies from using resources or institutions for the purpose of enforcing federal immigration laws.[86] In 1987, Oregon passed a law that prohibits state and local law enforcement agencies from using agency moneys, equipment or personnel for the purpose of detecting or apprehending foreign citizens based on violation of federal immigration law.[87] Oregon law, however, does permit their law enforcement officers to exchange information with federal authorities to verify the immigration status of an individual arrested for criminal offenses.

According to proponents, the movement to provide coverage for unauthorized aliens stems from the belief that the enforcement of immigration law is the responsibility of federal authorities, and that state resources should not be used for this purpose. Some view these policies to be at odds with §642 of IIRIRA, which permits the sharing of information between agencies and requires state and local agencies to share information with INS and prohibits such information from being restricted. They argue that requiring the reporting of unauthorized aliens to federal authorities infringes on states' tenth amendment right to sovereignty.

On January 5, 2006, the President signed the Violence Against Women and Department of Justice Reauthorization Act of 2005 into law.[88] As part of this reauthorization, the Inspector General of the Department of Justice is required to conduct a study of cities and localities with sanctuary policies and provide the Congress with a list of such areas.

Access to Database

Under current practice, state and local law enforcement officials do not have direct access to information on the immigration status of an alien. In the course of their duties, if state and local law enforcement officials encounter an alien whose immigration status is in question, they can contact the LESC in Burlington, Vermont.[89] Immigration officials at the LESC query a database that contains information on an alien's immigration status. If the alien is unauthorized to be present in the country and the state or local law enforcement official has decided that the alien will be released from their jurisdiction, immigration officials are notified to come and pick up the alien.[90]

In addition to the LESC, state and local law enforcement officials can access the NCIC for those aliens who are listed as absconders.[91] Aliens listed on the absconder list can be detained by state and local law enforcement officials because they are in violation of the federal criminal code. It has been reported, however, that the FBI has a backlog with respect to entering the names of over 350,000 absconders in the database.[92]

State and local law enforcement officials, however, have reported a variety of problems with accessing LESC and soliciting the help of federal immigration officials once it has been determined that an alien is unauthorized to be present in the country.[93] According to some state and local law enforcement officials, it can take several hours to get the results of a single query.[94] DHS, however, has reported that, on average, an immigrant status query takes 15 minutes.[95] State and local law enforcement officials have also reported that federal authorities rarely cooperate once they have been contacted by a state or local law enforcement entity.[96] Whatever the facts may be, there is a perception on the part of state and local law enforcement personnel that cooperation could be improved.

Civil Rights

One of the overriding concerns with state and local police involvement in the enforcement of immigration law is the potential for civil rights violations. A person is afforded certain civil rights under the Fifth Amendment, which guarantees that "no person shall ... be deprived of life, liberty, or property, without the due process of law ...," and the Fourteenth Amendment, which prohibits a state from denying to "any person within its jurisdiction the equal protection of the laws." It should also be noted that courts have reviewed alleged police misconduct under the Fourth Amendment's prohibition against unreasonable searches and seizures.

Congress has also statutorily prohibited certain discriminatory actions and has made available various remedies to victims of such discrimination. For example, Title VI of the Civil Rights Act of 1964 prohibits "discrimination under federally assisted programs on the grounds of race," which can include federal and state law enforcement entities. 42 U.S.C. §1983, enacted as part of the Civil Rights Act of 1871, provides a monetary damages remedy for harm caused by deprivation of federal constitutional rights by state or local governmental officials. The Violent Crime and Control and Law Enforcement Act of 1994 included a provision, 42 U.S.C. §14141, which authorizes the DOJ (but not private victims) to bring civil actions for equitable and declaratory relief against any police agency engaged in unconstitutional "patterns or practices."

Because unauthorized aliens are likely to be members of minority groups, complications may arise in enforcing immigration law due to the difficulty in identifying illegal aliens while at the same time avoiding the appearance of discrimination based on ethnicity or alienage. Thus, a high risk for civil rights violations may occur if state and local police do not obtain the requisite knowledge, training, and experience in dealing with the enforcement of immigration laws.

Moreover, suspects of immigration violations may become victims of "racial profiling" — the practice of targeting individuals for police or security detention based on their race or ethnicity in the belief that certain minority groups are more likely to engage in unlawful behavior or be present in the United States illegally. The prevalence of alleged civil rights violations and racial profiling among federal, state, and local law enforcement agencies has already received a significant amount of attention from the public and the courts.[97]

Detention Space

The former INS has long lacked sufficient beds to house immigration violators. As a result of the lack of bed space, many aliens continue to be released from detention. Some contend that a possible unintended consequence of permitting state and local law enforcement entities to enforce immigration law would lead to more aliens being detained. These critics point to the fact that there are over 350,000 aliens with final orders of deportation present in the United States; and, according to the 2000 U.S. Census, there are approximately 8 million undocumented aliens present. By increasing the number of law enforcement officers to enforce immigration law, they argue, inevitably more undocumented aliens would be detained. States and local jurisdictions already face some of the same challenges the federal government has been experiencing with respect to the lack of facilities to house criminals and immigrant violators. Moreover, some argue that state and local law enforcement agencies may bear the cost of detaining unauthorized aliens.[98]

Pro/Con Analysis of State and Local Law Enforcement Officials Enforcing Immigration Law

Determining what the proper role of state and local law enforcement officials is in enforcing immigration law is not without controversy. Lawmakers, scholars, observers and law enforcement officials have all expressed their opposition or support for increasing the role of state and local law enforcement with respect to enforcing immigration law. Following is a discussion of a few of the issues.

Impact on Communities

Opponents argue that utilizing state and local law enforcement to enforce immigration law would undermine the relationship between local law enforcement agencies and the communities they serve. For example, potential witnesses and victims of crime may be reluctant to come forward to report crimes in fear of actions that might be taken against them by immigration officials. They assert that the trust between immigrants and local authorities is tenuous in many jurisdictions and that such a policy could exacerbate the negative relationship.

Proponents contend that state and local law enforcement officers would best be able to enforce such laws simply because they know their communities. They argue that state and local law enforcement officers already have the power to enforce criminal immigration violations and have not seen a reluctance on the part of the communities they serve to cooperate.

Resources

Opponents argue that state and local law enforcement resources should not be used to fund a federal responsibility. They contend that such action could result in the reduction of local law enforcement resources available for other purposes and constitute a cost shift onto state and local law enforcement agencies. According to some, local jurisdictions are already witnessing a depletion of traditional funding to fight crime. Moreover, they contend, many jurisdictions have not received funding for their first responders programs. These critics also contend that there could be a de-emphasis on certain types of criminal investigations in an effort to focus on enforcing immigration law, which would divert law enforcement authorities' from their primary duties.

Proponents in favor of utilizing state and local law enforcement to enforce immigration law argue that such assistance would help the federal government to enforce the immigration law deeper into the interior of the United States. Moreover, they contend that local law enforcement agencies would bring additional resources to assist the federal government with enforcing immigration law. Finally, they argue that the current atmosphere of terrorist threat adds impetus to any efforts that might reduce this threat.

National Security

Opponents argue that such a policy would undermine public safety and could force many undocumented aliens to go underground, thus making it more difficult to solicit their cooperation in terrorist-related and criminal investigations.

Proponents assert that permitting state and local law enforcement to enforce immigration law would make it easier to arrest potential terrorists and criminals who are illegally present in the country, thus providing an elevated level of security for the nation. They argue that these individuals could provide important tips in an investigation.

Application of Policy

Under current law, the Secretary of DHS could enter into separate agreements with states and localities. Opponents contend that separate agreements could lead to inconsistent application of immigration law across jurisdictions and possible legal claims of disparate treatment. Moreover, they contend that different applications could lead to allegations of racial profiling and discrimination.

Proponents argue that jurisdictions have different needs and that separate agreements that are designed to meet the need of each jurisdiction are critical. They contend that as long as the jurisdiction is abiding by the conditions set forth in its MOU with the federal government, then the propensity for abuse or misapplication is mitigated.

Training

Since federal immigration law is a complex body of law, it requires extensive training and expertise to adequately enforce. Some argue that there are a variety of documents that allow someone to be legally present in the United States and state and local law enforcement officials do not have the necessary training on how to differentiate between those documents. Additionally, opponents maintain that the use of fraudulent documents is a growing problem and immigration authorities must be familiar with the various techniques that are used to misrepresent a document.

Proponents argue that the current training that is outlined in policy is sufficient to adequately train state and local law enforcement officials to properly enforce immigration law. They contend that state and local law enforcement entities, as in the case of Alabama's MOU, can supplement the required training as they see fit.[99]

SELECTED POLICY OPTIONS

As Congress debates the use of state and local law enforcement officers to enforce immigration law, it may want to consider several policy options, which may represent a choice among the options listed below or a combination. Congress may also choose to take no action, which could leave it to the courts to define these boundaries.

Direct Access to Databases

Under current practice, state and local law enforcement officials have indirect access to the immigration status of aliens through LESC and direct access to absconders through the FBI's NCIC, (see discussion in "Legislation in the 108th Congress"). Some law enforcement officials argue that direct access to databases that contain information on the immigrant's status would assist them in carrying out their responsibilities more efficiently and effectively. Opponents, on the other hand, argue that providing state and local law enforcement officials with direct access to an alien's personal information could lead to abuse of such information by the law enforcement official. Some raise questions about the quality of the various databases and the potential for false positives, which could lead to the incarceration of innocent people. While there are critics on both sides of the issue, there may be a consensus that state and local law enforcement officials need access to certain information on aliens with whom they come into contact.

According to some, other issues arise when addressing state and local law enforcement's access to immigration databases: (1) how much access should be granted to state and local law enforcement officials; (2) who should have access to the databases; (3) what level of background clearance would be sufficient for the officers accessing the database; (4) what type of privacy protection should be given for individuals whose personal information is being accessed; and (5) how can the quality of the databases be improved to avoid potential problems such as "false positives" and individuals with similar names, which could potentially clog up the system.

Funding for State Cooperation

Congress could appropriate additional funding to state and local law enforcement agencies for their cooperation with enforcing immigration law. A common argument made by local law enforcement officials against enforcing immigration law is the lack of resources.[100] Many states are facing budget crises and police departments have seen decreases in federal funding for some law enforcement programs. Moreover, there have been complaints from some jurisdictions that they are not receiving first responder funding.

State Criminal Alien Assistance Program (SCAAP)

In addition to some reduction in traditional funding for law enforcement-related purposes, states and localities have also seen a reduction in federal reimbursement for the SCAAP. SCAAP provides payment assistance to states and localities for the costs incurred for incarcerating undocumented aliens being held as a result of state or local charges.[101] SCAAP funding decreased from $564 million in FY2002 to $250 million in FY2003. In FY2004, SCAAP funding increased to $300 million. Congress appropriated an additional $5 million in FY2005 (a total of $305 million). For FY2006, Congress appropriated $405 million for SCAAP.

Criminalizing Civil Immigration Violations

At the center of the current debate to permit state and local law enforcement to enforce immigration law is whether state and local law enforcement has the inherent authority to enforce *civil* immigration violations, such as a nonimmigrant who overstays his visa. While this issue still appears somewhat unclear from a legal perspective (see earlier discussion in "Authorities to Enforce Immigration Law" and "State Involvement in the Enforcement of Immigration Law"), by criminalizing all *civil* immigration violations, state and local law enforcement agencies could seemingly arrest and detain all immigration violators.

While some view this option as closing the existing loophole, others express concern that state and local law enforcement officials are not adequately trained to ascertain the difference between a bonafide asylum seeker and an individual who may be fraudulently trying to circumvent the system. Others express concern that the pool of violators is great (8 million undocumented aliens)[102] and the immigration system is already overburdened. Observers question that if civil immigration violations were to become criminal would it be retroactive, and if so to what date; and would it preempt aliens who have civil immigration violations from adjusting their status.

REFERENCES

[1]   Michael Garcia, Director of the ICE, speech at the Heritage Foundation, July 23, 2003.
[2]   See discussion under "State Involvement in the Enforcement of Immigration Law."

[3]   For FY1999, Congress appropriated $21.8 million for INS to establish QRTs (see H.Rept. 105-825; P.L. 105-277). For FY2001, Congress appropriated $11 million for 23 additional QRTs (see H.Rept. 106-1005; P.L. 106-553).

[4]   The names of aliens with final orders of deportation was included in the NCIC, which includes both criminal aliens and aliens who violated civil immigration law.

[5]   Under current practice in most jurisdictions, state and local law enforcement officials can inquire into an alien's immigration status if the alien is being questioned by an officer as a result of a criminal investigation or other related matters (i.e., traffic violation). The LESC is discussed in "Selected Issues," under "Access to Database."

[6]   6 Charles Gordon, et. al, Immigration Law and Procedure §72.02[2][b], at 72-27 (Matthew Bender and Co., Inc. 2000) (citing *Abel v. United States*, 362 U.S. 217 (1960); *United States v. Cruz*, 559 F.2d 30 (5ᵗʰ Cir. 1977)).

[7]   U.S. Const., Art. I, §8, cl. 3, 4.

[8]   8 U.S.C. §1227(a)(1)(B). Other examples of civil violations include §1253(c) (penalties relating to vessels and aircraft) and §1324d (penalties for failure to depart).

[9]   Other criminal provisions include §1253(a) disobeying a removal order, §1306 offenses relating to registration of aliens, and §1324a(f) engaging in a pattern or practice of hiring illegal aliens.

[10] The federal authority to set rules on the entry of aliens and the conditions of their stay still leaves limited room for state law aimed at the alien community. If a state regulation is consistent with federal law and the equal protection requirements of the Fourteenth Amendment, it may stand. See generally *De Canas v. Bica*, 424 U.S. 351, 355 (1976).

[11] U.S. Const. Art. VI, cl.2.

[12] See, e.g., Gade v. National Solid Wastes Management Ass'n, 505 U.S. 88, 96 (1992).

[13] *English v. General Elec. Co.*, 496 U.S. 72, 78-79 (1990). Complete occupation of a field can be inferred from a "scheme of federal regulation ... so pervasive as to make reasonable the inference that Congress left no room for the States to supplement it," or where an act of Congress "touches a field in which the federal interest is so dominant that the federal system will be assumed to preclude enforcement of state laws on the same subject." Ibid., (quoting *Rice v. Santa Fe Elevator Corp.*, 331 U.S. 218, 230 (1947)). Conflict preemption occurs where it is "impossible for a private party to comply with both state and federal requirements," Ibid., citing *Florida Lime and Avocado Growers, Inc. v. Paul*, 373 U.S. 132, 142-43 (1963)), or where state law "stands as an obstacle to the accomplishment and execution of the full purposes and objectives of Congress." Ibid., (quoting *Hines v. Davidowitz*, 312 U.S. 52, 67 (1941)).

[14] Celica Renn, Selected Comment on 1986 Immigration Reform: *State and Local Enforcement of the Criminal Immigration Statutes and the Preemption Doctrine*, 41 U. Miami L. Rev. 999, 1023 (1987) (hereafter cited as Renn, Selected Comment); see also Linda R. Yanez and Alfonso Soto, *Local Police Involvement in the Enforcement of Immigration Law*, 1 Tex. Hisp. J.L. and Pol'y 9, 29 (1994).

[15] Renn, Selected Comment, at 30.

[16] See generally, *Printz v. United States*, 521 U.S. 898, 922 (1997); see, e.g., INA §287(g)(9) ("Nothing in this subsection shall be construed to require an agreement under this subsection in order for any State or political subdivision of a State to enter into an agreement with the Attorney General (AG) under this subsection.").

[17] *De Canas v. Bica*, 424 U.S. 351, 355 (1976); *Gonzalez v. City of Peoria*, 722 F. 2d 468, 474 (9ᵗʰ Cir. 1983).

[18] See *Gonzalez*, 722 F. 2d at 474 (9ᵗʰ Cir. 1983).

[19] Yanez, *supra* note 14, at 28-29. *Cf People* v. *Barajas*, 81 Cal. App. 3d 999 (1978) (concluding that "the supremacy clause is a two-edged sword, and in the absence of a limitation, the states are bound by it to enforce violations of the federal immigration laws."). Ibid., at 1006.

[20] Gonzalez, 722 F.2d at 474-75; see also Assistance by State and Local Police in Apprehending Illegal Aliens, 1996 OLC Lexis 76, at 2 (Feb. 5, 1996); Jeff Lewis, et al., Authority of State and Local Officers to Arrest Aliens Suspected of Civil Infractions of Federal Immigration Law, 7 Bender's Immigration Bulletin No. 15, p. 944 (Aug. 1, 2002).

[21] Illegal entry is a misdemeanor under INA §275. Because many encounters between local police and undocumented aliens involve warrantless arrests, an officer's authority to apprehend a person in violation of §275 will necessarily depend on whether state arrest statutes permit an arrest for a misdemeanor occurring outside the officer's presence, since the misdemeanor of illegal entry is apparently completed at the time of entry, and is not a "continuing" offense that occurs in the presence of the officer. A continuing offense may be found under INA §276, which applies to aliens previously deported who enter or are found in the United States.

[22] *Vasquez-Alvarez*, 176 F.3d at 1295; 84 Op. Atty. Gen. Cal. 189 (Nov. 16, 2001) 2001 Cal. AG Lexis 46, at *15; 2000 Op. Atty Gen. N.Y. 1001 (Mar. 21, 2000) 2000 N.Y. AG Lexis 2, at *11-12.

[23] Interpreter Releases, vol. 55, Aug. 9, 1978, p. 306 (quoting DOJ press release).

[24] Interpreter Releases, vol. 60, Mar. 4, 1983, pp. 172-73 (quoting Feb. 10, 1983, statement).

[25] Dep't of Justice, Office of Legal Counsel, *Handling of INS Warrants of Deportation in Relation to NCIC Wanted Person File*, at 4, 5, and n.11 (Apr. 11, 1989).

[26] Dep't of Justice, Office of Legal Counsel, *Assistance by State and Local Police in Apprehending Illegal Aliens*, 1996 OLC Lexis 76, at 2 (Feb. 5, 1996). (Hereafter cited as 1996 OLC Opinion).

[27] Federal News Service, Press Conference With U.S. AG John Ashcroft and James Ziglar, Commissioner, INS, Re: Tracking of Foreign Visitors (June 5, 2002).

[28] Nat'l Council of La Raza v. Dep't of Justice, 411 F.3d 350 (2ⁿᵈ Cir. 2005).

[29] Dep't of Justice, Office of Legal Counsel, *Non-preemption of the authority of state and local law enforcement officials to arrest aliens for immigration violations*, (Apr. 3, 2002) (Hereafter cited as 2002 OLC opinion) available at [http://www.aclu.org/ FilesPDFs/ ACF27DA.pdf].

[30] For example, the 2002 opinion states that the issue at hand does not fit under the typical preemption scenario, but instead, presents the question of whether states can *assist* the federal government by arresting aliens who have violated *federal law* (emphasis in original). As such, relying on the dictum discussed in the *Gonzales v. City of Peoria* case (see text under Case Law) was "entirely misplaced," according to the opinion.

[31] American Civil Liberties Union, Refutation of 2002 DOJ Memo, (Sept. 6, 2005) available at [http://www.aclu.org/FilesPDFs/ACF3189.pdf].

[32] For example, it has been suggested that the 2002 OLC opinion could support state and local arrests for violations of federal tax, environmental, finance, food safety, and education laws. See ibid.

[33] *Christensen* v. *Harris County*, 529 U.S. 576, 587 (2000).

[34] *Gonzalez* v. *City of Peoria*, 722 F.2d 468, 474 (9th Cir. 1983).

[35] The plaintiffs alleged that the city police engaged in the practice of stopping and arresting persons of Mexican descent without reasonable suspicion or probable cause and based only on their race. Furthermore, they alleged that those persons stopped under this policy were required to provide identification of legal presence in the U.S. and that anyone without acceptable identification was detained at the jail for release to immigration authorities.

[36] 8 U.S.C. §1324 prohibits the bringing in and harboring of certain undocumented aliens (see later discussion under "Express Authorization").

[37] See *Gonzalez*, 722 F. 2d at 475 (citing H.R. 1505, 82nd Cong., 2d sess, reprinted in 1952 U.S.C.C.A.N. 1358, 1360-61).

[38] *Gonzalez*, 722 F.2d at 475.

[39] Ibid., at 474-75.

[40] See, e.g., 1996 OLC Opinion; 84 Op. Atty. Gen. Cal. 189 (Nov. 16, 2001) 2001 Cal. AG Lexis 46; 2000 Op. Atty Gen. N.Y. 1001 (Mar. 21, 2000) 2000 N.Y. AG Lexis 2.

[41] *Gonzalez*, 722 F.2d at 474-75.

[42] Ibid., at 476.

[43] Linda R. Yanez and Alfonso Soto, *Local Police Involvement in the Enforcement of Immigration Law*, 1 Tex. Hisp. J.L. and Pol'y 9 (1994), at 28-29.

[44] CLEAR Act Hearing, H.R. 2671 (Oct. 1, 2003) (testimony of Kris W. Kobach, Professor of Law, Univ. of Missouri-Kansas City).

[45] *United States v. Salinas-Calderon*, 728 F.2d. 1298 (10th Cir. 1984).

[46] *Salinas-Calderon*, 728 F. 2d. at 1302 n. 3.

[47] See CLEAR Act Hearing, H.R. 2671 (Oct. 1, 2003) (testimony of Kris W. Kobach, Professor of Law, Univ. of Missouri-Kansas City).

[48] *United States v. Vasquez-Alvarez*, 176 F. 3d 1294 (10th Cir. 1999).

[49] Ibid., at 1295.

[50] Ibid., at 1296 (*citing Salinas-Calderon*, 728 F.2d at 1301-02 and n.3 (10th Cir. 1984)).

[51] Ibid., at 1299.

[52] Ibid., at 1297 (*citing* 11 Okla. Op. Att'y Gen. 345 (1979), 1979 WL 37653). See also *United States v. Daigle*, 2005 U.S. Dist. LEXIS 14533 (D. Me. July 19, 2005) (finding state statutory authority for the stop of a person suspected of the federal immigration offense of entering the country without inspection because (1) the immigration offense was the functional equivalent to a state Class E or Class D offense and (2) state law authorizes an officer to make a warrantless arrest for an analogous offense if, among other things, the stop and arrest are made upon a "fresh pursuit" or "reasonable time" after the commission of the offense (Me. Rev. Stat. Ann. tit. 17-A, §15(2)).

[53] *United States v. Santana-Garcia*, 264 F.3d 1188 (10th Cir. 2001).

[54] Ibid., at 1194. The court, nonetheless, cited Utah's peace officer statute (Utah Code Ann. §77-7-2) which empowers Utah state troopers to make warrantless arrests for "any public offense." The court also found Defendant's acknowledgment in *Vasquez-Alvarez*

that Oklahoma law specifically authorized local law enforcement officials to make arrests for violations of federal law unnecessary to that decision. Ibid., at 1194 n. 7.

[55] Citing *Salinas-Calderon*, 728 F. 2d 1298 (10th Cir. 1984); *United States* v. *Janik*, 723 F. 2d 537, 548 (7th Cir. 1983); *United States* v. *Bowdach*, 561 F. 2d 1160, 1167 (5th Cir. 1977).

[56] *Santana-Garcia*, 264 F. 3d at 1194 n. 8 (*citing* Utah Code Ann. §77-7-2).

[57] Conversely, state action may be preempted where Congress explicitly manifests its intent in law. Such an intent is evidenced in INA §274A(h)(2) (8 U.S.C. §1324A(h)(2)), which explicitly prohibits states from imposing civil or criminal sanctions upon those who employ, recruit, or refer unauthorized aliens. Other provisions that expressly consider the role of states are INA §287(d) (state and local police are requested to report to INS arrests related to controlled substances when the suspect is believed to be unlawfully in the country) and INA §288 (instructing INS to rely on state and local police for the enforcement of local laws within immigrant stations).

[58] Jay T. Jorgensen, Comment, The Practical Power of State and Local Governments to Enforce Federal Immigration Laws, 1997 B.Y.U. L. Rev. 899, 925 (1997).

[59] INA §287(g)(5).

[60] INA §287(g)(7)(8).

[61] Codified at 28 C.F.R. §65.84; see also 67 *Federal Register* 48354.

[62] Abbreviation or Waiver of Training for State or Local Law Enforcement Officers Authorized To Enforce Immigration Law During a Mass Influx of Aliens, 68 *Fed. Reg.* 8820-8822 (Feb. 26, 2003) (codified at 28 C.F.R. §65.84(a)(4)).

[63] P.L. 104-132, §439. See 142 *Congressional Record* 4619 (Rep. Doolittle offering amend.no. 7 to H.R. 2703).

[64] *Vasquez-Alvarez*, 176 F. 3d at 1299.

[65] *Vasquez-Alvarez*, 176 F. 3d at 1299, n. 4.

[66] 98 Cong. Rec. 810, 813 (1952) (emphasis added).

[67] Conf. Rep. No. 1505, 82 Cong., 2d (1952). Former Representative Walter offered the amendment to strike the words "of the United States." He stated that the purpose of the amendment was "to make it possible for any law enforcement officer to make an arrest." 98 Cong. Rec. 1414-15 (1952).

[68] As previously discussed, the 9th Circuit in *Gonzalez* used the legislative history of §1324(c) to conclude that local law enforcement officers are authorized to enforce all criminal immigration matters.

[69] U.S. Department of Justice, Attorney General Prepared Remarks on the National Security Entry-Exit Registration System, June 6, 2002.

[70] Local law enforcement was used to enforce immigration law prior to the 2002 DOJ initiative. In 1997, the then-INS and the police department in Chandler, Arizona conducted a joint operation wherein individuals in the community who were suspected of being illegally present in the United States were investigated. The city was sued due to allegations of profiling and settled the law suit with members in the community who were involved in the operation.

[71] P.L. 109-90.

[72] The MOU was renewed on Nov. 26, 2003.

[73] Under the MOU, law enforcement officers have the following authorities: (1) interrogate an alien in order to determine if there is probable cause for an immigration arrest; (2) arrest an alien without warrant for civil and criminal immigration violations; (3) complete required arrest reports and forms; (4) prepare affidavits and take sworn statements; (5) transport aliens; (6) assist in pre-trial and post-arrest case processing of aliens taken into custody by the ICE; (7) detain arrested aliens in ICE approved detention facilities.

[74] Available at [http://www.un.org/law/ilc/texts/consul.htm].

[75] The evaluation should include statistical evaluation, reports, records, officer evaluation, case reviews, complaint records, site visits, media coverage and community interaction.

[76] On Oct. 3, 2003, 21 Alabama state troopers completed training under the MOU.

[77] The aforementioned functions are usually performed by ICE agents in preparation for possible deportation proceedings and/or deportation.

[78] SCAAP is a federal grant program that reimburses states and localities for correctional officers' salary costs incurred for incarcerating undocumented criminal aliens.

[79] Under the MOU, *correctional officers* have the following authorities: (1) interrogate an alien in order to determine if there is probable cause for an immigration violation; (2) complete required arrest reports and forms; (3) prepare affidavits and take sworn statements; (4) prepare immigration detainers and I-213 Record of Deportable/Inadmissable Alien reports; and (5) prepare Notice to Appear or other removal charging documents.

[80] 28 U.S.C. §§2671-2680.

[81] 5 U.S.C. §§8101 *et seq.*

[82] Legislation discussed in this part is limited to provisions that pertain to state and local law enforcement's role in enforcing immigration law.

[83] Additional legislation contain a similar provision including, H.R. 3137, S. 1362, H.R. 3333, S. 1438, and H.R. 3938.

[84] Provisions in the Gang Deterrence and Community Protection Act of 2005 (H.R. 1279), as passed by the House, would also require information on certain immigration violators to be entered into the National Crime Information Center.

[85] Cities and counties currently that have sanctuary policies are; Anchorage, AK, Fairbanks, AK, Chandler, AZ, Fresno, CA, Los Angeles, CA, San Diego, CA, San Francisco, CA, Sonoma County, CA, Evanston, IL, Cicero, IL, Cambridge, MA, Orleans, MA, Portland, ME, Baltimore, MD, Takoma Park, MD, Ann Arbor, MI, Detroit, MI, Minneapolis, MN, Durham, NC, Albuquerque, NM, Aztec, NM, Rio Arriba, County, NM, Sante Fe, NM, New York, NY, Ashland, OR, Gaston, OR, Marion County, OR, Austin, TX, Houston, TX, Katy, TX, Seattle, WA, and Madison, WI.

[86] H.J.Res. 22, 23rd Leg., 1st sess., (Ak. 2003).

[87] Or. Rev. Stat. §181.850.

[88] P.L. 109-162; 119 Stat 2960.

[89] LESC was established in 1994 and is administered by ICE. It operates 24 hours a day, seven days a week. LESC gathers information from eight databases and several law enforcement databases, including the NCIC. In July 2003, LESC processed 48,007 inquiries.

[90] Section 642(c) of IIRIRA required the former INS to respond to inquiries from local law enforcement agencies that sought to ascertain the immigration status of an individual within the jurisdiction of the agency for any purpose authorized under law.

[91] Absconders are unauthorized or criminal aliens or nonimmigrants who violated immigration law and have been ordered deported by an immigration court.

[92] Testimony of INS Commissioner James Zigler, in U.S. Congress, House Appropriations Committee, Subcommittee on Commerce, Justice, State and the Judiciary, Hearing on the President's FY2003 Budget Request, Mar. 7, 2002.

[93] In some cases, local law enforcement may pick up an alien for questioning and determine that the alien could be released under normal circumstances, but because the alien has an illegal status, the officer should turn the alien over to federal authorities.

[94] U.S. Congress, House Subcommittee on Immigration, Border Security, and Claims, *H.R. 2671, The Clear Law Enforcement for Criminal Alien Removal Act*, 108th Cong., 1st sess., Oct. 1, 2003.

[95] Congressional Research Service interview with an ICE congressional liaison and official in Dec. 2003.

[96] Reportedly, this is more of a problem in rural areas where the closest immigration official may be in another state. U.S. Congress, House Subcommittee on Immigration, Border Security, and Claims, *H.R. 2671, The Clear Law Enforcement for Criminal Alien Removal Act*.

[97] See Department of Homeland Security Transition: Bureau of Immigration and Customs Enforcement: Hearing Before the Subcommittee on Immigration, Border Security, and Claims of the House Comm. on the Judiciary, 108th Cong. 66-69 (2003) (statement of the Mexican American Legal Defense and Education Fund) (citing various examples of racial profiling among federal and state officers).

[98] For additional information on aliens in detention, see CRS Report RL31606, *Detention of Noncitizens in the United States*, by Alison Siskin and Margaret Mikyung Lee.

[99] According to a 2002 rule, the AG could waive the required training for state or local law enforcement officers who may deputized to enforce immigration law.

[100] Local law enforcement officials have also made other arguments against enforcing immigration law as discussed in "Pro/Con Analysis of State and Local Law Enforcement Officials Enforcing Immigration Law."

[101] Section 241 of the INA created SCAAP.

[102] The 2000 Census Bureau estimated that there are approximately 8 million undocumented aliens in the United States.

In: Immigration Crisis: Issues, Policies and Consequences   ISBN: 978-1-60456-096-1
Editors: P. W. Hickman and T. P. Curtis, pp. 73-106   © 2008 Nova Science Publishers, Inc.

Chapter 3

U.S. Immigration Policy on Permanent Admissions[*]

Ruth Ellen Wasem

Abstract

When President George W. Bush announced his principles for immigration reform in January 2004, he included an increase in permanent immigration as a key component. President Bush has stated that immigration reform is a top priority of his second term and has prompted a lively debate on the issue. Of an array of bills to revise permanent admissions introduced, only one was enacted in the 109th Congress: A provision in P.L. 109-13 (H.R. 1268, the emergency FY2005 supplemental appropriation) makes up to 50,000 employment-based visas available for foreign nationals coming to work as medical professionals. There is a widely held expectation that the 110th Congress will consider immigration reform.

During the 109th Congress, the Comprehensive Immigration Reform Act (S. 2611) would have substantially increased legal immigration and would have restructured the allocation of these visas. S. 2611 would have doubled the number of family-based and employment-based immigrants admitted over the next decade, as well as expanded the categories of immigrants who may come without numerical limits. The Senate passed S. 2611 on May 25, 2006. The major House-passed immigration bill (H.R. 4437) did not revise family-based and employment-based immigration. Proposals to alter permanent admissions were included in several other immigration proposals (S. 1033/H.R. 2330, S. 1438, H.R. 3700, H.R. 3938, S. 1919). Thus far in the 110th Congress, H.R. 75, H.R. 938, H.R. 1645, and S. 1348 would revise categories for permanent admissions.

Four major principles underlie current U.S. policy on permanent immigration: the reunification of families, the admission of immigrants with needed skills, the protection of refugees, and the diversity of admissions by country of origin. These principles are embodied in the Immigration and Nationality Act (INA). The INA specifies a complex set of numerical limits and preference categories that give priorities for permanent

---

[*] Excerpted from CRS Report RL32235, dated May 11, 2007.

immigration reflecting these principles. Legal permanent residents (LPRs) refer to foreign nationals who live lawfully and permanently in the United States.

During FY2005, a total of 1,122,373 aliens became LPRs in the United States. Of this total, 57.8% entered on the basis of family ties. Additional major immigrant groups in FY2005 were employment-based preference immigrants (including spouses and children) at 22.0%, and refugees and asylees adjusting to immigrant status at 12.7%. Mexico led all countries with 161,445 aliens who became LPRs in FY2005. India followed at a distant second with 84,681 LPRs. China came in third with 69,967. These three countries comprise 30% of all LPRs in FY2005.

Significant backlogs are due to the sheer volume of aliens eligible to immigrate to the United States. Citizens and LPRs first file petitions for their relatives. After the petitions are processed, these relatives then wait for a visa to become available through the numerically limited categories. The siblings of U.S. citizens are waiting 11 years. Prospective LPRs from the Philippines have the most substantial waiting times; consular officers are now considering the petitions of the brothers and sisters of U.S. citizens from the Philippines who filed more than 22 years ago.

LATEST LEGISLATIVE DEVELOPMENTS

Legal immigration reform is likely to come up during the 110th Congress.[1] Senate Majority Leader Reid has indicated that S. 1348, which reportedly is virtually identical to S. 2611 as passed by the 109th Congress, will be the marker for Senate debate on comprehensive immigration reform. The Senate Majority Leader has publicly affirmed his commitment to begin floor debate on comprehensive immigration reform the week of May 14.[2] The House Judiciary Subcommittee on Immigration, Citizenship, Refugees, Border Security, and International Law held two hearings weekly in April and intends to continue this pace through May on various aspects of comprehensive immigration reform.[3]

OVERVIEW

Four major principles currently underlie U.S. policy on legal permanent immigration: the reunification of families, the admission of immigrants with needed skills, the protection of refugees, and the diversity of admissions by country of origin. These principles are embodied in federal law, the Immigration and Nationality Act (INA) first codified in 1952. The Immigration Amendments of 1965 replaced the national origins quota system (enacted after World War I) with per-country ceilings, and the statutory provisions regulating permanent immigration to the United States were last revised significantly by the Immigration Act of 1990.[4]

The two basic types of legal aliens are *immigrants* and *nonimmigrants*. As defined in the INA, immigrants are synonymous with legal permanent residents (LPRs) and refer to foreign nationals who come to live lawfully and permanently in the United States. The other major class of legal aliens are nonimmigrants — such as tourists, foreign students, diplomats, temporary agricultural workers, exchange visitors, or intracompany business personnel — who are admitted for a specific purpose and a temporary period of time. Nonimmigrants are required to leave the country when their visas expire, though certain classes of nonimmigrants may adjust to LPR status if they otherwise qualify.[5]

The conditions for the admission of immigrants are much more stringent than nonimmigrants, and many fewer immigrants than nonimmigrants are admitted. Once admitted, however, immigrants are subject to few restrictions; for example, they may accept and change employment, and may apply for U.S. citizenship through the naturalization process, generally after five years.

Petitions for immigrant (i.e., LPR) status are first filed with U.S. Citizenship and Immigration Services (USCIS) in the Department of Homeland Security (DHS) by the sponsoring relative or employer in the United States. If the prospective immigrant is already residing in the United States, the USCIS handles the entire process, which is called "adjustment of status" because the alien is moving from a temporary category to LPR status. If the prospective LPR does not have legal residence in the United States, the petition is forwarded to the Department of State's (DOS) Bureau of Consular Affairs in their home country after USCIS has reviewed it. The Consular Affairs officer (when the alien is coming from abroad) and USCIS adjudicator (when the alien is adjusting status in the United States) must be satisfied that the alien is entitled to the immigrant status. These reviews are intended to ensure that they are not ineligible for visas or admission under the grounds for inadmissibility spelled out in INA.[6]

Many LPRs are adjusting status from within the United States rather than receiving visas issued abroad by Consular Affairs.[7] As discussed more fully below, 65.8% of all LPRs adjusted to LPR status in the United States while only 34.2% arrived from abroad in FY2005.

The INA specifies that each year countries are held to a numerical limit of 7% of the worldwide level of U.S. immigrant admissions, known as per-country limits. The actual number of immigrants that may be approved from a given country, however, is not a simple percentage calculation. Immigrant admissions and adjustments to LPR status are subject to a complex set of numerical limits and preference categories that give priority for admission on the basis of family relationships, needed skills, and geographic diversity, as discussed below.[8]

CURRENT LAW AND POLICY

Worldwide Immigration Levels

The INA provides for a permanent annual worldwide level of 675,000 legal permanent residents (LPRs), but this level is flexible and certain categories of LPRs are permitted to exceed the limits, as described below.[9] The permanent worldwide immigrant level consists of the following components: family-sponsored immigrants, including immediate relatives of U.S. citizens and family-sponsored preference immigrants (480,000 plus certain unused employment-based preference numbers from the prior year); employment-based preference immigrants (140,000 plus certain unused family preference numbers from the prior year); and diversity immigrants (55,000).[10] Immediate relatives[11] of U.S. citizens as well as refugees and asylees who are adjusting status are exempt from direct numerical limits.[12]

The annual level of family-sponsored preference immigrants is determined by subtracting the number of immediate relative visas issued in the previous year and the number of aliens paroled[13] into the United States for at least a year from 480,000 (the total family-sponsored level) and — when available — adding employment preference immigrant numbers unused during the previous year. By law, the family-sponsored preference level may not fall below 226,000. In recent years, the 480,000 level has been exceeded to maintain the 226,000 floor on family-sponsored preference visas after subtraction of the immediate relative visas.

Within each family and employment preference, the INA further allocates the number of LPRs issued visas each year. As table 1 summarizes the legal immigration preference system, the complexity of the allocations becomes apparent.

Note that in most instances unused visa numbers are allowed to roll down to the next preference category.[14]

Table 1. Legal Immigration Preference System

Category		Numerical limit
Total Family-Sponsored Immigrants		480,000
Immediate relatives	Aliens who are the spouses and unmarried minor children of U.S. citizens and the parents of adult U.S. citizens	Unlimited
Family-sponsored Preference Immigrants		Worldwide Level 226,000
1st preference	Unmarried sons and daughters of citizens	23,400 plus visas not required for 4th preference
2nd preference	(A) Spouses and children of LPRs (B) Unmarried sons and daughters of LPRs	114,200 plus visas not required for 1st preference
3rd preference	Married sons and daughters of citizens	23,400 plus visas not required for 1st or 2nd preference
4th preference	Siblings of citizens age 21 and over	65,000 plus visas not required for 1st, 2nd, or 3rd preference
Employment-Based Preference Immigrants		Worldwide Level 140,000
1st preference	Priority workers: persons of extraordinary ability in the arts, science, education, business, or athletics; outstanding professors and researchers; and certain multi-national executives and managers	28.6% of worldwide limit plus unused 4th and 5th preference
2nd preference	Members of the professions holding advanced degrees or persons of exceptional abilities in the sciences, art, or business	28.6% of worldwide limit plus unused 1st preference
3rd preference — skilled	Skilled shortage workers with at least two years training or experience, professionals with baccalaureate degrees	28.6% of worldwide limit plus unused 1st or 2nd preference
3rd preference — "other"	Unskilled shortage workers	10,000 (taken from the total available for 3rd preference)
4th preference	"Special immigrants," including ministers of religion, religious workers other than ministers, certain employees of the U.S. government abroad, and others	7.1% of worldwide limit; religious workers limited to 5,000
5th preference	Employment creation investors who invest at least $1 million (amount may vary in rural areas or areas of high unemployment) which will create at least 10 new jobs	7.1% of worldwide limit; 3,000 *minimum* reserved for investors in rural or high unemployment areas

Source: CRS summary of §§ 203(a), 203(b), and 204 of INA; 8 U.S.C. § 1153.

Employment-based allocations are further affected by § 203(e) of the Nicaraguan and Central American Relief Act (NACARA), as amended by § 1(e) of P.L. 105-139. This provision states that when the employment 3rd preference "other worker" (OW) cut-off date reached the priority date of the latest OW petition approved prior to November 19, 1997, the 10,000 OW numbers available for a fiscal year are to be reduced by up to 5,000 annually beginning in the following fiscal year. This reduction is to be made for as long as necessary to offset adjustments under NACARA. Since the OW cut-off date reached November 19, 1997 during FY2001, the reduction in the OW limit to 5,000 began in FY2002.

Employers who seek to hire prospective employment-based immigrants through the second and third preference categories also must petition the U.S. Department of Labor (DOL) on behalf of the alien. The prospective immigrant must demonstrate that he or she meets the qualifications for the particular job as well as the preference category. If DOL determines that a labor shortage exists in the occupation for which the petition is filed, labor certification will be issued. If there is not a labor shortage in the given occupation, the employer must submit evidence of extensive recruitment efforts in order to obtain certification.[15]

As part of the Immigration Act of 1990, Congress added a fifth preference category for foreign investors to become LPRs. The INA allocates up to 10,000 admissions annually and generally requires a minimum $1 million investment and employment of at least 10 U.S. workers. Less capital is required for aliens who participate in the immigrant investor pilot program, in which they invest in targeted regions and existing enterprises that are financially troubled.[16]

Per-Country Ceilings

As stated earlier, the INA establishes per-country levels at 7% of the worldwide level.[17] For a dependent foreign state, the per-country ceiling is 2%. The per-country level is not a "quota" set aside for individual countries, as each country in the world, of course, could not receive 7% of the overall limit. As the State Department describes, the per-country level "is not an entitlement but a barrier against monopolization."

Two important exceptions to the per-country ceilings have been enacted in the past decade. Foremost is an exception for certain family-sponsored immigrants. More specifically, the INA states that 75% of the visas allocated to spouses and children of LPRs (2nd A family preference) are not subject to the per-country ceiling.[18] Prior to FY2001, employment-based preference immigrants were also held to per-country ceilings. The American Competitiveness in the Twenty-First Century Act of 2000 (P.L. 106-313) enabled the per-country ceilings for employment-based immigrants to be surpassed for individual countries that are oversubscribed as long as visas are available within the worldwide limit for employment-based preferences. The impact of these revisions to the per-country ceilings is discussed later in this report.

The actual per-country ceiling varies from year to year according to the prior year's immediate relative and parolee admissions and unused visas that roll over. In FY2003, the per-country ceiling was set at 27,827 and in FY2002 was 25,804. According to the Department of State's Bureau of Consular Affairs, the ceiling for FY2004 was expected to be about 30,000. Processing backlogs, discussed later in this report, also inadvertently reduced the number of LPRs in FY2003. Only 705,827 people became LPRs in FY2003. USCIS was only able to process 161,579 of the potential 226,000 family-sponsored LPRs in FY2003, and thus 64,421 LPR visas rolled over to the FY2004 employment-based categories.[19]

Other Permanent Immigration Categories

There are several other major categories of legal permanent immigration in addition to the family-sponsored and employment-based preference categories. These classes of LPRs cover a variety of cases, ranging from aliens who win the Diversity Visa Lottery to aliens in removal (i.e., deportation) proceedings granted LPR status by an immigration judge because of exceptional and extremely unusual hardship. Table 2 summarizes these major classes and identifies whether they are numerically limited.

Table 2. Other Major Legal Immigration Categories

Nonpreference Immigrants		Numerical Limit
Asylees	Aliens in the United States who have been granted asylum due to persecution or a well-founded fear of persecution and who must wait one year before petitioning for LPR status	No limits on LPR adjustments as of FY2005. (Previously limited to 10,000)
Cancellation of Removal	Aliens in removal proceedings granted LPR status by an immigration judge because of exceptional and extremely unusual hardship	4,000 (with certain exceptions)
Diversity Lottery	Aliens from foreign nations with low admission levels; must have high school education or equivalent or minimum two years work experience in a profession requiring two years training or experience	55,000
Refugees	Aliens abroad who have been granted refugee status due to persecution or a well-founded fear of persecution and who must wait one year before petitioning for LPR status	Presidential Determination for refugee status, no limits on LPR adjustments
Other	Various classes of immigrants, such as Amerasians, parolees, and certain Central Americans, Cubans, and Haitians who are adjusting to LPR status	Dependent on specific adjustment authority

Source: CRS summary of §§ 203(a), 203(b), 204, 207, 208, and 240A of INA; 8 U.S.C. § 1153.

ADMISSIONS TRENDS

Immigration Patterns, 1900-2005

Immigration to the United States is not totally determined by shifts in flow that occur as a result of lawmakers revising the allocations. Immigration to the United States plummeted in the middle of the 20th Century largely as a result of factors brought on by the Great Depression and World War II. There are a variety of "pushpull" factors that drive immigration. Push factors from the immigrant-sending countries include such circumstances as civil wars and political unrest, economic deprivation and limited job opportunities, and catastrophic natural disasters. Pull factors in the United States include such features as strong employment conditions, reunion with family, and quality of life considerations. A corollary factor is the extent that aliens may be able to migrate to other "desirable" countries that offer circumstances and opportunities comparable to the United States.

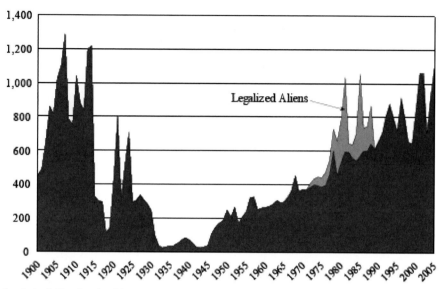

Source *Statistical Yearbook of Immigration.* Department of Homeland Security, Office of Immigration Statistics, multiple fiscal year liens legalizing through the Immigration Reform and Control Act of 1986 are depicted by year of arrival.

Figure 1. Annual Immigration Admissions and Status Adjustments, 1990-2005.

The annual number of LPRs admitted or adjusted in the United States rose gradually after World War II, as figure 1 illustrates. However, the annual admissions have not reached the peaks of the early 20th century. The DHS Office of Immigration Statistics (OIS) data present those admitted as LPRs or those adjusting to LPR status. The growth in immigration after 1980 is partly attributable to the total number of admissions under the basic system, consisting of immigrants entering through a preference system as well as immediate relatives of U.S. citizens, that was augmented considerably by legalized aliens.[20] The Immigration Act of 1990 increased the ceiling on employment-based preference immigration, with the provision that unused employment visas would be made available the following year for family preference immigration. In addition, the number of refugees admitted increased from 718,000 in the period 1966-1980 to 1.6 million during the period 1981-1995, after the enactment of the Refugee Act of 1980.

Many LPRs are adjusting status from within the United States rather than receiving visas issued abroad by Consular Affairs before they arrive in the United States. In the past decade, the number of LPRs arriving from abroad has remained somewhat steady, hovering between a high of 421,405 in FY1996 and a low of 358,411 in FY2003. Adjustments to LPR status in the United States has fluctuated over the same period, from a low of 244,793 in FY1999 to a high of 738,302 in FY2005. As figure 2 shows, most of the variation in total number of aliens granted LPR status over the past decade is due to the number of adjustments processed in the United States rather than visas issued abroad.

In FY2005, 65.8% of all LPRs were adjusting status within the United States. Most (89%) of the employment-based immigrants adjusted to LPR status within the United States. Many (61%) of the immediate relatives of U.S. citizens also did so. Only 33% of the other family-preference immigrants adjusted to LPR status within the United States.

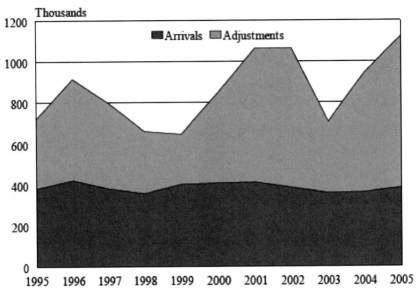

Source *Statistical Yearbook of Immigration*, U.S. Department of Homeland Security, Office of Immigration Statistics, (multiple years).

Figure 2. Legal Permanent Residents: New Arrivals and Adjustments of Status, FY1995-FY2005.

In any given period of United States history, a handful of countries have dominated the flow of immigrants, but the dominant countries have varied over time. Figure 3 presents trends in the top immigrant-sending countries (together comprising at least 50% of the immigrants admitted) for selected decades and illustrates that immigration at the close of the 20th century is not as dominated by a few countries as it was earlier in the century. These data suggest that the per-country ceilings established in 1965 had some effect. As figure 3 illustrates, immigrants from only three or four countries made up more then half of all LPRs prior to 1960. By the last two decades of the 20th century, immigrants from seven to eight countries comprised about half of all LPRs and this patterns has continued into the 21st century.

Although Europe was home to the countries sending the most immigrants during the early 20th century, Mexico has been a top sending country for most of the 20th century. Other top sending countries from the Western Hemisphere are the Dominican Republic and most recently — El Salvador and Cuba. In addition, Asian countries — notably the Philippines, India, China, Korea, and Vietnam — have emerged as top sending countries today.

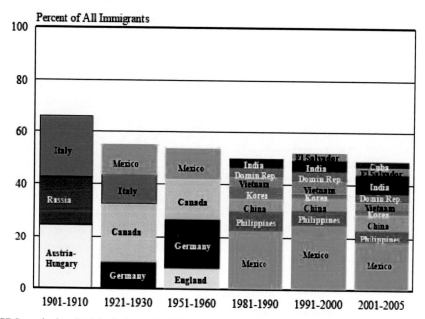

Source: CRS analysis of table 2, Statistical Yearbook of Immigration, U.S. Department of Homeland Security, Office of Immigration Statistics, FY2004 (June 2005).

Figure 3. Top Sending Countries (Comprising More Than Half of All LPRs): Selected Periods.

FY2005 Admissions

During FY2005, a total of 1,122,373 aliens became LPRs in the United States. The largest number of immigrants are admitted because of a family relationship with a U.S. citizen or resident immigrant, as figure 4 illustrates. Of the total LPRs in FY2005, 57.8% entered on the basis of family ties. Immediate relatives of U.S. citizens made up the single largest group of immigrants, as table 3 indicates. Family preference immigrants — the spouses and children of immigrants, the adult children of U.S. citizens, and the siblings of adult U.S. citizens — were the second largest group. Additional major immigrant groups in FY2005 were employment-based preference immigrants (including spouses and children) at 22.0%, and refugees and asylees adjusting to immigrant status at 12.7%.[21]

Table 3. FY2005 Immigrants by Category

Total	
Immediate relatives of citizens	436,231
Family preference	212,970
Employment preference	246,878
Refugee and asylee adjustments	142,962
Diversity	46,234
Other	37,098

Source: *Statistical Yearbook of Immigration*, FY2005, DHS Office of Immigration Statistics, Dec. 2006. For a more detailed summary of FY2005 immigration by category, see Appendix C.

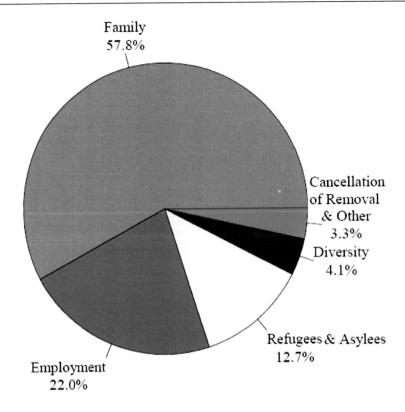

Family
57.8%

Cancellation
of Removal
& Other
3.3%
Diversity
4.1%

Refugees & Asylees
12.7%

Employment
22.0%

1.12 million

Source: CRS presentation of FY2005 data from the DHS Office of Immigration Statistics.

Figure 4. Legal Immigrants by Major Category, FY2005.

As figure 5 presents, Mexico led all countries with 161,445 aliens who became LPRs in FY2005. India followed at a distant second with 84,681 LPRs. China came in third with 69,967. These three countries comprise 30% of all LPRs in FY2005 and exceeded the per-country ceiling for preference immigrants because they benefitted from special exceptions to the per-country ceilings. Mexico did so as a result of the provision in INA that allows 75% of family second preference (i.e., spouses and children of LPRs) to exceed the per-country ceiling, while India and China exceeded the ceiling through the exception to the employment-based per-country limits.

The top 12 immigrant-sending countries depicted in figure 5 accounted for half of all LPRs in FY2005. The top 50 immigrant-sending countries contributed 87% of all LPRs in FY2005. Appendix A provides detailed data on the top 50 immigrant-sending countries by major category of legal immigration.

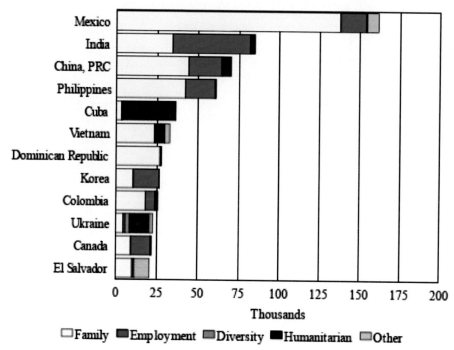

Source: CRS presentation of FY2005 data from the DHS Office of Immigration Statistics.

Figure 5. Top Twelve Immigrant-Sending Countries, FY2005.

BACKLOGS AND WAITING TIMES

Visa Processing Dates

According to the INA, family-sponsored and employment-based preference visas are issued to eligible immigrants in the order in which a petition has been filed. Spouses and children of prospective LPRs are entitled to the same status, and the same order of consideration as the person qualifying as principal LPR, if accompanying or following to join (referred to as derivative status). When visa demand exceeds the per-country limit, visas are prorated according to the preference system allocations (detailed in table 1) for the oversubscribed foreign state or dependent area. These provisions apply at present to the following countries oversubscribed in the family-sponsored categories: China, Mexico, the Philippines, and India.

Table 4. Priority Dates for Family Preference Visas[22]

Category	Worldwide	China	India	Mexico	Philippines
Unmarried sons and daughters of citizens	May 1, 2001	May 1, 2001	May 1, 2001	Jan. 1, 1994	Jan. 22, 1992
Spouses and children of LPRs	Mar. 22, 2002	Mar. 22, 2002	Mar. 22, 2002	Aug. 15, 2000	Mar. 22, 2002
Unmarried sons and daughters of LPRs	July 1, 1997	July 1, 1997	July 1, 1997	Mar. 1, 1992	Oct. 1, 1996
Married sons and daughters of citizens	Mar. 1, 1999	Mar. 1, 1999	Mar. 1, 1999	Aug. 1, 1994	Sept. 1, 1990
Siblings of citizens age 21 and over	Mar. 22, 1996	Aug. 22, 1995	Nov. 8, 1995	May 1, 1994	Sept. 1, 1984

Source: U.S. Department of State, Bureau of Consular Affairs, *Visa Bulletin for March 2007.*

As table 4 evidences, relatives of U.S. citizens and LPRs are waiting in backlogs for a visa to become available, with the brothers and sisters of U.S. citizens now waiting about 11 years. "Priority date" means that unmarried adult sons and daughters of U.S. citizens who filed petitions on May 1, 2001, are now being processed for visas. Married adult sons and daughters of U.S. citizens who filed petitions eight years ago (March 1, 1999) are now being processed for visas. Prospective family-sponsored immigrants from the Philippines have the most substantial waiting times before a visa is scheduled to become available to them; consular officers are now considering the petitions of the brothers and sisters of U.S. citizens from the Philippines who filed more than 22 years ago.

Because of P.L. 106-313's easing of the employment-based per-country limits, few countries and categories are currently oversubscribed in the employment-based preferences. As table 5 presents, however, some employment-based visa categories are once again unavailable. The Department of State's *Visa Bulletin for July 2005*, offered the following explanation: "The Employment Third and Third Other Worker categories have reached their annual limits and no further FY2005 allocations are possible for the period July through September. With the start of the new fiscal year in October, numbers will once again become available in these categories."[23] The *Visa Bulletin for September 2005* offered further information: "The backlog reduction efforts of both Citizenship and Immigration Services, and the Department of Labor continue to result in very heavy demand for Employment-based numbers. It is anticipated that the amount of such cases will be sufficient to use all available numbers in many categories...demand in the Employment categories is expected to be far in excess of the annual limits, and once established, cut-off date movements are likely to be slow."[24]

When the *Visa Bulletin for October 2005* became available, it was evident that third preference visas (professional, skilled, and unskilled) were oversubscribed on a worldwide level. The countries that are particularly affected by the oversubscription of the employment-based preference categories are China and India. The visa waiting times have eased somewhat over the summer of 2006, as indicated by the data from the *Visa Bulletin for March 2007.* "Visa retrogression" has occurred again for third preference visas (professional, skilled, and unskilled) as presented in table 5. Prospective immigrants from China, India, Mexico, and the Philippines are particularly affected.

Table 5. Priority Dates for Employment Preference Visas[25]

Category	Worldwide	China	India	Mexico	Philippines
Priority workers	current	current	current	current	current
Advanced degrees/ exceptional ability	current	Apr. 22, 2005	Jan. 8, 2003	current	current
Skilled and professional	Aug. 1, 2002	Aug. 1, 2002	May 8, 2001	May 15, 2001	Aug. 1, 2002
Unskilled	Oct. 1, 2001	Oct. 1, 2001	Oct. 1, 2001	Oct. 1, 2001	Oct. 1, 2001
Schedule Aa	current	current	current	current	current
Special immigrants	current	current	current	current	current
Investors	current	current	current	current	current

Source: U.S. Department of State, Bureau of Consular Affairs, *Visa Bulletin for March 2007*.

a. Schedule A refers to §502 of Division B, Title V of P.L. 109-13, which makes up to 50,000 permanent employment-based visas available for foreign nationals coming to work as nurses.

Petition Processing Backlogs

Distinct from the visa priority dates that result from the various numerical limits in the law, there are significant backlogs due to the sheer volume of aliens eligible to immigrate to the United States. In December 2003, USCIS reported 5.3 million immigrant petitions pending.[26] USCIS decreased the number of immigrant petitions pending by 24% by the end of FY2004, but still had 4.1 million petitions pending. As FY2005 drew to a close there were over 3.1 million immigration petitions pending.[27] The latest processing dates for immediate relative, family preference, and employment-based LPR petitions are presented in Appendix B for each of the four USCIS Regional Service Centers.

Even though there are no numerical limits on the admission of aliens who are immediate relatives of U.S. citizens, such citizens petitioning for their relatives are waiting at least a year and in some parts of the country, more than two years for the paperwork to be processed. Citizens and LPRs petitioning for relatives under the family preferences are often waiting several years for the petitions to be processed. Appendix B is illustrative, but not comprehensive because some immigration petitions may be filed at USCIS District offices and at the National Benefits Center.

Aliens with LPR petitions cannot visit the United States. Since the INA presumes that all aliens seeking admission to the United States are coming to live permanently, nonimmigrants must demonstrate that they are coming for a temporary period or they will be denied a visa. Aliens with LPR petitions pending are clearly intending to live in the United States permanently and thus are denied nonimmigrant visas to come temporarily.[28]

RECENT LEGISLATIVE HISTORY

Issues in the 108th Congress

Legislation reforming permanent immigration came from a variety of divergent perspectives in the 108th Congress. The sheer complexity of the current set of provisions makes revising the law on permanent immigration a daunting task. This discussion focuses only on those bills that would have revised the permanent immigration categories and the numerical limits as defined in §201-§203 of the INA.[29]

On January 21, 2004, Senators Chuck Hagel and Thomas Daschle introduced legislation (S. 2010) that would, if enacted, potentially yield significant increases in legal permanent admissions. The Immigration Reform Act of 2004 (S. 2010), would have among other provisions: no longer deduct immediate relatives from the overall family-sponsored numerical limits; treat spouses and minor children of LPRs the same as immediate relatives of U.S. citizens (exempt from numerical limits); and reallocate the 226,000 family preference numbers to the remaining family preference categories. In addition, many aliens who would have benefited from S. 2010's proposed temporary worker provisions would be able to adjust to LPR status outside the numerical limits of the per country ceiling and the worldwide levels.

Several bills that would offer more targeted revisions to permanent immigration were offered in the House. Representative Robert Andrews introduced H.R. 539, which would have exempted spouses of LPRs from the family preference limits and thus treated them similar to immediate relatives of U.S. citizens. Representative Richard Gephardt likewise included a provision that would have treated spouses of LPRs outside of the numerical limits in his "Earned Legalization and Family Unity Act" (H.R. 3271). Representative Jerrold Nadler introduced legislation (H.R. 832) that would have amended the INA to add "permanent partners" after "spouses" and thus would have enabled aliens defined as permanent partners to become LPRs through the family-based immigration categories as well as to become derivative relatives of qualifying immigrants.

Legislation that would have reduced legal permanent immigration was introduced early in the 108th Congress by Representative Thomas Tancredo. The "Mass Immigration Reduction Act" (H.R. 946) would have zeroed out family sponsored immigrants (except children and spouses of U.S. citizens), employment-based immigrants (except certain priority workers) and diversity lottery immigrants through FY2008. It also would have set a numerical limit of 25,000 on refugee admissions and asylum adjustments. Representative J. Gresham Barrett introduced an extensive revision of immigration law (H.R. 3522) that also included a significant scaling back of permanent immigration.

Legislation Passed in the 109th Congress

Recaptured Visa Numbers for Nurses

Section 502 of Division B, Title V of P.L. 109-13 (H.R. 1268, the emergency FY2005 supplemental appropriation) amends the American Competitiveness in the Twenty-first Century Act of 2000 (P.L. 106-313) to modify the formula for recapturing unused employment-based immigrant visas for employment-based immigrants "whose immigrant worker petitions were approved based on schedule A." In other words, it makes up to 50,000 permanent employment-based visas available for foreign nationals coming to work as nurses. This provision was added to H.R. 1268 as an amendment in the Senate and was accepted by the conferees.

Recaptured Employment-Based Visa Numbers

On October 20, 2005, the Senate Committee on the Judiciary approved compromise language that, among other things, would have recaptured up to 90,000 employment-based visas that had not been issued in prior years (when the statutory ceiling of 140,000 visas was not met). An additional fee of $500 would have been charged to obtain these recaptured visas. This language was forwarded to the Senate Budget Committee for inclusion in the budget reconciliation legislation. On November 18, 2005, the Senate passed S. 1932, the Deficit Reduction Omnibus Reconciliation Act of 2005, with these provisions as Title VIII. These provisions, however, were not included in the House-passed Deficit Reduction Act of 2005 (H.R. 4241).

The conference report (H.Rept. 109-362) on the Deficit Reduction Act of 2005 (S. 1932) was reported during the legislative day of December 18, 2005. It did not include the Senate provisions that would have recaptured employment-based visas unused in prior years. On December 19, the House agreed to the conference report by a vote of 212-206. On December 21, the Senate removed extraneous matter from the legislation pursuant to a point of order raised under the "Byrd rule" and then, by a vote of 51-50 (with Vice President Cheney breaking a tie vote), returned the amended measure to the House for further action.

USCIS Funding Trends

USCIS funds the processing and adjudication of immigrant, nonimmigrant, refugee, asylum, and citizenship benefits largely through monies generated by the Examinations Fee Account.[30] The Administration increased the fees charged to U.S. citizens and legal permanent residents petitioning to bring family or employees into the United States and to foreign nationals in the United States seeking immigration benefits.[31] In FY2004, 86% of USCIS funding came from the Examinations Fee Account. In FY2005, USCIS has budget authority for $1.571 billion from the Examinations Fee Account.[32] Congress provided a direct appropriation of $60 million in FY2005 to reduce the backlog of applications and to strive for a six-month processing standard for all applications by FY2006.[33]

FY2006

The Administration sought $1.81 billion for USCIS for FY2006. This figure would have been an additional $79 million for FY2006, a 5% increase over FY2005. For direct appropriations, the Administration requested $80 million — a cut of $80 million from FY2005 and a cut of $155 million from the $235 million Congress appropriated in FY2004. A decrease of 26% in backlog reduction and customer service activities was proposed for FY2006. The House-passed bill making FY2006 appropriations for the Department of Homeland Security (H.R. 2360) would have provided an increase of $40 million above the President's request for a total of $120 million, which would have been $40 million less than FY2005.

The Senate-reported version of H.R. 2360 would have provided $80 million for USCIS in direct appropriations, recommending $40 million less than provided in H.R. 2360 as passed by the House, and $80 million less than enacted in FY2005.

On September 29, 2005, the conference committee approved and filed the conference report (H.Rept. 109-241) to H.R. 2360. The conferees recommend a total of $1,889 million for USCIS, of which 94% comes from fees. The remaining 6% is a direct appropriation of $115 million, which includes $80 million for backlog reduction initiatives as well as $35 million to support the information technology transformation effort and to convert immigration records into digital format. The FY2006 appropriations amount is a decrease of 28% from the $160 million appropriated in FY2005. As a result of a 10% increase in revenue budgeted from fees, the FY2006 total is 6% greater than the FY2005 total. The President signed H.R 2360 as P.L. 109-90 on October 18, 2005.

FY2007

In terms of direct appropriations, the Administration requested $182 million — an increase of $68 million from FY2006. The Administration requested a total of $1,986 million for USCIS (an increase of 5% over the enacted FY2006 level of $1,888 million), the bulk of the funding coming from fees paid by individuals and businesses filing petitions. For FY2007, USCIS expects to receive a total of $1,804 million from the various fee accounts, most of which ($1,760 million) would be coming from the Examinations Fee Account. According to the USCIS Congressional Justification documents, funds from the Examinations Fee Account alone comprise 91% of the total USCIS FY2007 budget request. The FY2007 Budget also included $13 million from the H-1B Nonimmigrant Petitioner Account[34] and $31 million from the H-1B and L Fraud Prevention and Detection Account.[35] The Administration proposed to use the $31 million generated from the fee on H-1B and L petitions to expand its Fraud Detection and National Security Office.[36]

The House-passed FY2007 DHS appropriations bill, H.R. 5441, would have appropriated $162 million for USCIS in FY2007. The Senate would have provided USCIS $135 million in direct appropriations for FY2007. Among the Senate floor amendments to H.R. 5441 was one that would direct DHS, notably through USCIS, to increase its fees charged to noncitizens to produce an additional $350 million in receipts for FY2007. Most of the funds collected by the fee increases would have gone to CBP and ICE, but $85 million would have remained with USCIS for business transformation ($47 million) and fraud detection and national security ($38 million).[37]

The conferees (H.Rept. 109-699) provide USCIS with $182 million in direct appropriations, $47 million of which is contingent on USCIS obtaining approval from the Committees on Appropriations of the USCIS plan for "business system and information technology transformation plan." As enacted, P.L. 109-295 provides $114 million for expansion of the Employment Eligibility Verification system and $21 million for the Systematic Alien Verification for Entitlements (SAVE) system, automated database systems to ascertain immigration status. In terms of USCIS income from fees, current estimates are $1,804 million, giving USCIS $1,986 million in total resources.

Major Issues in the 109th Congress

President Bush's Immigration Reform Proposal

When President George W. Bush announced his principles for immigration reform in January 2004, he included an increase in permanent legal immigration as a key component. The fact sheet that accompanied his remarks referred to a "reasonable increase in the annual limit of legal immigrants."[38] When the President spoke, he characterized his policy recommendation as follows:

> The citizenship line, however, is too long, and our current limits on legal immigration are too low. My administration will work with the Congress to increase the annual number of green cards that can lead to citizenship. Those willing to take the difficult path of citizenship — the path of work, and patience, and assimilation — should be welcome in America, like generations of immigrants before them.[39]

Some commentators are speculating the President is promoting increases in the employment-based categories of permanent immigration, but the Bush Administration has not yet provided specific information on what categories of legal permanent admissions it advocates should be increased. Details on the level of increases the Administration is seeking also have not been provided.

The President featured his immigration reform proposal in the 2004 State of the Union address, and a lively debate has ensued. Most of the attention has focused on the new temporary worker component of his proposal and whether the overall proposal constitutes an "amnesty" for aliens living in the United States without legal authorization.

President Bush continues to state that immigration reform is a top priority. In an interview with the Washington Times, the President responded to a question about where immigration reform ranks in his second term agenda by saying, "I think it's high. I think it's a big issue." The President posited that the current situation is a "bureaucratic nightmare" that must be solved.[40]

Securing America's Borders Act (S. 2454)/Chairman's Mark

Title IV of S. 2454, the Securing America's Borders Act, which Senate Majority Leader Bill Frist introduced on March 16, 2006, as well as Title V in the draft of Senate Judiciary Chairman Arlen Specter's mark circulated March 6, 2006 (Chairman's mark) would have substantially increased legal immigration and would have restructured the allocation of these visas. The particular provisions in S. 2454 and the Chairman's mark were essentially equivalent.

Foremost, Title IV of S. 2454 and Title V of the Chairman's mark would have no longer deducted immediate relatives of U.S. citizens from the overall family-sponsored numerical limit of 480,000. This change would have likely added at least 226,000 more family-based admissions annually (based upon the current floor of 226,000 family-sponsored visas). The bills would have increased the annual number of employment-based LPRs from 140,000 to 290,000. They also would have no longer counted the derivative family members of employment-based LPRs as part of the numerical ceiling. If each employment-based LPR would be accompanied by 1.2 family members (as is currently the ratio), then an estimated 348,000 additional LPRs might have been admitted. The bills would have "recaptured" visa numbers from FY2001 through FY2005 in those cases when the family-based and employment-based ceilings were not reached.

Title IV of S. 2454 and Title V of the Chairman's mark would have raised the current per-country limit on LPR visas from an allocation of 7% of the total preference allocation to 10% of the total preference allocation (which would have been 480,000 for family-based and

290,000 for employment-based under this bill). Coupled with the proposed increases in the worldwide ceilings, these provisions would have eased the visa wait times that oversubscribed countries (i.e., China, India, Mexico, and the Philippines) currently have by substantially increasing their share of the overall ceiling.

Title IV of S. 2454 and Title V of the Chairman's mark would have further reallocated family-sponsored immigrants and employment-based visas. The numerical limits on immediate relatives of LPRs would have increased from 114,200 (plus visas not used by first preference) to 240,000 annually. They would have shifted the allocation of visas from persons of "extraordinary" and "exceptional" abilities and persons having advanced professional degrees (i.e., first and second preferences), and increased the number of visas to unskilled workers 10,000 to 87,000 — plus any unused visas that would roll down from the other employment-based preference categories. Employment-based visas for certain special immigrants would have no longer been numerically limited.[41]

Comprehensive Immigration Reform (S. 2611)

As the Senate was locked in debate on S. 2454 and the Judiciary Chairman's mark during the two-week period of March 28-April 7, 2006, an alternative was offered by Senators Chuck Hagel and Mel Martinez. Chairman Specter, along with Senators Hagel, Martinez, Graham, Brownback, Kennedy, and McCain introduced this compromise as S. 2611 on April 7, 2006, just prior to the recess. The identical language was introduced by Senator Hagel (S. 2612). Much like S. 2454 and S.Amdt. 3192, S. 2611 would have substantially increased legal permanent immigration and would have restructured the allocation of the family-sponsored and employment-based visas. After several days of debate and a series of amendments, the Senate passed S. 2611 as amended by a vote of 62-36 on May 25, 2006.

In its handling of family-based legal immigration, Title V of S. 2611 mirrored Title IV of S. 2454 and Title V of the Chairman's mark. It would have no longer deducted immediate relatives of U.S. citizens from the overall family-sponsored numerical limit of 480,000. This change would have likely added at least 226,000 more family-based admissions annually (based upon the current floor of 226,000 family-sponsored visas). The numerical limits on immediate relatives of LPRs would have increased from 114,200 (plus visas not used by first preference) to 240,000 annually.

Assuming that the trend in the number of immediate relatives of U.S. citizens continued at the same upward rate, the projected number of immediate relatives would have been approximately 470,000 in 2008. Assuming that the demand for the numerically limited family preferences continued at the same level, the full 480,000 would have been allocated. If these assumptions held, the United States would have likely admitted or adjusted an estimated 950,000 family-sponsored LPRs by 2009, as figure 6 projects.[42]

In terms of employment-based immigration, S. 2611 would have increased the annual number of employment-based LPRs from 140,000 to 450,000 from FY2007 through FY2016, and set the limit at 290,000 thereafter. S. 2611/S. 2612 also would have no longer counted the derivative family members of employment-based LPRs as part of the numerical ceiling. As in S. 2454, S. 2611 would have reallocated employment-based visas as follows: up to 15% to "priority workers"; up to 15% to professionals holding advanced degrees and certain persons of exceptional ability; up to 35% to skilled shortage workers with two years training or experience and certain professionals; up to 5% to employment creation investors; and up to 30% (135,000) to unskilled shortage workers.

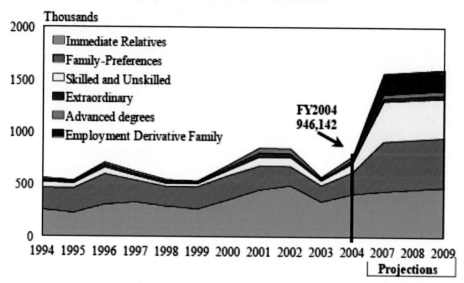

Note: Future Employment-based 4th preference special immigrants and 5th preference in have too many unknown factors to estimate.

Source: CRS analysis of data from the DHS Office of Immigration Statistics and the former INS.

Figure 6. Projected Flow of LPRs under S. 2611, FY2007 FY2009.

Employment-based visas for certain special immigrants would have no longer been numerically limited. S. 2611 also would have no longer counted the derivative family members of employment-based LPRs as part of the numerical ceiling. If each employment-based LPR would be accompanied by 1.2 family members (as is currently the ratio), then an estimated 540,000 additional LPRs might have been admitted. However, the Senate passed an amendment on the floor that placed an overall limit of 650,000 on employment-based LPRs and their accompanying family annually FY2007-FY2016, as figure 6 projects.[43]

In addition, special exemptions from numerical limits would have also been made for aliens who have worked in the United States for three years and who have earned an advanced degree in science, technology, engineering, or math. Certain widows and orphan who meet specified risk factors would have also been exempted from numerical limits. The bills would have further increased overall levels of immigration by reclaiming family and employment-based LPR visas when the annual ceilings were not met, FY2001-FY2005. As noted earlier, unused visas from one preference category in one fiscal year roll over to the other preference category the following year.

S. 2611 would have significantly expanded the number of guest worker and other temporary foreign worker visas available each year and would have coupled these increases with eased opportunities for these temporary workers to ultimately adjust to LPR status.[44] Whether the LPR adjustments of guest workers and other temporary foreign workers were channeled through the numerically limited, employment-based preferences or were exempt from numerical limits (as were the proposed F-4 foreign student fourth preference adjustments) obviously would have affected the projections and the future flows.[45]

S. 2611 included a provision that would have exempted from direct numerical limits those LPRs who are being admitted for employment in occupations that the Secretary of Labor has deemed there are insufficient U.S. workers "able, willing and qualified" to work. Such occupations are commonly referred to as Schedule A because of the subsection of the code where the Secretary's authority derives. Currently, nurses and physical therapists are listed on Schedule A, as are certain aliens deemed of exceptional ability in the sciences or arts (excluding those in the performing arts).

Title V of S. 2611 would have raised the current per-country limit on LPR visas from an allocation of 7% of the total preference allocation to 10% of the total preference allocation (which would be 480,000 for family-based and 450,000/290,000 for employment-based under this bill).[46] Coupled with the proposed increases in the worldwide ceilings, these provisions would have eased the visa wait times that oversubscribed countries (i.e., China, India, Mexico, and the Philippines) currently have by substantially increasing their share of the overall ceiling. The bill would have also eliminated the exceptions to the per-country ceilings for certain family-based and employment-based LPRs, which are discussed above.[47]

Secure America and Orderly Immigration Act (S. 1033/H.R. 2330)

On May 12, 2005, a bipartisan group of Senators and Congressmen[48] introduced an expansive immigration bill known as the Secure America and Orderly Immigration Act (S. 1033/H.R. 2330). Among other things, these bills would have made significant revisions to the permanent legal admissions sections of INA.[49] Specifically Title VI of the legislation would have

- removed immediate relatives of U.S. citizens from the calculation of the 480,000 annual cap on family-based visas for LPR status, thereby providing additional visas to the family preference categories;
- lowered the income requirements for sponsoring a family member for LPR status from 125% of the federal poverty guidelines to 100%;
- recaptured for future allocations those LPR visas that were unused due to processing delays from FY2001 through FY2005;
- increase the annual limit on employment-based LPR visa categories from 140,000 to 290,000 visas; and
- raised the current per-country limit on LPR visas from an allocation of 7% of the total preference allocation to 10% of the total preference allocation (which would be 480,000 for family-based and 290,000 for employment-based under this bill).

Comprehensive Enforcement and Immigration Reform Act of 2005

The Comprehensive Enforcement and Immigration Reform Act of 2005 (S. 1438), introduced by Senators John Cornyn and Jon Kyl on July 20, 2005, had provisions that would have restructured the allocation of employment-based visas for LPRs. Among the various proposals, Title X of this legislation would have made the following specific changes to the INA provisions on permanent admissions:

- reduced the allocation of visas to persons of "extraordinary" and "exceptional" abilities and persons having advanced professional degrees (i.e., first and second preferences);

- increased the number of visas to unskilled workers from a statutory cap of 10,000 annually to a level of 36% of the 140,000 ceiling for employment-based admissions (plus any other unused employment-based visas);
- eliminated the category of diversity visas; and ! recaptured for future allocations those employment-based visa numbers that were unused from FY2001 through FY2005.

Immigration Accountability Act of 2005

As part of a package of four immigration reform bills, Senator Chuck Hagel introduced the Immigration Accountability Act of 2005 (S. 1919), which would have provided for "earned adjustment of status" for certain unauthorized aliens who met specified conditions and would have expanded legal immigration. In terms of permanent legal admissions, S. 1919 would have among other provisions:

- no longer deducted immediate relatives from the overall family-sponsored numerical limits of 480,000;
- treated spouses and minor children of LPRs the same as immediate relatives of U.S. citizens (i.e., exempt from numerical limits); and
- reallocated the 226,000 family preference numbers to the remaining family preference categories.

The Hagel immigration reform proposal also included legislation revising the temporary worker programs, border security efforts, and employment verification.

Enforcement First Immigration Reform Act of 2005

Title VI of the Enforcement First Immigration Reform Act of 2005 (H.R. 3938), introduced by Representative J.D. Hayworth, focused on revising permanent admissions. H.R. 3938 would have increased employment-based admissions and decreased family-based admissions. More specifically, it would have

- increased the worldwide ceiling for employment-based admissions by 120,000 to 260,000 annually;
- within the employment-based third preference category, doubled unskilled admission from 10,000 to 20,000;
- eliminated the family-based fourth preference category (i.e., adult sibling of U.S. citizens); and
- eliminated the diversity visa category.

H.R. 3938 also had two provisions aimed at legal immigration from Mexico: §604 would have placed a three-year moratorium on permanent family-preference (not counting immediate relatives of U.S. citizens) and employment-based admissions from Mexico; and §605 would have amended the INA to limit family-based immigration from Mexico to 50,000 annually.

Reducing Immigration to a Genuinely Healthy Total (RIGHT) Act of 2005

On September 8, 2005, Representative Thomas Tancredo introduced the "Reducing Immigration to a Genuinely Healthy Total (RIGHT) Act of 2005" (H.R. 3700), which would have substantially overhauled permanent admissions to the United States. Among other provisions, H.R. 3700 would have

- reduced the worldwide level of employment-based immigrants from 140,000 to 5,200 annually;
- limited the 5,200 employment-based visas to persons of "extraordinary" and "exceptional" abilities and persons having advanced professional degrees (i.e., first and second preferences);
- eliminated the family preference visa categories; and
- eliminated the category of diversity visas.

Additional Immigration Reduction Legislation

Representative J. Gresham Barrett introduced an extensive revision of immigration law (H.R. 1912) that also included a significant scaling back of permanent immigration. This legislation was comparable to legislation he introduced in the 108th Congress.

Permanent Partners

Representative Jerrold Nadler introduced legislation (H.R. 3006) that would have amended the INA to add "permanent partners" after "spouses" and thus would have enabled aliens defined as permanent partners to become LPRs through the family-based immigration categories as well as to become derivative relatives of qualifying immigrants. This bill was comparable to legislation he introduced previously.

LEGISLATION IN THE 110TH CONGRESS

Key Issues

Balancing the Priorities

The challenge inherent in reforming legal immigration is balancing employers' hopes to increase the supply of legally present foreign workers, families' longing to re-unite and live together, and a widely-shared wish among the various stakeholders to improve the policies governing legal immigration into the country. President Bush emphasized the importance he places on comprehensive immigration reform in his recent tour of Latin American countries,[50] and there is a commonly-held expectation that the 110th Congress will consider immigration reform.

Broader Issues of Debate

As Congress debates immigration control (i.e., border security and interior enforcement) and legal reform (i.e., temporary and permanent admissions), the proposals that remain contentious include expanding the number of guest worker and other temporary foreign worker visas available each year and a concurrent easing of opportunities for these temporary workers to ultimately adjust to LPR status.[51] Whether the LPR adjustments of guest workers and other temporary foreign workers are channeled through the numerically limited, employment-based preferences or are exempt from numerical limits will affect the future flow of LPRs. Whether the legislation also contains the controversial provisions that would permit aliens currently residing in the United States without legal status to adjust to LPR status, to acquire "earned legalization," or to obtain a guest worker visa also has affects on future legal permanent admissions.[52] Although guest workers and other temporary foreign workers options, as well as legalization proposals, are not topics of this report, the issues have become inextricably linked to the debate on legal permanent admissions.

Preference System Versus Point System[53]

Replacing or supplementing the current preference system (discussed earlier in this report) with a point system is garnering considerable interest for the first time in over a decade. Briefly, point systems such as those of Australia, Canada, Great Britain, and New Zealand assign prospective immigrants with credits if they have specified attributes, most often based upon educational attainment, shortage occupations, extent of work experience, language proficiency, and desirable age range. Proponents of point systems maintain that such merit-based approaches are clearly defined and based upon the nation's economic needs and labor market objectives. A point system, supporters argue, would be more acceptable to the public because the government (rather than employers or families) would be selecting new immigrants and this selection would be based upon national economic priorities. Opponents of point systems state that the judgement of individual employers are the best indicator of labor market needs and an immigrant's success. Opponents warn that the number of people who wish to immigrate to the United States would overwhelm a point system comparable to Australia, Canada, Great Britain, and New Zealand. In turn, this predicted high volume of prospective immigrants, some say, would likely lead to selection criteria so rigorous that it would be indistinguishable from what is now the first preference category of employment-based admissions (persons of extraordinary ability in the arts, science, education, business, or athletics; outstanding professors and researchers; and certain multi-national executives and managers) and ultimately would not result in meaningful reform.[54]

Comprehensive Immigration Reform Legislation

Senate Majority Leader Harry Reid has introduced S. 9 as the Comprehensive Immigration Reform Act of 2007. The bill's expressed purpose is "to recognize the heritage of the United States as a nation of immigrants and to amend the Immigration and Nationality Act to provide for more effective border and employment enforcement, to prevent illegal immigration, and to reform and rationalize avenues for legal immigration, and for other purposes." Reportedly, the Senate's comprehensive immigration reform package is expected to come to the Senate floor as early as the week of May 14, 2007.[55] Senate Majority Leader Reid has indicated that S. 1348, which reportedly is virtually identical to S. 2611 as passed by the 109th Congress, will be the marker for Senate debate on comprehensive immigration reform.[56]

STRIVE (H.R. 1645)

Congressmen Luis Gutierrez and Jeff Flake have introduced a bipartisan immigration reform bill, H.R. 1645, know as the Security Through Regularized Immigration and a Vibrant Economy Act of 2007 or STRIVE. This legislation is similar, but not identical, to S. 2611 of the 109th Congress. Specifically, H.R. 1645 would no longer deduct immediate relatives of U.S. citizens from the overall family-sponsored numerical limit of 480,000. This change would likely add at least 226,000 more family-based admissions annually (based upon the current floor of 226,000 family-sponsored visas). Family-sponsored immigrants would be reallocated as follows: up to 10% to unmarried sons and daughters of U.S. citizens; up to 50% to spouses and unmarried sons and daughters of LPRs, (of which 77% would be allocated to spouses and minor children of LPRs); up to 10% to the married sons and daughters of U.S. citizens; and, up to 30% to the brothers and sisters of U.S. citizens.

STRIVE would increase the annual number of employment-based LPRs from 140,000 to 290,000 and would no longer count the derivative family members of employment-based LPRs as part of the numerical ceiling. It would, however, cap the total employment-based LPRs and their derivatives at 800,000 annually. It would reallocate employment-based visas as follows: up to 15% to "priority workers"; up to 15% to professionals holding advanced degrees and certain persons of exceptional ability; up to 35% to skilled shortage workers with two years training or experience and certain professionals; up to 5% to employment creation investors; and up to 30% (135,000) to unskilled shortage workers.

Congresswoman Sheila Jackson-Lee has introduced H.R. 750, the Save America Comprehensive Immigration Act of 2007. Among its array of immigration provisions are those that would double the number of family-sponsored LPRs from 480,000 to 960,000 annually and would double the number of diversity visas from 55,000 to 110,000 annually.

Immigration Control and Reform Legislation

Nuclear Family Priority Act

H.R. 938, the Nuclear Family Priority Act would amend the INA to limit family sponsored LPRs the immediate relatives of U.S. citizens and LPRs. More specifically, it would eliminate the existing family-sponsored preference categories for the adult children and siblings of U.S. citizens and replace them with a single preference allocation for spouses and children of LPRs.

USCIS Funding and Backlogs

FY2008 Funding

The Administration requests a total of $2,569 million for USCIS in FY2008, an increase of 29% over the enacted FY2007 level of $1,986 million. To achieve this increase, the Administration recommends funding 99% of the USCIS budget from fees collected by the agency and has proposed a substantial increase in the user fees.[57] The Administration requests $30 million in direct appropriations to continue expanding the agency's employment eligibility verification program (previously known as basic pilot). Congress provided USCIS with $182 million in direct appropriations in FY2007.

The proposed fee increase is sparking considerable controversy as well as an oversight hearing in which concerns over many immigrants' ability to pay the higher fees arose.[58] A January 2004 GAO report had concluded that USCIS' fees were insufficient to fund its operations. GAO recommended that USCIS "perform a comprehensive fee study to determine the costs to process new immigration applications."[59] USCIS maintains that the agency loses $3 million a day the current fee schedule.[60]

Backlog Issues

Many in Congress have expressed concern and frustration about the backlogs and pending caseload, and Congress has already enacted statutory requirements for backlog elimination.[61] Former USCIS Director Eduardo Aguirre acknowledged the challenges his agency faces in testimony before the House Judiciary Subcommittee on Immigration, Border Security and Claims in 2004.

> We fully realize that the increased funding requested in the budget alone will not enable us to realize our goals. We must fundamentally change the way we conduct our business. We are aggressively working to modernize our systems and increase our capacity through the reengineering of processes, the development and implementation of new information technology systems, and the development of mechanisms to interact with customers in a more forward-reaching manner.[62]

Pending caseloads and processing backlogs continue to plague USCIS. The U.S. Government Accountability Office (GAO) concluded in 2005 that it was unlikely that USCIS would completely eliminate the backlog of pending adjudications by the 2006 deadline.[63] Despite progress in cutting the backlog of pending cases from 3.8 million in January 2004 to 1.2 million in June 2005, GAO speculated that USCIS may have difficulty eliminating its backlog for the more complex application types that constitute nearly three-quarters of the backlog.[64]

The agency's redefinition of what constitutes a backlog has emerged as an issue. The June 2006 report of the USCIS Ombudsman stated "...in July 2004, USCIS reported 1.5 million backlogged cases, which was an apparent reduction from the 3.5 million backlogged cases in March 2003. However, the agency also reclassified 1.1 million of the 2 million cases eliminated...." The Ombudsman went on to disclose that USCIS had again redefined the backlog in April 2006: "After the redefinition, the backlog supposedly declined from 1.08 million cases to 914,864 cases at the end of FY 05. Yet, individuals whose cases were factored out of the backlog still awaited adjudication of their applications and petitions."[65] This reclassification of pending cases arose at a recent oversight hearing of the House Committee on the Judiciary Subcommittee on Immigration, Citizenship, Refugees, Border Security, and International Law.[66]

The DHS Inspector General found problems in the background checks for which USCIS is now responsible. Among other findings, the report concluded that USCIS' security checks are overly reliant on the integrity of names and documents that applicants submit and that "USCIS has not developed a measurable, risk-based plan to define how USCIS will improve the scope of security checks." It further stated that "USCIS' management controls are not comprehensive enough to provide assurance that background checks are correctly completed."[67] GAO expanded on the concerns of the DHS Inspector General detailed in their report on USCIS.[68] The USCIS Ombudsman further concluded "FBI name checks, one of the security screening tools used by USCIS, significantly delay adjudication of immigration benefits for many customers, hinder backlog reductions efforts, and may not achieve their intended national security objectives."[69]

REFERENCES

[1]   CRS Report RS22574, Immigration Reform: Brief Synthesis of Issue, by Ruth Ellen Wasem.

[2]   CQ Today, "Senate Immigration Vote Turns Into a Gamble for Reid and His Caucus," by Michael Sandler, May 10, 2007.

[3]   For a listing of these hearings, see the website of the House Committee on the Judiciary at [http://judiciary.house.gov/], accessed May 9, 2007.

[4]   Congress has significantly amended the INA numerous times since 1952. Other major laws amending the INA are the Refugee Act of 1980, the Immigration Reform and Control Act of 1986, and Illegal Immigration Reform and Immigrant Responsibility Act of 1996. 8 U.S.C. §1101 et seq.

[5]   Nonimmigrants are often referred to by the letter that denotes their specific provision in the statute, such as H-2A agricultural workers, F-1 foreign students, or J-1 cultural exchange visitors. CRS Report RL31381, U.S. Immigration Policy on Temporary Admissions, by Ruth Ellen Wasem.

[6]   These include criminal, national security, health, and indigence grounds as well as past violations of immigration law. § 212(a) of INA.

[7]   For background and analysis of visa issuance and admissions policy, see CRS Report RL31512, Visa Issuances: Policy, Issues, and Legislation, by Ruth Ellen Wasem.

[8]   Immigrants are aliens who are admitted as LPRs or who adjust to LPR status within the United States.

[9]   § 201 of INA; 8 U.S.C. § 1151.

[10]   For more information, see CRS Report RS21342, Immigration: Diversity Visa Lottery, by Ruth Ellen Wasem and Karma Ester.

[11]   "Immediate relatives" are defined by the INA to include the spouses and unmarried minor children of U.S. citizens, and the parents of adult U.S. citizens.

[12]   CRS Report RL31269, Refugee Admissions and Resettlement Policy, by Andorra Bruno.

[13]   "Parole" is a term in immigration law which means that the alien has been granted temporary permission to be present in the United States. Parole does not constitute formal admission to the United States and parolees are required to leave when the terms of their parole expire, or if otherwise eligible, to be admitted in a lawful status.

[14]   Employment-based allocations are further affected by § 203(e) of the Nicaraguan and Central American Relief Act (NACARA), as amended by § 1(e) of P.L. 105-139. This provision states that when the employment 3rd preference "other worker" (OW) cut-off date reached the priority date of the latest OW petition approved prior to November 19, 1997, the 10,000 OW numbers available for a fiscal year are to be

reduced by up to 5,000 annually beginning in the following fiscal year. This reduction is to be made for as long as necessary to offset adjustments under NACARA. Since the OW cut-off date reached November 19, 1997 during FY2001, the reduction in the OW limit to 5,000 began in FY2002.

[15] See CRS Report RS21520, Labor Certification for Permanent Immigrant Admissions, by Ruth Ellen Wasem.

[16] CRS Report RL33844, Foreign Investor Visas: Policies and Issues, by Chad C. Haddal.

[17] § 202(a)(2) of the INA; 8 U.S.C. § 1151.

[18] § 202(a)(4) of the INA; 8 U.S.C. § 1151.

[19] Telephone conversation with DOS Bureau of Consular Affairs, February 13, 2004.

[20] The Immigration Reform and Control Act of 1986 legalized several million aliens residing in the United States without authorization.

[21] The largest group in the "other category" are aliens who adjusted to LPR status through cancellation of removal and through §202 and §203 of the Nicaraguan and Central American Relief Act of 1997.

[22] Table prepared by LaVonne Mangan, CRS Knowledge Service's Group

[23] The archived copies of the U.S. Department of State, Bureau of Consular Affairs, Visa Bulletin, is available at [http://travel.state.gov/visa/frvi/bulletin/bulletin_1360.html].

[24] The U.S. Department of State, Bureau of Consular Affairs, Visa Bulletin, is available at [http://travel.state.gov/visa/frvi/bulletin/bulletin_1360.html].

[25] Table prepared by LaVonne Mangan, CRS Knowledge Service's Group

[26] According to USCIS, other immigration-related petitions, such as applications for work authorizations or change of nonimmigrant status, filed bring the total cases pending to over 6 million. Telephone conversation with USCIS Congressional Affairs, February 12, 2004.

[27] DHS Office of Immigration Statistics. For USCIS workload statistics, see [http://www.dhs.gov/ximgtn/statistics/publications/index.shtm#6], accessed March 13, 2007. The FY2006 data are not yet available.

[28] §214(b) of INA. Only the H-1 workers, L intracompany transfers, and V family members are exempted from the requirement that they prove that they are not coming to live permanently.

[29] For discussion of other major immigration legislation, see CRS Report RL32169, Immigration Legislation and Issues in the 108th Congress, coordinated by Andorra Bruno. Other CRS reports on the reform of other immigration provisions are available at [http://www.crs.gov/products/browse/is-immigration.shtml].

[30] § 286 of the Immigration and Nationality Act. 8 U.S.C. § 1356.

[31] For example, the I-130 petition for family members went from $130 to $185, the I-140 petition for LPR workers went from $135 to $190, the I-485 petition to adjust statuswent from $255 to $315, and the N-400 petition to naturalize as a citizen went from $260 to $320. Federal Register, vol. 69, no. 22, February 3, 2004, pp. 5088-5093.

[32] P.L. 108-334, conference report to accompany H.R. 4567, H.Rept. 108-774.

[33] The President's Budget request for FY2002 proposed a five-year, $500 million initiative to reduce the processing time for all petitions to six months. Congress provided $100 in budget authority ($80 direct appropriations and $20 million from fees)

for backlog reduction in FY2002. P.L. 107-77, conference report to accompany H.R. 2500, H.Rept. 107-278.

[34] §286(s) of INA; 8 U.S.C. §1356(s).

[35] §286(v) of INA; 8 U.S.C. §1356(v).

[36] USCIS added a Fraud Detection and National Security Office to handle duties formerly done by the INS's enforcement arm, which is now part of DHS's ICE Bureau. CRS Report RL33319, Toward More Effective Immigration Policies: Selected Organizational Issues, by Ruth Ellen Wasem.

[37] For complete analysis, see CRS Report RL33428, Homeland Security Department: FY2007 Appropriations, coordinated by Jennifer Lake and Blas Nunez-Neto.

[38] The White House, Fact Sheet: Fair and Secure Immigration Reform, January 7, 2004, available at [http://www.whitehouse.gov/news/releases/2004/01/20040107-1.html].

[39] President George W. Bush, "Remarks by the President on Immigration Policy," January 7, 2004, available at [http://www.whitehouse.gov/news/releases/2004/01/20040107-3.html].

[40] Washington Times, January 12, 2005.

[41] For analysis of immigration trends and projections under S. 2454, see CRS Congressional Distribution Memorandum, "Legal Immigration: Modeling the Principle Components of Permanent Admissions," by Ruth Ellen Wasem, March 28, 2006.

[42] 20 CFR §656.

[43] 20 CFR §656.

[44] For an analysis of guest worker and other temporary foreign worker visas legislation, see CRS Report RL32044, Immigration: Policy Considerations Related to Guest Worker Programs, by Andorra Bruno; and, CRS Report RL30498, Immigration: Legislative Issues on Nonimmigrant Professional Specialty (H-1B) Workers, by Ruth Ellen Wasem.

[45] In S. 2611/S. 2612, unauthorized aliens who have been residing in the United States prior to April 5, 2001, and meet specified requirements would be eligible to adjust to LPR status outside of the numerical limits of INA. An estimated 60% of the 11 to 12 million unauthorized aliens residing in the United States may be eligible to adjust through this provision, according to calculations based upon analysis by demographer Jeffrey Passel. "The Size and Characteristics of the Unauthorized Migrant Population in the U.S.: Estimates Based on the March 2005 Current Population Survey," by Jeffrey S. Passel, Senior Research Associate, Pew Hispanic Center, available at [http://pewhispanic.org/files/reports/61.pdf].

[46] The per-country ceiling for dependent states are raised from 2% to 7%.

[47] For analysis of immigration trends and projections under S. 2611/, see CRS Congressional Distribution Memorandum, "Legal Immigration: Modeling the Principle Components of Permanent Admissions, Part 2," by Ruth Ellen Wasem, May 10, 2006.

[48] In the Senate, the co-sponsors are Senators John McCain, Ted Kennedy, Sam Brownback, Ken Salazar, Lindsey Graham and Joe Lieberman. In the House, the co-sponsors are lead by Representatives Jim Kolbe, Jeff Flake, and Luis Gutierrez.

[49] For an analysis of other major elements of these bills, see CRS Report RL32044, Immigration: Policy Considerations Related to Guest Worker Programs, by Andorra Bruno.

[50] For examples of news coverage, see Houston Chronicle, "Immigration tops agenda as Bush meets with Calderon," March 14, 2007; New York Times, "From Mexico Also, the Message to Bush Is Immigration," March 14, 2007; Washington Times, "Calderon condemns border fence," March 14, 2007.

[51] For an analysis of other major elements of these bills, see CRS Report RL32044, Immigration: Policy Considerations Related to Guest Worker Programs, by Andorra Bruno; and, CRS Report RL30498, Immigration: Legislative Issues on Nonimmigrant Professional Specialty (H-1B) Workers, by Ruth Ellen Wasem.

[52] An estimated 60% of the 11 to 12 million unauthorized aliens residing in the United States have been here for at least five years, according to calculations based upon analysis by demographer Jeffrey Passel. "The Size and Characteristics of the Unauthorized Migrant Population in the U.S.: Estimates Based on the March 2005 Current Population Survey," by Jeffrey S. Passel, Senior Research Associate, Pew Hispanic Center, available at [http://pewhispanic.org/files/reports/61.pdf].

[53] A point system approach is also being offered for the adjustment of status of unauthorized aliens in the United States. For example, see the Immigrant Accountability Act of 2007 (S. 1225).

[54] U.S. House of Representatives, Committee on the Judiciary, Subcommittee on Immigration, Citizenship, Refugees, Border Security, and International Law, Hearing on An Examination of Point Systems as a Method for Selecting Immigrants, May 1, 2007.

[55] CQ Today, "Reid Readies Senate Immigration Debate Despite Chamber's Changed Views," by Michael Sandler, May 8, 2007.

[56] CQ Today, "Senate Immigration Vote Turns Into a Gamble for Reid and His Caucus," by Michael Sandler, May 10, 2007.

[57] Federal Register, vol. 72, no. 21, February 1, 2007, pp. 4888-4915.

[58] U.S. House Committee on the Judiciary Subcommittee on Immigration, Citizenship, Refugees, Border Security, and International Law, Hearing on Proposal to Adjust the Immigration Benefit Application and Petition Fee Schedule, February 14, 2007.

[59] U.S. Government Accountability Office, Immigration Application Fees: Current Fees are Not Sufficient to Fund U.S. Citizenship and Immigration Services' Operations, GAO-04 — 309R, January 5, 2004.

[60] U.S. House Committee on the Judiciary Subcommittee on Immigration, Citizenship, Refugees, Border Security, and International Law, Hearing on Proposal to Adjust the Immigration Benefit Application and Petition Fee Schedule, Testimony of Emilio T. Gonzalez, February 14, 2007.

[61] For example, see §§ 451-461 of the Homeland Security Act of 2002 (P.L. 107-296). the development of mechanisms to interact with customers in a more forward-reaching manner.

[62] U.S. Congress, House Committee on the Judiciary, Subcommittee on Immigration, Border Security and Claims, Hearing on Backlog Reduction Plan for Immigration Applications, June 17, 2004.

[63] The Immigration Services and Infrastructure Improvements Act of 2000 (§ 205(a) of P.L. 106-313, 8 U.S.C. § 1574(a)) defines backlog as the period of time in excess of 180 days that an immigration benefit application has been pending before the agency. USCIS defines backlog as the number of pending applications (i.e., the number of

applications awaiting adjudication) in excess of the number of applications received in the most recent six months.

[64] U.S. Government Accountability Office, Immigration Benefits: Improvements Needed to Address Backlogs and Ensure Quality of Adjudications, GAO-06-20, November 2005.

[65] U.S. Citizenship and Immigration Services Ombudsman, 2006 Annual Report to Congress, June 2006. Available at [http://www.dhs.gov/xabout/structure/ editorial_0890.shtm], accessed March 14, 2007.

[66] U.S. House Committee on the Judiciary Subcommittee on Immigration, Citizenship, Refugees, Border Security, and International Law, Hearing on Proposal to Adjust the Immigration Benefit Application and Petition Fee Schedule, February 14, 2007.

[67] U.S. Department of Homeland Security, Office of Inspector General, A Review of U.S. Citizenship and Immigration Services' Alien Security Checks, OIG 06-06, November 2005, p .2.

[68] U.S. Government Accountability Office, Immigration Benefits: Additional Controls and a Sanctions Strategy Could Enhance DHS's Ability to Control Benefit Fraud, GAO-06-259, March 2006, p. 5.

[69] U.S. Citizenship and Immigration Services Ombudsman, 2006 Annual Report to Congress, June 2006. Available at [http://www.dhs.gov/xabout/structure/ editorial_0890.shtm], last accessed March 14, 2007.

APPENDIX A. TOP FIFTY SENDING COUNTRIES IN FY2005 BY CATEGORY OF LPR

Region and Country of Birth	Total	Family Sponsored Preferences	Employment Based Preferences	Immediate Relatives of U.S. Citizens	Diversity	Refugees and Asylees	Cancellation of Removal and Other
Mexico	161,44 5	65,369	16,347	72,435	11	240	7,043
India	84,681	15,256	47,705	19,108	60	2,331	221
China, People's Republic	69,967	17,082	20,626	26,852	32	5,335	40
Philippines	60,748	14,975	18,332	27,157	6	85	193
Cuba	36,261	1,478	18	1,759	371	32,555	80
Vietnam	32,784	12,220	304	11,379	5	5,818	3,058
Dominican Republic	27,504	15,813	444	11,134	6	49	58
Korea	26,562	1,997	15,929	8,598	8	7	23
Colombia	25,571	2,725	5,976	15,413	12	1,270	175
Ukraine	22,761	198	1,235	4,346	2,745	12,421	1,816
Canada	21,878	761	12,296	8,483	72	28	238
El Salvador	21,359	3,847	1,243	6,234	D	D	9,476
United Kingdom	19,800	594	10,753	8,237	113	33	70
Jamaica	18,346	5,032	1,214	12,049	D	D	45
Russia	18,083	172	2,574	8,767	613	5,335	622
Guatemala	16,825	1,949	1,071	7,518	D	D	5,586
Brazil	16,664	335	8,866	7,105	170	99	89
Peru	15,676	2,264	2,301	8,911	1,128	900	172
Poland	15,352	2,953	3,241	5,768	3,259	60	71
Pakistan	14,926	3,203	4,798	5,789	12	967	157
Haiti	14,529	4,363	192	6,032	4	1,118	2,820
Bosnia-Herzegovina	14,074	D	71	650	44	13,298	D
Iran	13,887	1,986	1,024	3,922	407	6,480	68
Ecuador	11,608	2,547	2,323	6,366	193	77	102
Bangladesh	11,487	3,118	1,520	4,625	1,753	405	66
Venezuela	10,645	454	4,929	4,573	133	520	36
Nigeria	10,598	900	1,383	5,383	2,379	502	51

Appendix A. (Continued).

Region and Country of Birth	Total	Family Sponsored Preferences	Employment Based Preferences	Immediate Relatives of U.S. Citizens	Diversity	Refugees and Asylees	Cancellation of Removal and Other
Ethiopia	10,573	378	182	2,771	3,427	3,802	13
Guyana	9,318	5,360	279	3,655	5	4	15
Germany	9,264	167	3,516	4,473	602	464	42
Taiwan	9,196	2,749	3,001	3,101	326	6	13
Japan	8,768	135	3,451	4,885	271	11	15
Egypt	7,905	897	995	2,548	2,478	938	49
Romania	7,103	295	1,714	3,322	1,585	163	24
Argentina	7,081	195	3,382	3,129	69	279	27
Honduras	7,012	1,889	589	4,174	7	158	195
Trinidad and Tobago	6,568	1,413	955	4,119	D	D	53
Ghana	6,491	534	487	4,100	1,049	289	32
Albania	5,947	125	207	2,036	2,438	1,137	4
Somalia	5,829	D	29	260	46	5,478	D
Israel	5,755	262	2,437	2,805	192	31	28
Bulgaria	5,635	80	792	1,713	2,854	163	33
Thailand	5,505	337	1,084	3,370	60	414	240
Kenya	5,348	147	967	1,963	1,536	718	17
Sudan	5,231	28	59	269	248	4,619	8
Serbia and Montenegro	5,202	120	353	1,400	208	3,078	43
Liberia	4,880	178	55	712	373	3,548	14
Afghanistan	4,749	143	16	517	16	4,049	8
Turkey	4,614	167	1,439	1,869	1,043	89	7
South Africa	4,536	78	3,017	1,291	128	18	4
Morocco	4,411	137	373	1,922	1,958	4	17
Totals	970,942	197,405	216,094	368,997	34,455	119,393	33,277

Source: CRS analysis of data from the U.S. Department of Homeland Security, *FY2005 Statistical Yearbook of Immigration*, 2006.

Note: "D" means that data disclosure standards are not met; " — " represents zero.

APPENDIX B. PROCESSING DATES FOR IMMIGRANT PETITIONS

Immigrant Category	California	Regional Service Centers			Vermont
		Nebraska	Texas		
Immediate relatives	August 21, 2006	N/A	N/A		Mar. 12, 2006
Unmarried sons and daughters of citizens	Jan. 17, 2003	N/A	N/A		Feb. 26, 2006
Spouses and children of LPRs	Jan. 1, 2005	N/A	N/A		Oct. 22, 2005
Unmarried sons and daughters of LPRs	Feb. 7, 2005	N/A	N/A		Mar. 12, 2006
Married sons and daughters of citizens	April 30, 2001	N/A	N/A		Mar. 12, 2006
Siblings of citizens age 21 and over	April 30, 2001	N/A	N/A		Oct. 7, 2000
Priority workers — extraordinary	N/A	June 6, 2006	August 21, 2006		April 1, 2006
Priority workers — outstanding	N/A	June 8, 2006	August 21, 2006		April 1, 2006
Priority workers — executives	N/A	June 16, 2006	August 21, 2006		April 1, 2006
Persons with advanced degrees or exceptional abilities	N/A	July 19, 2006	August 21, 2006		April 1, 2006
Skilled workers (at least two years experience) or professionals (B.A.)	N/A	August 2, 2006	August 21, 2006		April 1, 2006
Unskilled shortage workers	N/A	August 21, 2006	June1, 2006		April 1, 2006

Source: CRS presentation of USCIS information dated February 20, 2007; available online at [https://egov.immigration.gov/cris/jsps/ptimes.jsp/]. Table prepared by LaVonne Mangan, CRS Knowledge Service's Group.

APPENDIX C. FY2005 IMMIGRANTS BY PREFERENCE CATEGORY

Type and Class of Admission	2001	2002	2003	2004	2005
Family-sponsored preferences	231,699	186,880	158,796	214,355	212,970
First	Unmarried sons/daughters of U.S. citizens and their children	27,003	23,517	21,471	26,380	24,729
Second	Spouses, children, and unmarried sons/daughters of alien residents	112,015	84,785	53,195	93,609	100,139
Third	Married sons/daughters of U.S. citizens and their spouses and children	24,830	21,041	27,287	28,695	22,953
Fourth	Brothers/sisters of U.S. citizens (at least 21 years of age) and their spouses and children	67,851	57,537	56,843	65,671	65,149
Employment-based preferences	178,702	173,814	81,727	155,330	246,878
First	Priority workers and their spouses and children	41,672	34,168	14,453	31,291	64,731
Second	Professionals with advanced degrees or aliens of exceptional ability and their spouses and children	42,550	44,316	15,406	32,534	42,597
Third	Skilled workers, professionals, and unskilled workers and their spouses and children	85,847	88,002	46,415	85,969	129,070
Fourth	Special immigrants and their spouses and children	8,442	7,186	5,389	5,407	10,134
Fifth	Employment creation (investors)and their spouses and children	191	142	64	129	346
Immediate relatives of U.S. citizens	439,972	483,676	331,286	417,815	436,231
Spouses	268,294	293,219	183,796	252,193	259,144
Children	91,275	96,941	77,948	88,088	94,974
Parents	80,403	93,516	69,542	77,534	82,113
Refugees	96,870	115,601	34,362	61,013	112,676
Asylees	11,111	10,197	10,402	10,217	30,286
Diversity	41,989	42,820	46,335	50,084	46,234
Cancellation of removal	22,188	23,642	28,990	32,702	20,785
Parolees	5,349	6,018	4,196	7,121	7,715
Nicaraguan Adjustment and Central American Relief Act (NACARA)	18,663	9,307	2,498	2,292	1,155
Haitian Refugee Immigration Fairness Act (HRIFA)	10,064	5,345	1,406	2,451	2,820
Other	2,295	2,056	3,544	4,503	4,623
Total	1,058,902	1,059,356	703,542	957,883	1,122,373

Source: CRS analysis of data from the U.S. Department of Homeland Security, *FY2005 Statistical Yearbook of Immigration*, 2006.

In: Immigration Crisis: Issues, Policies and Consequences   ISBN: 978-1-60456-096-1
Editors: P. W. Hickman and T. P. Curtis, pp. 107-127 © 2008 Nova Science Publishers, Inc.

Chapter 4

IMMIGRATION POLICY ON EXPEDITED REMOVAL OF ALIENS[*]

Alison Siskin and Ruth Ellen Wasem

ABSTRACT

Expedited removal, an immigration enforcement strategy originally conceived to operate at the borders and ports of entry, is being expanded, raising a set of policy, resource, and logistical questions. Expedited removal is a provision under which an alien who lacks proper documentation or has committed fraud or willful misrepresentation of facts may be removed from the United States without any further hearings or review, unless the alien indicates a fear of persecution. Congress added expedited removal to the Immigration and Nationality Act (INA) in 1996, making it mandatory for arriving aliens, and giving the Attorney General the option of applying it to aliens in the interior of the country who have not been admitted or paroled into the United States and who cannot affirmatively show that they have been physically present in the United States continuously for two years. Until recently, expedited removal was only applied to aliens at ports of entry.

In the 110th Congress, H.R. 519 would require that expedited removal be applied to all aliens eligible for expedited removal under the statute. Proponents of expanding expedited removal point to the lengthy procedural delays and costs of the alien removal process. They cite statistics that indicate that the government is much more successful at removing detained aliens (aliens in expedited removal must be detained) than those not detained. They argue that aliens who entered the country illegally should not be afforded the due process and appeals that those who entered legally are given under the law. They point to the provision added to INA in 1996 that clarified that aliens who are in the United States without inspection are deemed to be "arriving" (i.e., not considered to have entered the United States and acquired the legal protections it entails). Advocates for requiring mandatory expedited removal maintain that it is an essential policy tool to handle the estimated 12 million unauthorized aliens in the United States.

Opponents of the expansion of mandatory expedited removal to the interior argue that it poses significant logistical problems, and cite increased costs caused by mandatory

---

[*] Excerpted from CRS Report RL33109, dated January 24, 2007.

detention and the travel costs of repatriation. They also express concern that apprehended aliens will not be given ample opportunity to produce evidence that they are not subject to expedited removal, and argue that expedited removal limits an alien's access to relief from deportation. Some predict diplomatic problems if the United States increases repatriations of aliens who have not been afforded a judicial hearing. The Bush Administration is taking a an incremental approach to expanding expedited removal. From April 1997 to November 2002, expedited removal only applied to arriving aliens at ports of entry. In November 2002, it was expanded to aliens arriving by sea who are not admitted or paroled. Subsequently, in August 2004, expedited removal was expanded to aliens who are present without being admitted or paroled, are encountered by an immigration officer within 100 air miles of the U.S. southwest land border, and can not establish to the satisfaction of the immigration officer that they have been physically present in the United States continuously for the 14-day period immediately preceding the date of encounter. In January 2006, expedited removal was reportedly expanded along all U.S. borders. This report will be updated.

BACKGROUND

Overview

Expedited removal, an immigration enforcement strategy originally conceived to operate at the borders and ports of entry, recently has been expanded in certain border regions. Whether the policy should be made mandatory and extended into the interior of the country is emerging as an issue. Expanding expedited removal raises a set of policy, resource, and logistical questions.

Expedited removal is a provision in the Immigration and Nationality Act (INA),[1] under which an alien who lacks proper documentation or has committed fraud or willful misrepresentation of facts to gain admission into the United States is inadmissible[2] and may be removed from the United States without any further hearings or review,[3] unless the alien indicates either an intention to apply for asylum[4] or a fear of persecution. Aliens who receive negative "credible fear" determinations may request that an immigration judge review the case.[5] Under expedited removal, both administrative and judicial review are limited generally to cases in which the alien claims to be a U.S. citizen or to have been previously admitted as a legal permanent resident, a refugee, or an asylee.[6]

Aliens subject to expedited removal must be detained until they are removed and may only be released due to medical emergency or if necessary for law enforcement purposes. In addition, aliens who have been expeditiously removed are barred from returning to the United States for five years.[7] Although under law, the Attorney General[8] may apply expedited removal to any alien who has not been admitted or paroled into the United States and cannot show that they have been continuously present for two years,[9] expedited removal has been applied in a more limited manner.

Under regulation, expedited removal only applied to arriving aliens at ports of entry from April 1997 to November 2002.[10] In November 2002, the Bush Administration extended expedited removal to aliens arriving by sea who are not admitted or paroled.[11] Subsequently, in August 2004, expedited removal was expanded to aliens who are present without being admitted or paroled, are encountered by an immigration officer within 100 air miles of the U.S. international southwest land border, and have not established to the satisfaction of an immigration officer that they have been physically present in the United States continuously for the 14-day period immediately preceding the date of encounter.

Legislative History

Failure to have valid documents has long been a ground for exclusion from the United States.[12] With regard to fraudulent entry in general, the INA provides that "any alien who, by fraud or willfully misrepresenting a material fact, seeks to procure (or has sought to procure or has procured) a visa, other documentation, or admission into the United States or other benefit provided under this Act is inadmissible."[13]

The policy option known as expedited removal was proposed in the early 1980s under the name "summary exclusion." The proposal was triggered largely by the mass migration of approximately 125,000 Cubans and 30,000 Haitians to South Florida in 1980. While this dramatic influx of asylum seekers, commonly known as the Mariel boatlift, lasted only a few months, it cast a long shadow over U.S. immigration policy. At that time, aliens arriving at a port of entry to the United States without proper immigration documents were eligible for a hearing before an Executive Office for Immigration Review (EOIR) immigration judge to determine whether the aliens were admissible.[14] If the alien received an unfavorable decision from the immigration judge, he or she also could seek administrative and judicial review of the case. The goal of "summary exclusion" was to stymie unauthorized migration by restricting the hearing, review, and appeal process for aliens arriving without proper documents at ports of entry. It was included and then deleted from legislation that became the Immigration Reform and Control Act of 1986.[15]

In 1993, during the 103rd Congress, the Clinton Administration proposed "summary exclusion" in S. 1333/H.R. 2836, the "Expedited Exclusion and Alien Smuggling Enhanced Penalties Act of 1993," to address the problem of aliens arriving at ports of entry without proper documents. The goal of these provisions was to target the perceived abuses of the asylum process by restricting the hearing, review, and appeal process for aliens at the port of entry. The bill would have instituted a "summary exclusion" procedure for such aliens who did not articulate a plausible asylum claim. The House took no action on H.R. 2836, but approved H.R. 2602, a similar bill that would have created a summary exclusion process.

During the 104th Congress, the House-passed version of H.R. 2202 "The Immigration in the National Interest Act of 1995" (which subsequently became the Illegal Immigration Reform and Immigrant Responsibility Act of 1996) had language providing for the "expedited removal of arriving aliens" and deemed aliens who were in the United State without inspection to be arriving.[16] H.R. 2202 also restructured the laws on deportation and exclusion into a single "removal" process. During the debate on its related bill, S. 1664, however, the Senate eliminated the bill's "expedited removal" provisions, replacing them with a more limited special exclusion process to be used only in "extraordinary migration situations."[17] The Illegal Immigration Reform and Immigrant Responsibility Act of 1996 (IIRIRA; P.L. 104-208, Division C) established the expedited removal policy that is in place today.[18]

CURRENT POLICY

Basics of Expedited Removal

An immigration officer can summarily exclude an alien arriving without proper documentation or an alien present in the United States for less than two years, unless the alien expresses an intent to apply for asylum or has a fear of persecution or torture. According to DHS immigration policy and procedures, Customs and Border Protection (CBP) inspectors, as well as other DHS immigration officers, are required to ask each individual who may be subject to expedited removal (i.e., arriving aliens who lack proper immigration documents) a series of "protection questions" to identify anyone who is afraid of return.[19]

If the alien expresses a fear of return, the alien is supposed to be detained by the Immigration and Customs Enforcement (ICE) Bureau and interviewed by an asylum officer from DHS' Bureau of Immigration and Citizenship Services (USCIS).[20] The asylum officer then makes the "credible fear" determination of the alien's claim. Those found to have a "credible fear" are referred to an EOIR immigration judge, which places the asylum seeker on the *defensive* path to asylum.[21] In those cases in which the alien requests it, an immigration judge may review the USCIS asylum officer's determination that the alien does not have a credible fear of persecution. Under IIRIRA, the review must be concluded "as expeditiously as possible, to the maximum extent practicable within 24 hours, but in no case later than 7 days" after the asylum officer's finding of no credible fear.[22]

The law states that expedited removals are not subject to administrative appeals; however, those in expedited removal who claim a legal right to reside in the United States based on citizenship, legal permanent residence, asylee or refugee status are to be provided with additional procedural protections, rather than being immediately returned. Aliens whose visas have been revoked by the Department of State are subject to expedited removal. The expedited removal provisions provide very limited circumstances for administrative and judicial review of those aliens who are summarily excluded or removed.[23] Additionally, those in expedited removal are subject to mandatory detention.[24]

When expedited removal initially went into effect in April 1997, the INS applied the provisions only to "arriving aliens" as defined in 8 CFR §1.1(q).[25] The discussion accompanying the regulation defining expedited removal procedures and "arriving aliens" clarifies:

> The [Justice] Department acknowledges that application of the expedited removal provisions to aliens already in the United States will involve more complex determinations of fact and will be more difficult to manage, and therefore wishes to gain insight and experience by initially applying these new provisions on a more limited and controlled basis.
> The Department does, however, reserve the right to apply the expedited removal procedures to additional classes of aliens within the limits set by the statute, if, in the [INS] Commissioner's discretion, such action is operationally warranted. It is emphasized that a proposed expansion of the expedited removal procedures may occur at any time and may be driven either by specific situations such as a sudden influx of illegal aliens motivated by political or economic unrest or other events or by a general need to increase the effectiveness of enforcement operations at one or more locations.[26]

Expedited Removal Procedure at the Ports of Entry

The logistics of expedited removal at ports of entry are fairly straightforward. Aliens placed in expedited removal proceedings are detained pending a determination of their removability. At land ports of entry, the aliens who are issued expedited removal orders are denied entry to the United States. After the expedited removal order is issued at an air or sea port of entry, the airline or sea carrier is required to take the inadmissible alien back on board or have another vessel or aircraft operated by the same company return the alien to the country of departure.[27]

Arrivals at Sea

On November 13, 2002, INS published a notice clarifying that certain aliens arriving by sea who are not admitted or paroled are to be placed in expedited removal proceedings.[28] This notice concluded that illegal mass migration by sea threatens national security because it diverts the Coast Guard and other resources from their homeland security duties.[29] This expansion of expedited removal was in response to a vessel that sailed into Biscayne Bay, Florida on October 29, 2002, carrying 216 aliens from Haiti and the Dominican Republic who were attempting to enter the United States illegally.[30]

Expansion Along the Border

In addition, on August 11, 2004, DHS published a notice potentially expanding the use of expedited removal by authorizing the agency to place in expedited removal proceedings aliens who:

- are determined to be inadmissible because they lack proper documents;
- are present in the United States without having been admitted or paroled following inspection by an immigration officer at a designated port of entry;
- are encountered by an immigration officer within 100 air miles of the U.S. international land border; and
- have not established to the satisfaction of an immigration officer that they have been physically present in the United States continuously for the 14-day period immediately preceding the date of encounter.

The notice was given effect with respect to apprehensions made within the border patrol sectors of Laredo, Rio Grande Valley (McAllen), Del Rio, Marfa, El Paso, Tucson, Yuma, El Centro, San Diego, Blaine, Spokane, Havre, Grand Forks, Detroit, Buffalo, Swanton, and Houlton. Expedited removal is only applied to nationals who are not from Mexico or Canada,[31] and Canadians and Mexicans with histories of criminal activities or immigration violations.[32] DHS stated that expanding expedited removal on the border "will enhance national security and public safety by facilitating prompt immigration determinations, enabling DHS to deal more effectively with the large volume of persons seeking illegal entry, and ensure the removal from the country of those not granted relief, while at the same time protecting the rights of the individuals affected."[33] DHS also maintains that the expansion of expedited removal will the interfere operation of human trafficking and smuggling organizations.[34]

Nonetheless, DHS states that expedited removal currently can not be applied to the nearly one million aliens who are apprehended annually on the southwest border, as it is not possible to initiate formal removal proceedings against all of the aliens. The majority of aliens apprehended along the southwest border are Mexican nationals who are "voluntarily" returned to Mexico without a formal removal hearing.[35] Nationals from countries other than Mexico (often referred to as Other-than Mexicans or OTMs)[36] must be returned to their home county by aircraft (when apprehended at a airport) or placed into removal proceedings.[37]

Although the August 2004 notice stated that expedited removal could be applied to numerous border patrol sectors along the southwest and northern borders, *it was only expanded to all eligible southwest border patrol sections in September 2005, and to the northern and coastal borders in January 2006.* Beginning in August 2004, expedited removal was piloted in the Laredo, Texas and Tucson, Arizona sectors, and then expanded to the Rio Grande Valley, Texas sector. In addition, expedited removal was used in the Yuma and El Centro Arizona, and the San Diego, California sectors only for aliens who met the criteria for expedited removal and had illegally reentered the United States while being subject to prior orders of exclusion, removal, or deportation.[38] On September, 14, 2005, the Secretary of Homeland Security stated that border patrol agents had been trained in the application of expedited removal and expanded the use of expedited removal to the entire southwest border. The Secretary also reported, that because of support from Congress, DHS would acquire the additional detention space needed to detain the increased number of aliens subject to expedited removal.[39] Lastly, on January 30, 2006, the Secretary announced the expansion of expedited removal along the northern and coastal borders.[40]

STATISTICS

Although expedited removal has recently been expanded, the currently available data on expedited removal only includes expedited removals at the ports of entry. As figure 1 indicates, many aliens subject to expedited removal are given the opportunity to withdraw their application for admission, and thus they are not subject to any of the bars from reentry caused by a formal removal from the United States. Of the 177,040 aliens subject to expedited removal in FY2003, almost three-quarters (72.5%) withdrew their application. That same year, 3% were referred to USCIS for a credible fear determination. During the four-year period spanning FY2000-FY2003, 93% of all the aliens who were referred for a credible fear determination were approved.[41]

More than 264 million aliens were inspected in FY2003. The majority of travelers (approximately 80%) enter the United States at a land port of entry, and, as a result, the majority of expedited removals are issued at land ports of entry. Over the years, the southwest border has seen the highest volume of travelers seeking entry into the United States, and the largest number of expedited removals.[42]

Mexicans comprised 85.1% of all aliens issued expedited removal orders from FY2000-FY2003. They received a total of 199,079 orders during these four years. Aliens from Brazil followed at a distant second with 2.0% (4,705) and aliens from the Dominican Republic were third with 1.5% (3,602) of all expedited removal orders from FY2000-FY2003.[43] An earlier study found that Mexicans made up 91% of the approximately 190,000 persons removed pursuant to expedited removal from FY1997-FY1999.[44]

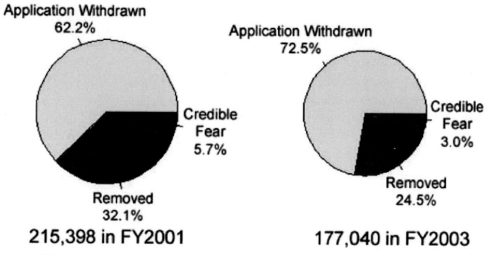

Sources: CRS presentation of data compiled by the U.S. Commission on International Religious Freedom from Immigration and Customs Enforcement, Customs and Border Protection, and U.S. Citizenship and Immigration Services.

Figure 1. Aliens Subject to Expedited Removal: Comparative Outcomes in FY 2001 and FY 2003.

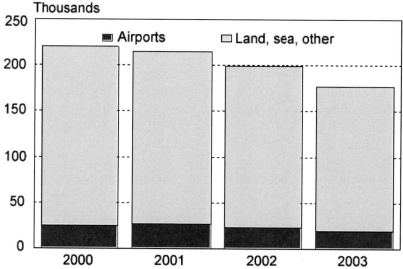

Sources: CRS presentation of data compiled by the U.S. Commission on International Religious Freedom from Immigration and Customs Enforcement, Customs and Border Protection, and U.S. Citizenship and Immigration Services.

Figure 2. Aliens Expeditory Removed, FY2000-FY2003.

ISSUES

Due Process

In terms of procedural due process under the Fifth Amendment, critics of expedited removal maintain that immigration law has long made a distinction between those aliens seeking admission to the United States and those who are already within the United States, irrespective of the legality of the entry.[45] In the latter instance, they observe, the Supreme Court has recognized additional rights and privileges not extended to those in the former category, who are merely "on the threshold of initial entry."[46] Some legal scholars continue to question whether the Constitution applies at all to aliens seeking entry at the border or a port of entry, particularly in determining an alien's right to be here.[47]

Proponents of expedited removal state that it is well settled in the courts that aliens seeking admission have no constitutional rights with respect to their applications for admission. Accordingly, they cite the 1998 U.S. District Court decision in *AILA* v. *Reno*, in which the court concluded that the aliens "cannot avail themselves of the protections of the Fifth Amendment to guarantee certain procedures with respect to their admission."[48] Proponents similarly reject arguments based upon equal protection claims for discrimination.[49]

Protections for Asylum Seekers

Proponents of expedited removal reference the provisions giving aliens who express a fear of persecution or an intention to seek asylum the opportunity for a credible fear determination. They usually cite statistics indicating that more than 90% of aliens who express a fear are deemed to be credible (pass their credible fear hearing) and are able to bring their cases to an immigration judge. They also note that the U.S. Commission on International Religious Freedom (USCIRF) study found that DHS has mandatory procedures in place to ensure that asylum seekers are protected under expedited removal.[50] Testifying on the issue of expedited removal, C. Stewart Verdery, Jr., formerly Assistant Secretary for Border and Transportation Security Policy and Planning in DHS, concluded, "I am heartened to see that internal and external reviews of the asylum process largely have concluded that DHS has handled this subset of cases appropriately."[51]

Critics of expedited removal maintain that a low-level immigration officer's authority to order removal is virtually unchecked. The officer's decision to place the person in expedited rather than regular removal proceedings, they argue, can result in the person losing substantive rights. Indeed, they assert that there have been reports of abuse of the procedure since it was first implemented at the ports of entry and many individuals with valid claims have been erroneously removed.[52] Critics refer to one investigation that found cases where aliens had requested the opportunity to apply for asylum but were refused and "pushed back" at primary inspection.[53]

Mandatory Detention of Asylum Seekers

As discussed, IIRIRA requires that aliens in expedited removal be detained, and thus aliens in expedited removal who claim asylum are detained while their "credible fear" cases are pending.[54] Prior to IIRIRA, most aliens arriving without proper documentation who applied for asylum were released on their own recognizance into the United States (and given work authorization), a practice which enabled inadmissable aliens falsely claiming persecution to enter the country. As a result, many argued that the only way to deter fraudulent asylum claims was to detain asylum seekers rather than releasing them on their own recognizance. Indeed the practice of detaining asylum seekers has reduced the number of fraudulent asylum claims.[55]

However, others contend that the policy of detaining all asylum seekers who enter without proper documentation is too harsh. The position of the United Nations High Commission on Refugees is that detention of asylum seekers is "inherently undesirable."[56] They argue that detention may be psychologically damaging to an already fragile population such as those who are escaping from imprisonment and torture in their countries. Often the asylum seeker does not understand why they are being detained. Additionally, asylum seekers are often detained with criminal aliens. From April 1, 1997, through September 30, 2001, there were 34,736 aliens in expedited removal who made a claim of credible fear. Of these, 33,551 were detained, and 1,185 were paroled.[57]

Coordination Across Agencies

Concerns about the coordination across agencies involved in expedited removal are arising, an issue that some observers argue has been exacerbated by the dispersal of immigration functions into four different agencies.[58] While one evaluation points to longstanding immigration management issues,[59] another study that focused on expedited removal concludes "[t]he impediments to communication and information sharing within DHS ... are serious." This study further maintains:

> Some procedures were applied with reasonable consistency, but compliance with others varied significantly, depending upon where the alien arrived, and which immigration judges or inspectors addressed the alien's claim. Most procedures lacked effective quality assurance measures to ensure that they were consistently followed.[60]

Supporters of expedited removal point to evidence of cooperation among the agencies and maintain that proper training has been a key part of the expedited removal deployment.[61] The Administration states that all immigration officers who conduct expedited removal proceedings have been trained in how to implement the statutory provisions and regulations. It further argues that it "developed extensive, detailed regulations and procedures that go far beyond the statutory requirements to ensure fair and consistent application of the law," and adds that these regulations, "were developed following public comment and input from various immigrant, legal and community-based groups...."[62]

Expansion of Expedited Removal

There have been discussions about expanding expedited removal to include all groups authorized under statute. In other words, aliens who had illegally entered the United States and could not prove that they had been continuously present for more than two years would be detained and removed without hearings or review unless they claimed asylum. Proponents argue that expedited removal is necessary to stretch enforcement resources.[63] Opponents note that there are other ways to accelerate the removal process (such as, the Institutional Removal Program)[64] which are efficient and do not sacrifice the aliens rights.[65]

Protection of Rights

When aliens are placed in expedited removal, they do not have access to relief from deportation other than asylum protections and protections under the torture convention, unless they claim a legal right to reside in the United States based on citizenship, or legal permanent resident status. For example, those in expedited removal would not be eligible for relief from deportation under the Violence Against Women Act, Temporary Protected Status, or as trafficking victims.[66] As discussed above, aliens in full removal proceedings (under INA §240, see Appendix A for a discussion of §240 removal proceedings) have access to more types of relief from removal than those in expedited removal.

Opponents of expanding expedited removal argue that aliens in the United States have a fundamental right to due process and other constitutional protections, and that the expansion would deprive aliens of significant rights and safeguards (including the opportunity to apply for immigration benefits for which they are eligible), and would be constitutional unsound.[67] In addition, those opposed to the expansion of expedited removal express concerns that since there is no review by EOIR and only limited judicial review, the immigration officer's authority to order the alien removed is almost unchecked, and that there have been reports of abuse of the expedited removal procedure since its inception, including aliens with valid legal status who were expeditiously removed.[68]

Proponents of expanding expedited removal point to the law which states that aliens subject to expedited removal have not "entered" the United States, and therefore are not entitled to these rights. In addition, aliens in primary and secondary inspection do not have a right to representation unless the alien has become the focus of a criminal investigation.[69] Proponents reiterate that all expedited removal orders are reviewed by the immigration officers' supervisors, providing a built-in check to the system, and that there are safeguards built into the expedited removal system for those who fear persecution.[70]

Cost and Resources

Arguments for and against the expansion of expedited removal invoke the issue of resources. While expanding expedited removal will increase the need for some resources, it will also lessen the need for others. As a result, it is difficult to ascertain whether the expansion of expedited removal will increase or decrease the cost of removing aliens. Since expedited removal accelerates the removal of aliens by limiting the aliens' access to judicial hearings and reviews, it can reduce the costs of the DHS lawyers who represent the government's position in removal cases, the EOIR courts, and detention — both staff and bed space — , as the aliens are detained for shorter periods of time.[71] Similarly, as aliens in expedited removal are not eligible for bond, they are also, unlike aliens in formal removal procedures, ineligible for bond redetermination hearings[72] in front of an immigration judge. In addition, there is evidence that the most recent expansion of expedited removal along the southwest border has decreased the apprehensions of OTMs along the border,[73] which may imply that the expansion of expedited removal has been a deterrent to those trying to enter the country illegally.

However, both the availability of detention bed space and transportation of aliens placed in expedited removal (i.e., transporting the aliens to detention facilities, and returning the alien to their home country) present barriers to expanding expedited removal.[74] Aliens placed in expedited removal are subject to mandatory detention, yet many of these individuals do not have criminal records, multiple re-entries, or other characteristics that would make them subject to mandatory detention absent expedited removal. Since aliens under expedited removal are subject to mandatory detention while noncriminal aliens in removal proceedings are often not detained, expanding expedited removal may raise detention costs (including transporting aliens to the detention facilities), and make fewer beds available for other aliens to go through removal proceedings.[75] Notably, ICE has been at or above their detention capacity for several years.[76] In addition, expanding expedited removal would increase the need for deportation officers to arrange the physical removal of the aliens, and USCIS asylum officers, to conduct the additional credible fear hearings.

Removal Proceeding Delays

Proponents of expanding expedited removal note the delays imposed by immigration judges in adjudicating removal cases, as well additional postponements resulting from the appeals process, which can take years.[77] In addition, they contend that aliens use frivolous appeals to postpone deportation.[78] Some note that any improvement that can reduce the delays in the removal process, including both the courts and the actual deportation, can enhance the government's ability to enforcement immigration laws.[79] Opponents of expanding expedited removals contend that removing EOIR's role in removal proceedings infringes on the rights of aliens and creates a situation where there is little oversight, noting that recent changes in EOIR have helped streamline the removal procedures.[80]

Logistics

Expanding expedited removal raises questions about how the policy would be implemented. As discussed previously, the process of expedited removal at ports of entry is fairly straightforward, but there are issues that need to be explored to expand expedited removal into the interior. For example, if an alien is arrested and placed in expedited removal, would he have a chance to collect documents, or contact family or friends? Would the alien be released to gather documents to prove that he is not subject to expedited removal?[81] Since those in expedited removal are subject to mandatorily detention, would the alien be detained?[82] In addition, what happens to aliens who are unable to be returned to their home countries because the country will not produce travel documents? Would these aliens be subject to the same post-order-custody reviews as those who were given final orders of removal and are unable to be returned to their native country?[83] For example, in 1999, INS published an advance notice that it intended to apply expedited removal on a pilot basis to certain criminal aliens beings held in three correctional facilities in Texas.[84] The program was never implemented. Under this pilot program expedited removal would have only been applied when the federal courts had affirmatively determined that the alien fell within the illegal entry criteria for expedited removal.[85]

As discussed above, the INS wrote in the interim rule on expedited removal that the " application of the expedited removal provisions to aliens already in the United States will involve more complex determinations of fact and will be more difficult to manage...."[86] Nonetheless, expedited removal has been in practice for eight years, providing DHS with insight on the process, and presumably putting DHS in a better position to expand expedited removal than when the policy was new. Furthermore, to expand expedited removal, proper training would have to be provided to immigration officers implementing expedited removal. DHS stated that training was one of the reasons that expedited removal was implemented in stages along the southwest border.[87]

LEGISLATION IN THE 109TH CONGRESS

There were several bills in the 109th Congress that would have expanded the application of expedited removal. In the House, H.R. 4437, as passed by the House on December 16, 2005,[88] and H.R. 4312, as reported by the House Homeland Security Committee on December 6, 2005,[89] would have mandated that expedited removal be applied to alien nationals of countries other than Canada, Mexico, and Cuba encountered within 100 miles of an international land border who have not been in the United States more than 14 days. The provisions in H.R. 4437 and H.R. 4312 were similar to those in S. 2454, introduced by Senator William H. Frist on March 16, 2006, S.Amdt. 3192, and S. 2611/S. 2612. S.Amdt. 3192 was introduced by Senator Arlen Specter on the floor as an amendment to S. 2454, and the provisions as introduced were identical to those contained in the version of Chairman Specter's mark reported out of the Senate Judiciary Committee on March 27, 2006. Two other versions of the Comprehensive Immigration Reform Act of 2006 were introduced in the Senate on April 24, 2006, and were commonly referred to as the Hagel/Martinez proposal. One version of the Hagel/Martinez proposal was introduced by Senator Specter as S. 2611 and was passed by the Senate on May 25, 2006. The other version was introduced by Senator Chuck Hagel as S. 2612 and was referred to the Senate Judiciary Committee. In other words, H.R. 4437, H.R. 4312, S. 2454, S.Amdt. 3192, and S. 2611/S. 2612 would have codified DHS' current policy regarding expedited removal along the U.S. land borders.

In addition, H.R. 4032, introduced by Representative John T. Doolittle on October 7, 2005, would have required that expedited removal be applied to all aliens eligible for expedited removal under the statute. Dissimilarly, H.R. 257 and H.R. 2092, both introduced by Representative Sheila Jackson-Lee,[90] would have eliminated the mandatory detention of aliens subject to expedited removal.

LEGISLATION IN THE 110TH CONGRESS

Representative John T. Doolittle introduced H.R. 519 on January 17, 2007. Comparable to H.R. 4032 in the 109th Congress, H.R. 519 would require that expedited removal be applied to all aliens eligible for expedited removal under the statute. Thus, unlike current policy, aliens in the interior of the country who have not been admitted or paroled into the United States and who cannot affirmatively show that they have been physically present in the United States continuously for two years, would be subject to expedited removal. The bill was referred to the House Judiciary Committee.

APPENDIX A. OVERVIEW OF §240 FORMAL REMOVAL PROCEDURES

When DHS encounters an alien that DHS thinks should be removed from the United States, the alien is presented a Notice-to-Appear (NTA),[91] which commences the removal proceeding.[92] The NTA is comparable to a charging document in criminal courts. The NTA outlines the charges against the alien, and identifies which part of the immigration statute the alien is being charged with violating.

If the alien's NTA is issued by the border patrol and the alien is not taken into custody, the alien is released on his own recognizance. If the NTA is issued by ICE, an alien not subject to mandatory detention may be released on bond. If the alien is not a mandatory detainee and is not released on bond, the alien may request a bond redetermination hearing before an immigration judge to have the bond lowered, or to be given bond. During the bond hearing, the alien must prove that he is not a flight risk or a danger to society.[93] Bond hearings are not considered part of the removal process.

The alien's first appearance in immigration court is at the master calendar hearing, a preliminary hearing to review the case. *In absentia* cases,[94] and cases where the respondent concedes removability and does not apply for relief, are decided at the master calender hearing. Relief from deportation can be granted at the master calender hearing if both the government and the alien agree to the relief. Frequently the cases of detained aliens are also concluded at the master calender hearing. Nonetheless, under most circumstances, at the master calender hearing, a time is set for an individual merit hearing. The individual merit hearing is the time when the government's attorney must prove the charges on the NTA, witnesses are presented, and the judge rules on whether the alien is removable from the United States and is eligible for relief from removal.[95] Within 30 days after the hearing, the government's attorney or the alien may appeal the decision to the Board of Immigration Appeals (BIA). After the BIA decision the alien may appeal to a federal court.

The first step in a court removal proceeding is that DHS must establish that the person in court is indeed an alien.[96] Then, if the alien establishes that he/she was admitted, then the burden shifts back to DHS to prove that the alien is deportable. The alien has the burden to prove that he/she is eligible for any form of relief. An alien who fails to appear for a removal hearing (absent exceptional circumstances) can be removed in absentia and is ineligible for relief from removal for 10 years.[97] In addition, the alien becomes inadmissible for five years.[98]

The courts have ruled that removal proceedings are civil not criminal, and that deportation is not punishment. Thus, there is no right to counsel, no right to a jury trial, and the due process protections are less than in a criminal trial. Furthermore, a decision on removablity does not have to be proven beyond a reasonable doubt. In addition, because deportation is not punishment, Congress may impose new immigration consequences for actions that previously occurred (i.e., actions which would not have made the alien deportable when they occurred, may make the alien deportable at a later date if Congress changes the law). IIRAIRA limited the time and number of motions to reopen[99] and reconsider[100] removal cases for the alien.

REFERENCES

[1]   INA §235(b)(1)(A)(i); 8 U.S.C. §1225(b)(1)(A)(i).

[2]   All aliens must satisfy to immigration inspectors upon entry to the United States that they are not ineligible for admission under the so-called "grounds for inadmissibility" of INA §212. These categories are: health-related grounds; criminal history; national security and terrorist concerns; public charge; seeking to work without proper labor certification; illegal entrants and immigration law violations; lacking proper documents; ineligible for citizenship; and, aliens previously removed.

[3]   Aliens from Western Hemisphere countries with which the United States does not have full diplomatic relations (e.g., Cuba) are excluded from expedited removal. In addition, a former Immigration and Naturalization Service (INS) policy memorandum (Aug. 1997), stated that unaccompanied minors should be placed in expedited removal in limited circumstances.

[4]   The INA provides immigration protections to aliens who have a well-founded fear of persecution, most notably in the form of asylum status. Aliens seeking asylum must demonstrate a well-founded fear that if returned home, they will be persecuted based upon one of five characteristics: race, religion, nationality, membership in a particular social group, or political opinion.

[5]   Aliens who are in expedited removal and claim asylum are given a "credible fear" hearing to determine if there is support for their asylum claim. The INA states that "the term credible fear of persecution means that there is a significant possibility, taking into account the credibility of the statements made by the alien in support of the alien's claim and such other facts as are known to the officer, that the alien could establish eligibility for asylum..."(INA §235(b)(1)(B)(v); 8 U.S.C. §1225). Those who pass the credible fear hearing are placed into formal removal proceedings under INA §240. For a discussion of removal under §240 see *Appendix A*. For more on credible fear, see CRS Report RL32621, *U.S. Immigration Policy on Asylum Seekers*, by Ruth Ellen Wasem.

[6]   The INA states that judicial review of an expedited removal order is available in habeas corpus proceedings, but the review is limited to whether the petitioner is an alien, was ordered expeditiously removed, or was previously granted legal permanent resident (LPR), refugee or asylee status.

[7]   INA §212(a)(9)(i).

[8]   The Homeland Security Act of 2002 (P.L. 107-296) abolished the INS and transferred most of its functions to various bureaus in the new Department of Homeland Security (DHS) effective Mar. 1, 2003. Expedited removal policy is being administered by the Secretary of Homeland Security.

[9]   Under regulation, any absence from the United States breaks the period of continuous presence (8 C.F.R. 325.3(b)(1)(ii)).

[10] Department of Justice, "Inspection and Expedited Removal of Aliens; Detention and Removal of Aliens; Conduct of Removal Proceedings; Asylum Procedures; Final Rule," 62 *Federal Register* 10311, Mar. 6, 1997.

[11] "Parole" is a term in immigration law that means the alien has been granted temporary permission to enter and be present in the United States. Parole does not constitute formal admission to the United States and parolees are required to leave when the parole expires, or if eligible, to be admitted in a lawful status. Department of Justice, "Notice Designating Aliens Subject to Expedited Removal Under §235(b)(1)(A)(iii) of the Immigration and Nationality Act; Notice," 67 *Federal Register* 68923, Nov. 13, 2002.

[12] INA §212(a)(7).

[13] INA §212(a)(6)(C).

[14] In addition to an inadmissibility hearing, aliens lacking proper documents could request asylum in the United States at that time.

[15] P.L. 99-603, S. 1200.

[16] §302 of H.R. 2202 in the 104th Congress.

[17] §141 of S. 1664 in the 104th Congress. In the Senate version of a related bill (S. 269), as introduced, §141 was characterized as "special port-of-entry exclusion procedure for aliens using documents fraudulently or failing to present documents, or excludable aliens apprehended at sea."

[18] The IIRIRA provisions amended §235 of the INA. For an earlier enacted version of expedited removal see The Antiterrorism and Effective Death Penalty Act of 1996 (AEDPA; P.L. 104-132, §422).

[19] The required "protection questions" are Why did you leave your home country or country of last residence? Do you have any fear or concern about being returned to your home country or being removed from the United States? Would you be harmed if you were returned to your home country or country of last residence? Do you have any questions or is there anything else you would like to add?

[20] For further discussions of expedited removal, see CRS Report RL32621, *U.S. Immigration Policy on Asylum Seekers*, by Ruth Ellen Wasem.

[21] For more information, see *Obtaining Asylum in the United States: Two Paths to Asylum,* at the USCIS website [http://uscis.gov/graphics/services/asylum/ aths.htm seekers].

[22] INA §235(b)(1)(B)(iii)(III).

[23] INA §235(b)(1)(C).

[24] For more information on mandatory detention of aliens see CRS Report RL31606, *Detention of Noncitizens in the United States*, by Alison Siskin and Margaret Mikyung Lee; and CRS Report RL32369, *Immigration-Related Detention: Current Legislative Issues,* by Alison Siskin.

[25] "The term *arriving alien* means an applicant for admission coming or attempting to come into the United States at a port-of-entry, or an alien seeking transit through the United States at a port-of-entry, or an alien interdicted in international or United States waters and brought into the United States by any means, whether or not to a designated port-of-entry, and regardless of the means of transport. An arriving alien remains such even if paroled pursuant to §212(d)(5) of the act, except that an alien who was paroled before Apr. 1, 1997, or an alien who was granted advance parole which the alien

applied for and obtained in the United States prior to the alien's departure from and return to the United States, shall not be considered an arriving alien for purposes of §235(b)(1)(A)(i) of the act." 8 CFR §1.1(q).

[26] Department of Justice, "Inspection and Expedited Removal of Aliens; Detention and Removal of Aliens; Conduct of Removal Proceedings; Asylum Procedures; Final Rule," 62 *Federal Register* 10313, Mar. 6, 1997.

[27] INA §241(c), (d).

[28] Department of Justice, "Notice Designating Aliens Subject to Expedited Removal Under §235(b)(1)(A)(iii) of the Immigration and Nationality Act," 67 *Federal Register* 68923, Nov. 13, 2002.

[29] 23 I and N Dec. 572 (A.G. 2003).

[30] For more information on Haitian migration and this incident, see CRS Report RS21342, *U.S. Immigration Policy on Haitian Migrants*, by Ruth Ellen Wasem.

[31] Nonetheless, Mexican nationals have historically been the largest group subject to expedited removal. From FY2000-FY2003, Mexicans comprised 85.1% of all aliens issued expedited removal orders. U.S. Commission on International Religious Freedom, *Study on Asylum Seekers in Expedited Removal, Statistical Report on Expedited Removal, Credible Fear, and Withdrawal, FY 2000-2003*, Feb. 2005.

[32] Cubans are not subject to expedited removal under this regulation.

[33] Department of Homeland Security, "Designating Aliens for Expedited Removal," 69 *Federal Register* 48877, Aug. 11, 2004.

[34] Department of Homeland Security, "Designating Aliens for Expedited Removal," 69 *Federal Register* 48877-48881, Aug. 11, 2004.

[35] Voluntary departure is a cost saving measure as DHS does not have to pay for aliens to be returned to their home countries. Nonetheless, since aliens who agree to voluntary departure who are not at the border, agree to the leave the United States on their own, the aliens may not depart from the United States.

[36] For more information on the treatment of OTMs encountered on the southwest border, see CRS Report RL33097, *Border Security: Apprehensions of 'Other Than Mexican' Aliens*, by Blas Nuñez-Neto, Alison Siskin, and Stephen Viña.

[37] Department of Homeland Security, "Designating Aliens for Expedited Removal," 69 *Federal Register* 48877-48881, Aug. 11, 2004.

[38] Testimony of Chief, Office of the Border Patrol, David Aguilar, in U.S. Congress, House Committee on Appropriations, Subcommittee on Homeland Security, *Coping with Illegal Immigration on the Southwest Border*, hearings, 109th Cong., 2nd sess., July, 12, 2005. (Hereafter, Aguilar, *Coping with Illegal Immigration on the Southwest Border*.)

[39] Department of Homeland Security, "DHS Expands Expedited Removal Authority Along Southwest Border," Sept. 14, 2005, [http://www.dhs.gov/dhspublic/display?ontent=4816].

[40] Department of Homeland Security, "Department of Homeland Security Streamlines Removal Process Along Entire U.S. Border," Jan. 30, 2006, at [http://www.dhs.gov/dhspublic/display?content=5377].

[41] U.S. Commission on International Religious Freedom, *Study on Asylum Seekers in Expedited Removal*, Feb. 2005, pp. 32-33.

[42] For data analysis of immigration inspections, see CRS Report RL32399, *Border Security: Inspections Practices, Policies, and Issues*, coordinated by Ruth Ellen Wasem; for data analysis of expedited removal, see U.S. Commission on International Religious Freedom, *Study on Asylum Seekers in Expedited Removal, Statistical Report on Expedited Removal, Credible Fear, and Withdrawal, FY2000-FY2003*, Feb. 2005.

[43] Compilation of data from Immigration and Customs Enforcement, Customs and Border Protection, and U.S. Citizenship and Immigration Services presented in U.S. Commission on International Religious Freedom, *Study on Asylum Seekers in Expedited Removal, Statistical Report on Expedited Removal, Credible Fear, and Withdrawal, FY 2000-FY2003*, Feb. 2005.

[44] Center for Human Rights and International Justice, University of California, Hastings College of Law, *Report on the First Three Years of Implementation of Expedited Removal*, May 2000.

[45] For further analysis of legal issues, see CRS Report RL32399, *Border Security: Inspections Practices, Policies, and Issues*, by Ruth Ellen Wasem, Jennifer Lake, James Monke, Lisa Seghetti, and Stephen Viña.

[46] *Leng May Ma v. Barber*, 357 U.S. 185, 187 (1958) (articulating the "entry fiction" doctrine).

[47] For an example of this argument, see Mary Kenny, *DHS Announces Unprecedented Expansion of Expedited Removal to the Interior*, American Immigration Law Foundation Legal Action Center Practice Advisory, Aug. 13, 2004, available at [http://www.ailf.org/ lac/lac_pa_081704.asp]. (Hereafter Kenny, *DHS Announces Unprecedented Expansion of Expedited Removal to the Interior*.)

[48] *American Immigration Lawyers Association (AILA) v. Reno*, Nos. 97-0597, 97-1237, and 97-1229 (D.D.C. 1998).

[49] Ibid.

[50] U.S. Commission on International Religious Freedom, *Study on Asylum Seekers in Expedited Removal*, Feb. 2005

[51] U.S. Senate Committee on the Judiciary, Subcommittee on Terrorism, Technology and Homeland Security and Subcommittee on Immigration, Border Security and Citizenship, hearing on "The Southern Border in Crisis: Resources and Strategies to Improve National Security," June 7, 2005.

[52] For examples of this view, see American Immigration Law Foundation, *DHS Announces Unprecedented Expansion of Expedited Removal to the Interior*, by Mary Kenney, Aug. 13, 2004; and Center for Human Rights and International Justice, University of California, Hastings College of Law, *Report on the First Three Years of Implementation of Expedited Removal*, May 2000.

[53] CBP has stated that it is "very concerned and dismayed that this is happening contrary to policy, and is taking steps to address this." U.S. Commission on International Religious Freedom, *Study on Asylum Seekers in Expedited Removal*, Feb. 2005.

[54] H.R. 257, introduced on Mar. 2, 2005, and H.R. 2092, introduced on May 23, 2005, by Representative Sheila Jackson Lee, would remove the requirement that those in expedited removal are subject to mandatory detention.

[55] CRS Issue Brief IB93095, *Immigration: Illegal Entry and Asylum Issues*, coordinated by Ruth Ellen Wasem. This report is archived and available from the author.

[56] Office of the of the United Nations High Commissioner for Refugees. UNHRC Revised Guidelines on Applicable Criteria and Standards Relating to the Detention of Asylum Seekers, February 1999. p. 1.

[57] Phone call with Maureen Stanton, INS Congressional Affairs, Aug. 6, 2002.

[58] Homeland Security Act of 2002 (P.L. 107-296) abolished INS and transferred most of its functions from the Department of Justice (DOJ) to several bureaus in DHS. The responsibilities for expedited removal are spread across Customs and Border Protection (apprehensions and inspections), Immigration and Customs Enforcement (investigations, arrests, detention and deportation), U.S. Citizenship and Immigration Services (credible fear determination, as well as all other immigration and naturalization adjudications), and DOJ's Executive Office for Immigration Review (asylum, immigration and removal hearings).

[59] U.S. Government Accountability Office, Management Challenges Remain in Transforming Immigration Programs GAO-05-81, Oct. 2004.

[60] U.S. Commission on International Religious Freedom, *Study on Asylum Seekers in Expedited Removal,* Executive Summary, p. 4, Feb. 2005.

[61] U.S. Senate Committee on the Judiciary, Subcommittee on Terrorism, Technology and Homeland Security and Subcommittee on Immigration, Border Security and Citizenship, hearing on "The Southern Border in Crisis: Resources and Strategies to Improve National Security," June 7, 2005.

[62] U.S. Citizenship and Immigration Services, Fact Sheet, *Expedited Removal,* Nov. 8, 2002.

[63] Testimony of C. Stewart Verdery, Jr., in U.S. Congress, Senate Judiciary Committee, Subcommittees on Immigration, Border Security and Citizenship, and Terrorism, Technology and Homeland Security, *The Southern Border in Crisis: Resources and Strategies to Improve National Security*, hearing 109th Cong., 1st sess., June 7, 2005. (Hereafter, Verdery, *The Southern Border in Crisis: Resources and Strategies to Improve National Security.*)

[64] The Institutional Removal Program (IRP) is a program during which incarcerated criminal aliens undergo their removal proceedings while they are serving their criminal sentences. Once the alien has served his criminal sentence, he is taken into ICE custody and quicky deported from the country.

[65] Letter from Robert D. Evans, Director Governmental Affairs Office, American Bar Association, to Public Comment Clerk, regarding the Federal Register Notice of Expansion of Expedited Removal to Certain Jails in Texas, Nov 22, 1999.

[66] For more information on these types of relief, see CRS Report RS20844, *Temporary Protected Status: Current Immigration Policy and Issues*, by Ruth Ellen Wasem and Karma Ester, and CRS Report RL30559, *Immigration: Noncitizen Victims of Family Violence*, by Andorra Bruno and Alison Siskin.

[67] Letter from Robert D. Evans, Director Governmental Affairs Office, American Bar Association, to Public Comment Clerk, regarding the Federal Register Notice of Expansion of Expedited Removal to Certain Jails in Texas, Nov. 22, 1999.

[68] Kenny, DHS Announces Unprecedented Expansion of Expedited Removal to the Interior.

[69] Department of Justice, "Inspection and Expedited Removal of Aliens; Detention and Removal of Aliens; Conduct of Removal Proceedings; Asylum Procedures; Final Rule," 62 *Federal Register* 10319, Mar. 6, 1997.

[70] Department of Justice, "Inspection and Expedited Removal of Aliens; Detention and Removal of Aliens; Conduct of Removal Proceedings; Asylum Procedures; Final Rule," 62 *Federal Register* 10357, Mar. 6, 1997.

[71] Using expedited removal on these OTMs along the southwest border has reportedly reduced the average amount of time in detention from 90 to 26 days. Verdery, *The Southern Border in Crisis: Resources and Strategies to Improve National Security.*

[72] Aliens who are not subject to mandatory detention may be released on bond. The minimum bond amount is $1,500, and the bond amount may be set by ICE. Aliens given bond by ICE may request that an immigration judge have a hearing to redetermine the bond amount. In addition, aliens in detention who are not mandatory detainees, may have a hearing in front of an immigration judge to determine whether the alien will be released on bond.

[73] Aguilar, Coping with Illegal Immigration on the Southwest Border.

[74] Ibid.

[75] Verdery, The Southern Border in Crisis: Resources and Strategies to Improve National Security.

[76] Ibid.

[77] For an example of this argument, see Michelle Malkin, *The Deportation Abyss*, Center for Immigration Studies, Backgrounder, (Sept. 2002); and Testimony of the Former Acting Director of the Office of Detention and Removal Operations, David Venturella, in U.S. Congress, Senate Judiciary Committee, Subcommittees on Immigration, Border Security and Citizenship, and Terrorism, Technology and Homeland Security, *Strengthening Interior Enforcement*, hearing 109th Cong., 1st sess., Apr. 14, 2005. (Hereafter, Venturella, *Strengthening Interior Enforcement.*)

[78] Howard Mintz, "Fight for Refuge," *San Jose Mercury News*, Sept. 18, 2005, p. 1. (Hereafter, Mintz, *Fight for Refuge.*)

[79] Venturella, Strengthening Interior Enforcement.

[80] In 2002, the Board of Immigration Appeals (BIA) was streamlined. While some argue that this has increased the efficiency of the BIA and reduced the backlog, others note that, especially in the 9th U.S. Circuit Court of Appeals, there has been an increase in the number of cases being heard by the federal circuit court and being overturned and sent back to EOIR to begin the removal proceeding process all over again, which extends the time that an alien is in removal proceedings. Mintz, *Fight for Refuge*, p. 1.

[81] Interestingly, the issue of proving eligibility for expedited removal was addressed during the discussion of expanding expedited removal to three jails in Texas. Under the proposed program, expedited removal would only be applied to aliens that the Federal Courts had affirmatively determined have entered illegally. Since these aliens have been convicted of illegal entry, the court records and documentation in the file will clearly establish the time, place, and manner of entry, thereby establishing eligibility for expedited removal.

[82] Kenny, DHS Announces Unprecedented Expansion of Expedited Removal to the Interior.

[83] Detained aliens who have been ordered removed and have not been removed within six months after the 90 removal period has expired, are subject to a post-order-custody review to determine whether the alien can be removed in the foreseeable future. If the review rules that the alien can not be removed in the foreseeable future, in almost all cases the alien must be released. For more details on post-order-custody reviews, see CRS Report RL31606, *Detention of Noncitizens in the United States*, by Alison Siskin and Margaret Mikyung Lee.

[84] To have been subject to expedited removal under the pilot program, the aliens would have: (1) either had to have been convicted of illegal entry into the United States, or have had the court establish the time, place and manner of entry; (2) not to have been admitted or paroled into the United States; and (3) not to have been physically present for two years. The correctional facilities were Big Spring Correction Center, Eden Detention Center, or Reeves County Bureau of Prisons Contract Facility.

[85] Department of Justice, "Advance Notice of Expansion of Expedited Removal to Certain Criminal Aliens Held in Federal, State, and Local Jails," 64 *Federal Register* 51338, Sept. 22, 1999. The rational for the pilot program was that each year thousands of criminal aliens had undergone removal proceedings prior to their release from criminal custody. If the alien was removable, the alien was removed from the country upon completion of their criminal sentence, shortening the amount of time the alien would have to be in immigration custody, and lessening the cost of detaining the alien. Many incarcerated aliens had been convicted of illegal entry, and were given relatively short sentences that made it difficult to complete removal proceedings prior to the completion of their criminal sentences.

[86] *Federal Register*, vol. 62, no. 44, p. 10313 (Mar. 6, 1997).

[87] Department of Homeland Security, "DHS Expands Expedited Removal Authority Along Southwest Border," Sept. 14, 2005. Available at [http://www.dhs.gov/dhspublic/isplay? content=4816].

[88] The bill was introduced by Representative James Sensenbrenner and Peter T. King on Dec. 6, 2005.

[89] H.R. 4312 was introduced by Representative Peter T. King on Nov. 14, 2005.

[90] H.R. 257 was introduced on Mar. 2, 2005, and H.R. 2092 was introduced on May 4, 2005.

[91] CBP, the Bureau of Immigration and Customs Enforcement (ICE), and USCIS issue NTAs.

[92] As discussed above, IIRAIRA eliminated the distinction between exclusion and deportation proceedings, combining them into removal proceedings. Removal proceedings are generally the sole procedure for determining whether an alien is inadmissible, deportable, or eligible for relief from removal.

[93] In FY2004, 37% of those released on bond or on their own recognizance, and 40% of aliens who were never detained failed to appear for their removal hearings. Department of Justice, Executive Office of Immigration Review, *FY2004 Statistical Yearbook*, pp. 24-26.

[94] In absentia cases are where the alien does not attend the hearing, and thus the immigration judge summarily rules on removability.

[95] Examples of relief from deportation are voluntary departure, cancellation of removal, and asylum.

[96]   Gordon, Charles, et al. *Immigration Law and Procedure* §64.11.

[97]   INA §240(b)(7). Relief includes being able to adjust status or change nonimmigrant classification or take advantage of the registry.

[98]   An alien is inadmissible to the United States under §212(a)(6)(B) if he/she failed to attend his/her removal proceeding without "reasonable cause."

[99]   A motion to reopen is filed if there are new facts or law or intervening circumstances which may change the results of the hearing. With some exception, only one motion to reopen may be filed and it must be filed within 90 days of the final administrative order of removal. Gordon, Charles, et al. *Immigration Law and Procedure* §64.18.

[100] A motion to reconsider must be filed within 30 days of the final administrative order of removal, and may assert that the IJ or BIA made errors of law. Only one motion to reconsider may be filed. Charles Gordon, et al. *Immigration Law and Procedure* §64.19.

In: Immigration Crisis: Issues, Policies and Consequences   ISBN: 978-1-60456-096-1
Editors: P. W. Hickman and T. P. Curtis, pp. 129-152 © 2008 Nova Science Publishers, Inc.

Chapter 5

IMMIGRATION ISSUES IN TRADE AGREEMENTS[*]

Ruth Ellen Wasem

ABSTRACT

The connections between trade and migration are as longstanding as the historic movements of goods and people. The desire for commerce may often be the principal motivation, but the need to send people to facilitate the transactions soon follows. Recognition of this phenomenon is incorporated into the Immigration and Nationality Act (INA), which includes provisions for aliens who are entering the United States solely as "treaty traders" and "treaty investors." Although the United States has not created a common market for the movement of labor with our trading partners, there are immigration provisions in existing free trade agreements (FTAs) that spell out reciprocal terms regulating the "temporary entry of business persons."

Immigration issues often raised in the context of the FTAs include whether FTAs should contain provisions that expressly expand immigration between the countries as well as whether FTAs should require that the immigrant-sending countries restrain unwanted migration (typically expressed as illegal aliens). The question of whether the movement of people — especially temporary workers — is subsumed under the broader category of "provision of services" and thus an inherent part of any free trade agreement also arises. Even in FTAs that do not have explicit immigration provisions, such as the United States-Dominican Republic-Central America Free Trade Agreement (DR-CAFTA), there may be a debate over the effects that FTAs might have on future migration.

There are a variety of approaches to study the impact of trade agreements on migration, and this report draws on several different perspectives. The volume of trade that the United States has with its top trading partners correlates with the number of times foreign nationals from these countries enter the United States, regardless of whether there is an FTA. Research on the aftermath of the North American Free Trade Agreement (NAFTA) found upward trends in the temporary migration of business and professional workers between the United States and Canada during the years that followed the implementation of the Canada-United States FTA (later NAFTA). Another set of analyses revealed that the number of Mexican-born residents of the United States who

---

[*] Excerpted from CRS Report RL32982, dated January 25, 2007.

report that they came in to the country during the years after NAFTA came into force is substantial and resembles the "migration hump" that economists predicted. Many factors other than NAFTA, however, have been instrumental in shaping this trend in Mexican migration.

This report provides background and analysis on the complex nexus of immigration and trade. It does not track legislation and will not be regularly updated.

INTRODUCTION

The connections between trade and migration are as longstanding as the historic movements of goods and people. The desire for commerce may often be the principal motivation, but the need to send people to facilitate the transactions soon follows. Recognition of this phenomenon was incorporated into the Immigration Act of 1924, which included a provision for aliens who were entering the United States solely to carry on trade between the United States and the foreign state the alien was coming from, pursuant to a treaty of commerce and navigation.[1] Over 80 years later, a comparable provision of immigration law continues to enable foreign nationals, now known as "treaty traders" and "treaty investors," to enter the United States.[2]

In addition to the specific treaty trader/investor provisions of immigration law, there are often broader immigration issues raised in the context of the recent free trade agreements (FTAs).[3] These issues include whether FTAs should contain provisions that expressly expand immigration between the countries as well as whether FTAs should require that the immigrant-sending countries restrain unwanted migration (typically expressed as illegal aliens). The question of whether the movement of people — especially temporary workers — is subsumed under the broader category of "provision of services" and thus an inherent part of any free trade agreement also arises. Even in FTAs that do not have explicit immigration provisions, such as the U.S.-Dominican Republic-Central America Free Trade Agreement (DR-CAFTA), there is a debate over the effects that FTAs may have on future migration.

This report opens with an overview of the specific elements of immigration law and policythat are germane to trade-related immigration and follows with a summary of the recent FTAs that include changes to U.S. immigration law. An analysis of research on the interaction between trade and migration is discussed, with caveats on the limitations of such analysis. The report concludes with a set of immigration policy questions that arise in the context of FTAs.

BACKGROUND ON IMMIGRATION POLICY

Context of Policy Making

As a prologue to any discussion of the nexus of immigration and trade, it is important to acknowledge two key points of departure in policy making on these issues. Foremost is what branch of government — the legislative or executive — takes the lead in setting the policy. Secondly, is whether policies are set unilaterally and without special consideration of other countries or are developed bilaterally or multilaterally.

Although Congress has the ultimate Constitutional authority to regulate interstate and foreign commerce, it has shared the authority with the executive branch. The executive branch takes the lead in negotiating trade agreements under strictly defined conditions. Congress considers legislation implementing the trade agreements, according to the Trade Act of 1974, as amended.[4] Immigration policy, on the other hand, is traditionally spelled out by the Congress, not the executive branch. Congress has not shared its authority over immigration and naturalization law with the executive branch to the extent it has done so with trade policy.[5]

Bilateral and multilateral agreements with specific countries, a staple of trade negotiations, are quite rare in U.S. immigration policy. When the Immigration Amendments of 1965 replaced the national origins quota system (enacted after World War I) with per-country ceilings, U.S. immigration policy shifted to one that was applied neutrally across the countries of origin.[6] Not only did the admission of legal permanent residents (LPRs) become country-neutral at that time, but formal bilateral guest worker programs, such as the Bracero Program with Mexico, ended as well.[7]

Temporary Admissions in General

Foreign nationals seeking to come to the United States temporarily rather than to live permanently are known as nonimmigrants.[8] These aliens are admitted to the United States for a temporary period of time and an expressed reason. Currently, there are 24 major nonimmigrant visa categories, and 72 specific types of nonimmigrant visas issued. These visa categories are commonly referred to by the letter and numeral that denote their subsection in the Immigration and Nationality Act (INA).[9] Several visa categories that are designated for business and employment-based temporary admission are discussed below, as they are the most likely to correspond to trade-related temporary immigration.[10]

Treaty Traders and Treaty Investors

To qualify as an E-1 treaty trader or E-2 treaty investor, a foreign national first must be a citizen or national of a country with which the United States maintains a treaty of commerce and navigation.[11] The foreign national then must demonstrate that the purpose of coming to the United States is one of the following: to carry on substantial trade, including trade in services or technology, principally between the United States and the treaty country; or to develop and direct the operations of an enterprise in which the national has invested, or is in the process of investing a substantial amount of capital. Unlike most nonimmigrant visas, the E visa may be renewed indefinitely.

The regulations describe substantial trade as follows:

> Substantial trade is an amount of trade sufficient to ensure a continuous flow of international trade items between the United States and the treaty country. This continuous flow contemplates numerous transactions over time. Treaty trader status may not be established or maintained on the basis of a single transaction, regardless of how protracted or monetarily valuable the transaction.

The regulations define the related concept of principal trade as "when over 50 percent of the volume of international trade of the treaty trader is conducted between the United States and the treaty country of the treaty trader's nationality."[12]

For treaty investors, the investment must be sufficient to ensure the successful operation of a bona fide enterprise, and the investor must have control of the funds. Uncommitted funds in a bank account or similar security are not considered an investment. The investor must be coming to the United States to develop and direct the enterprise. If the applicant is not the principal investor, he or she must be employed in a supervisory, executive, or highly specialized skill capacity.

Other Business Personnel and Temporary Workers

Business Travelers

B-1 nonimmigrants are visitors for business and are required to be seeking admission for activities other than purely local employment or hire. The difference between a business visitor and a temporary worker depends also on the source of the alien's salary. To be classified as a visitor for business, an alien must receive his or her salary from abroad and must not receive any remuneration from a U.S. source other than an expense allowance and reimbursement for other expenses incidental to temporary stay.

Multinational Executives and Intracompany Transferees

Intracompany transferees who are employed by an international firm or corporation are admitted on the L visas.[13] To obtain an L visa, the alien must be employed in an executive capacity, a managerial capacity, or have specialized knowledge of the firm's product. To qualify as an executive, the regulations state that the alien must direct the management of the organization or a major component or function of the organization and receive only general supervision or direction from higher level executives, the board of directors, or stockholders of the organization. Those considered to be managerial staff supervise the work of other supervisory, professional, or managerial employees, or manage an essential function within the organization. The regulations define "specialized knowledge" as special knowledge possessed by an individual of the petitioning organization's product, service, research, equipment, techniques, management, or other interests and its application in international markets, or an advanced level of knowledge or expertise in the organization's processes and procedures.[14]

Temporary Workers[15]

The major nonimmigrant category for temporary workers is the H visa.[16] The current H-1 categories include professional specialty workers (H-1B) and nurses (H-1C). There are two visa categories for temporarily importing seasonal workers, i.e., guest workers: agricultural workers enter with H2A visas and other seasonal workers enter with H-2B visas. Temporary professional workers from Canada and Mexico may enter according to terms set by the North American Free Trade Agreement (NAFTA) on TN visas. The law sets numerical restrictions on annual admissions of the H-1B (65,000), the H-2B (66,000) and the H-1C (500) visas. There is no limit on TN visas.

Requirements for Employers of Temporary Foreign Workers

Labor Certification

The INA requires that employers of H-2 nonimmigrants conduct an affirmative search for available U.S. workers and that the Department of Labor (DOL) determine that admitting alien workers will not adversely affect the wages and working conditions of similarly employed U.S. workers. Under this process — known as labor certification — employers must apply to the DOL for certification that unemployed domestic workers are not available and that there will be not an adverse effect from the alien workers' entry. The H-2A visa has additional requirements aimed at protecting the alien H-2A workers from exploitive working situations and preventing the domestic work force from being supplanted by alien workers willing to work for sub-standard wages. Most notably, the employer must offer the H-2A workers wages according to the "adverse effect wage rate."[17]

Labor Attestation

The labor market test required for employers of H-1 workers, known as labor attestation, is less stringent than labor certification. Any employer wishing to bring in an H-1B worker must attest in an application to the DOL that the employer will pay the H-1B worker the greater of the actual wages paid other employees in the same job or the prevailing wages for that occupation; the employer will provide working conditions for the H-1B worker that do not cause the working conditions of the other employees to be adversely affected; and there is no strike or lockout. Employers recruiting the H-1C nurses must attest similarly to those recruiting H-1B workers, with the additional requirement that the facility attest that it is taking significant steps to recruit and retain U.S. registered nurses.

The INA does not require firms who wish to bring L intracompany transfers into the United States to meet any labor market tests (e.g., demonstrate that U.S. employees are not being displaced or that working conditions are not being lowered) in order to obtain a visa for the transferring employee.[18] Foreign nationals obtaining B-1 business visas are not held to any labor market tests, as they must receive their salary from abroad.

IMMIGRATION PROVISIONS IN FTAs

The United States is not a signatory to any trade agreements that provide for open borders or freedom of movement of individuals among the participating countries. Although the United States has not created a common market for the movement of labor with our trading partners, there are immigration provisions in several existing FTAs[19] that spell out reciprocal terms regulating the "temporary entry of business persons." These provisions are discussed below.

Negotiators for the Uruguay Round Agreements of the General Agreement on Tariffs and Trade (GATT), completed in 1994 and known as the General Agreement on Trade in Services (GATS), included specific language on temporary professional workers. This language references §101(a)(15)(H(i)(b) of INA and commits the United States to admitting 65,000 H-1B visa holders each year under the definition of H-1B specified in GATS.[20] In addition, GATS includes very specific language on "intra-corporate transfers."[21] This language is similar but not identical to the definitions of intracompany transferee found in the regulations governing the L visa.[22]

North American Free Trade Agreement

The provisions of the North American Free Trade Agreement (NAFTA) dealing with migration among Canada, Mexico, and the United States closely tracked those of the U.S.-Canadian Free Trade Agreement of 1988. The official summary of the four categories of "business persons" who may enter the three countries temporarily and on a reciprocal basis are as follows:

- business visitors engaged in international business activities for the purpose of conducting activities related to research and design, growth, manufacture and production, marketing, sales, distribution, after-sales service and other general services (B-1 visitors for business);
- traders who carry on substantial trade in goods or services between their own country and the country they wish to enter, as well as investors seeking to commit a substantial amount of capital in that country, provided that such persons are employed in a supervisory or executive capacity or one that involves essential skills (E-1 treaty traders and E-2 treaty investors);
- intracompany transferees employed by a company in a managerial or executive capacity or one that involves specialized knowledge and who are transferred within that company to another NAFTA country (L intracompany transferees); and
- certain categories of professionals who meet minimum educational requirements or who possess alternative credentials and who seek to engage in business activities at a professional level in that country (TN professionals under Section 214(e) of the INA).[23]

No party to NAFTA may impose numerical limits or labor market tests as a condition of entry for intracompany transferees.[24] The agreement, however, included a 10-year limitation, which expired last year, of 5,500 annually on Mexican professionals who could enter the United States under the TN category. To qualify as a TN, an alien must possess certain credentials included in a list of approximately 60 professions. An employer must certify that the alien is so qualified and is coming to a position which requires such a professional.

Chile and Singapore Free Trade Agreements

The legislation implementing the Chile and Singapore FTAs (P.L. 108-77 and P.L. 108-78, respectively) amended several sections of the INA. Foremost, the laws amended §101(a)(15)(H) of INA to carve out a portion of the H-1B visas — designated as the H-1B-1 visa — for professional workers entering through the FTAs. In many ways the FTA professional worker visa requirements parallel the H1B visa requirements, notably having similar educational requirements. The H-1B visa, however, specifies that the occupation require *highly* specialized knowledge, while the FTA professional worker visa specifies that the occupation require only specialized knowledge.

The laws also amended §212 of INA to add a labor attestation requirement for employers bringing in potential FTA professional worker nonimmigrants that is similar to the H-1B labor attestation statutory requirements. The additional attestation requirements for "H-1B dependent employers" currently specified in §212 are not included in the labor attestation requirements for employers of the FTA professional worker nonimmigrants.

P.L. 108-77 contains numerical limits of 1,400 new entries under the FTA professional worker visa from Chile, and P.L. 108-78 contains a limit of 5,400 from Singapore. The laws do not limit the number of times that an alien may renew the FTA professional worker visa on an annual basis, unlike H-1B workers, who are limited to a total of six years. The laws count an FTA professional worker against the H-1B cap the first year he/she enters and again after the fifth year he/she seeks renewal. Although the foreign national holding the FTA professional worker visa remains a temporary resident who is only permitted to work for employers who meet the labor attestation requirements, the foreign national with an FTA professional worker visa may legally remain in the United States indefinitely.

In addition to the immigration provisions in the implementing law, the U.S.Singapore Free Trade Agreement states that the United States shall not require labor certification or other similar procedures as a condition of entry and shall not impose any numerical limits on intracompany transfers from Singapore.[25] Similar language is also in the U.S.-Chile Free Trade Agreement.[26]

Australian Free Trade Agreement

The Australian FTA, signed on May 18, 2004, does not contain any explicit immigration provisions. However, the FY2005 supplemental appropriations for military operations in Iraq and Afghanistan, reconstruction in Afghanistan and other foreign aid (H.R. 1268, P.L. 109-16) includes a provision that touches on the nexus of H-1B visas and FTAs. Specifically, §501 of the legislation as reported by the conferees and enacted adds 10,500 visas for Australian nationals to perform services in specialty occupations under a new E-3 temporary visa. The Senate had adopted a provision during the floor debate on H.R. 1268 that created a new E-3 temporary visa and capped the number at 5,000 per year.[27]

Dominican Republic-Central America Free Trade Agreement

The U.S.-Dominican Republic-Central America Free Trade Agreement (DR-CAFTA) was signed on August 5, 2004, but must be approved by the legislatures of all seven countries before it becomes effective. Implementing legislation was sent to the U.S. Congress on June 23, 2005. Unlike NAFTA and the Chile and Singapore FTAs, the DR-CAFTA does not contain any explicit immigration provisions.

INTERACTION OF TRADE AND MIGRATION

Classical trade theory presents trade and migration as substitutes, that is, a country where labor is abundant and inexpensive is assumed to have the option of exporting either labor-intensive goods or its workers. Another construct — the multinational corporation — emphasizes the value of relocating managers and technical experts to facilitate production, which has led to the theory that trade liberalization increases the migration of knowledge-based workers. Obviously, the similarities of the economies of the trading partners (e.g., relative level of development and size of the economy) are factors that would affect the assumptions underlying any theory of the nexus between trade and migration. One analyst summed up the research on these relationships as follows:

> The question of whether trade and migration are complements or substitutes has been the focus of numerous studies, the results of which differ markedly according to the hypotheses selected. According to some authors free trade could lead to a reduction in migration flows. For others, it could have no visible effect on migration or it could bring about an increase of these flows (disruptive effect) by having a negative effect on small and medium-sized industries and by accelerating the drift from rural to urban areas.[28]

There are a variety of approaches to study the impact of trade agreements on migration, and this report draws on three of several different possible perspectives. The first explores the relationship between trade and temporary workers and business personnel among the United States' top trading partners. The second synthesizes the research on how NAFTA may have affected temporary migration of knowledge-based workers between the United States and Canada. The third analyzes possible effects of NAFTA on permanent migration from Mexico.

Trade Volume and Business-Based Temporary Admissions

The volume of trade that the United States has with its top trading partners correlates with the number of times foreign nationals from these countries enter the United States.[29] This positive relationship holds whether analyzing total nonimmigrant admissions or only those foreign nationals entering with the business-based visas discussed above (E, H, L and TN visas).[30] As table 1 details, the rankings of the top trading partners by total trade and by the number of their nationals entering with the business-based visas, while not identical, are similar. The relationship also appears when analyzing the alien admissions data with the balance of trade data.

This strong positive relationship between trade and temporary admissions appears to exist regardless of whether the United States has an FTA with the country. The specific relationship that one would expect between FTAs and the issuance of E visas for treaty traders and investors, however, is clearly illustrated in the growing use of E visas by foreign nationals from the United States' top trading partners and NAFTA signators — Canada and Mexico. As figure 1 illustrates, issuances of the E visas by the State Department to nationals of both countries accelerated as soon as the FTAs were implemented in 1989 and 1994, respectively. In 2004, U.S. issuances of E visas to Mexicans exceeded Canadian issuances for the first time.

Table 1. Comparative 2004 Rankings of Top U.S. Trading Partners and Entries of Persons with E, H, L and TN Visas

Total trade in U.S. dollars			Entries with E, H, L or TN visas		
Rank	Country	Dollars (millions)	Rank	Country	Entries
1	Canada	446,091	1	Mexico	133,427
2	Mexico	266,618	2	Canada	126,295
3	China	231,420	3	Japan	118,441
4	Japan	183,995	4	United Kingdom	117,303
5	Germany	108,617	5	India	111,355
6	United Kingdom	82,362	6	Thailand	104,642
7	Korea (South)	72,496	7	Germany	62,193
8	Taiwan	56,348	8	France	46,817
9	France	53,054	9	Korea (South)	28,940
10	Malaysia	39,082	10	China	26,477
11	Italy	38,800	11	Venezuela	24,028
12	Netherlands	36,891	12	Australia	23,434
13	Ireland	35,608	13	Brazil	22,954
14	Brazil	35,020	14	Colombia	21,507
15	Singapore	34,907	15	Italy	19,636
16	Venezuela	29,744	16	Netherlands	16,059
17	Belgium	29,325	17	Israel	15,593
18	Saudi Arabia	26,169	18	Spain	15,124
19	Hong Kong	25,123	19	Ireland	11,821
20	Thailand	23,940	20	Sweden	10,067
21	Israel	23,725	21	Philippines	9,751
22	Australia	21,815	22	South Africa	9,613
23	India	21,657	23	Russia	8,369
24	Switzerland	20,911	24	Switzerland	8,229
25	Nigeria	17,798	25	Belgium	6,795
26	Philippines	16,216	26	Malaysia	4,039
27	Sweden	15,952	27	Singapore	3,715
28	Russia	14,806	28	Hong Kong	2,588
29	Spain	14,116	29	Nigeria	1,873
30	Indonesia	13,480	30	Indonesia	1,621
31	Colombia	11,794	31	Saudi Arabia	256
32	Iraq	9,371	32	Iraq	6
33	South Africa	9,116	33	Taiwan	(in China)
World		2,289,573		World	1,181,799

Source: Table 6 in CRS Issue Brief IB96038, *U.S. International Trade: Data and Forecasts*, by Dick K. Nanto and Thomas Lum; and temporary admissions data from DHS Office of Immigration Statistics, Yearbook of Immigration Statistics: 2004.

Note: Trade data presented as millions of U.S. dollars, customs basis.

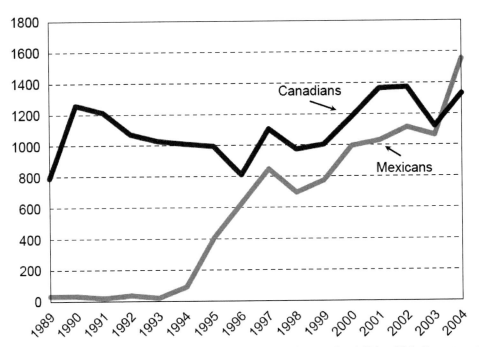

Source: CRS analysis of data from the Visa Office, Bureau of Consular Affairs, U.S. Department of State.

Figure 1. Issuances of E Visas to Treaty Traders and Investors from Canada and Mexico, FY1989-FY2004.

NAFTA: A Canadian Illustration

When Canada and the United States implemented an FTA in 1989, some Canadian policy makers expressed concern that the trade liberalization between the two nations would trigger a "brain drain" of knowledge-based workers from Canada. Others argued that the migration of professional and managerial workers is fundamental to economic integration, and that U.S. professional and managerial workers would likewise migrate to Canada. While some feared that labor flows would be economically damaging to Canada, others speculated that it would benefit Canada in the long run when these temporary workers returned to Canada with additional professional and technical skills acquired in the United States. The core migration questions were whether the FTA would stimulate the flow of professional workers to the United States and whether these workers returned or became permanent residents of the United States.

Ten years after the implementation of the Canada-United States FTA, the Canadian government asked a group of experts to assess its effects, and one of these research studies found that the migration of skilled workers increased during this time. In particular, Professor Steven Globerman, currently the Director of the Center for International Business at Western Washington University, reported that the number of Canadian professionals coming to the United States on TC/TN visas increased by approximately 3,000 to 4,000 visas each year over the period studied. Globerman noted that professional workers from the United States were emigrating to Canada in higher numbers, though at a slower rate than their Canadian counterparts. Globerman also found an increase in bilateral flows of L intracompany transfers.[31]

Figure 2 illustrates the upward trends in the temporary migration of all business and professional workers that Globerman observed between the United States and Canada during the years that followed the entry into force of the Canada-United States FTA. The data depicted in figure 2 include intracompany transferees, traders and investors as well as professional workers.[32]

When Globerman analyzed permanent migration flows between the two countries, he found that the patterns of permanent migration had been fairly consistent during the 1980s and 1990s. Globerman concluded that the trade liberalization per se had little impact on permanent migration between the United States and Canada. Although the magnitude of the permanent flow did not meaningfully change, the composition of the immigration did appear to change somewhat. Specifically, Globerman found some evidence that professional and managerial workers comprised a larger share of the immigration to the United States and a smaller share of the emigration from the United States over the period studied compared with the previous period.[33]

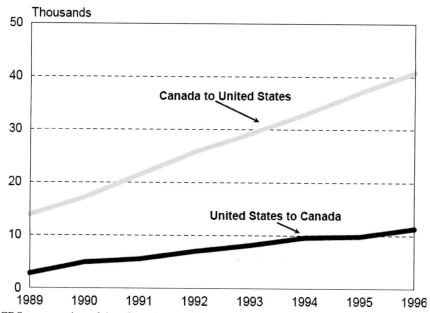

Source: CRS presentation of data from Steven Globerman (1999).

Figure 2. Temporary Migration of Business and Professional Workers between United States and Canada, 1989-1996.

NAFTA: A Mexican Illustration

During the debate over NAFTA, some asserted that the agreement would reduce unwanted migration (typically expressed as illegal aliens) from Mexico. They based this argument on the assumption that the NAFTA would bolster the Mexican economy, thereby improving employment opportunities. The result, some theorized, was that NAFTA would reduce the "push-pull" forces that draw workers from less developed countries to more developed countries because of better economic prospects. This view was presented by the U.S. International Trade Commission in its 1991 report to the House Ways and Means and the Senate Finance Committees:

> An FTA is likely to decrease slightly the gap between real United States wages and Mexican wages of both skilled and unskilled workers combined, but a greater share of the wage adjustment would occur in Mexico than in the United States. As wage differentials between the United States and Mexico narrow, the incentive for migration from Mexico to the United States will decline.[34]

Others asserted that NAFTA would stimulate unwanted migration from Mexico. This argument stemmed from the view that the NAFTA would destablize the Mexican economy as it tries to compete in a free market, dislocating many workers and farmers. The result, some theorized, was that — once these workers and farmers were uprooted — they would be forced to seek new employment opportunities and ultimately many would migrate to the United States.

These issues were weighed by the Commission for the Study of International Migration and Cooperative Economic Development (International Migration Commission) that Congress established in 1986 to examine the "push" factors in the major source countries for illegal migration. Although the International Migration Commission specifically recommended a U.S.-Mexican free trade agreement in its 1990 report, it stated that expanded trade and development was a long-term solution to the problem of unauthorized migration. It noted a major paradox: "[T]he development process itself tends to stimulate migration in the short to medium term by raising expectations and enhancing people's ability to migrate. Thus, the development solution to unauthorized migration is measured in decades — even generations."[35]

One widely discussed model, referred to as the "migration hump," incorporated these perspectives. Professor Philip Martin, chair of the Comparative Immigration and Integration Program at the University of California-Davis, proposed this migration model, depicted in figure 3, during the debate on NAFTA in the early 1990s. Martin theorized that migration would initially increase in the years immediately following the implementation of NAFTA and subsequently it would diminish. Martin predicted that migration levels would be at the point they would have been without NAFTA after about 15 years, and that over the course of 30 years migration would be at much lower levels.[36] In 2002, Philip Martin concluded "that NAFTA will reduce unwanted Mexico-US migration in the medium to long term, as trade becomes a substitute for migration."[37]

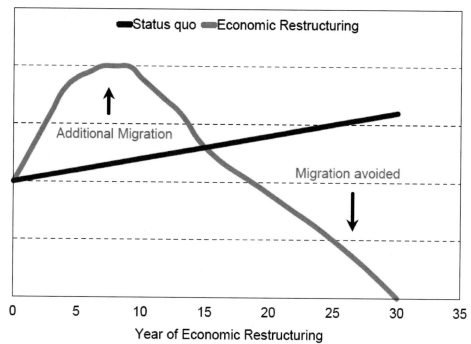

Source: CRS depiction of migration model developed by Phillip Martin (1993, 2002).

Figure 3. Theorized Model of Relationship Between NAFTA and Immigration to the United States from Mexico.

While there are no data that accurately measure the annual flow of all migrants from Mexico to the United States, the March Supplement of the Current Population Survey offers limited data on migration by year of arrival. The CPS is a sample of all persons living in the United States and, thus, includes unauthorized aliens, long-term nonimmigrants, and legal permanent residents, as well as U.S. citizens. Specifically, the CPS asks foreign-born residents: "When did you come to the U.S. to stay?" The CPS data represent a sample of those foreign born who remain in the United States. The data understate the earlier (pre-1996) migration trend because of the emigration and death of earlier migrants. As a result, the slope of the trend line depicted in figure 4 is biased upward.

As figure 4 illustrates, the number of Mexican-born residents of the United States who report that they came after 1995 (NAFTA went into force in October 1994) is substantial and resembles the "migration hump" that Philip Martin predicted. It would be naive, however, to not acknowledge the importance of other factors in shaping this surge. The dramatic drop in the value of the *peso* in 1995, for example, is often cited as a major "push" determinant in out-migration from Mexico. The growth of jobs in the U.S. economy during the mid- and late-1990s was an obvious "pull" variable.

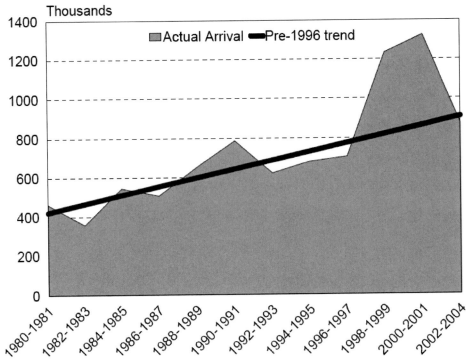

Source: CRS analysis of the March 2004 Supplement of the Current Population Survey.

Figure 4. Estimated Mexican-Born Residents of the United States by Reported Year of Arrival, 1980-2004.

Another factor that may have contributed to the increase in Mexican residents is a change in the INA provisions on legal permanent admission that now allows 75% of Mexicans coming as spouses and children of legal permanent residents (LPRs) to exceed the per-country ceiling set by law.[38] Immediate relatives[39] of U.S. citizens, moreover, are exempt from direct numerical limits. As a result, Mexico consistently ranks as the top LPR sending country, with 206,426 (19.4%) in 2001, 219,380 (20.6%) in 2002 and 115,864 (16.4%) in 2003.[40]

In terms of illegal migration, the research points to a constellation of factors that has contributed to the increase in unauthorized resident aliens, many of whom (an estimated 57%) are from Mexico. Historically, unauthorized migration is generally attributed to the "push-pull" of prosperity-fueled job opportunities in the United States in contrast to limited or nonexistent job opportunities in the sending countries.[41] Some observers maintain that lax enforcement of employer sanctions for hiring unauthorized aliens has facilitated this "push-pull," but it is difficult to empirically demonstrate this element. Although most policy makers have assumed that tighter border enforcement would reduce unauthorized migration, some researchers are now suggesting that the strengthening of the immigration enforcement provisions, most notably by the enactment of the Illegal Immigration Reform and Immigrant Responsibility Act of 1996 (IIRIRA), may have inadvertently *increased* the population of unauthorized resident aliens. This perspective argues that IIRIRA's increased penalties for illegal entry coupled with increased resources for border enforcement have raised the stakes in crossing the border illegally and created an incentive for those who succeed in entering the United States to stay.[42]

Another caveat to consider before embracing the "migration hump" model is that *all* migration to the United States dropped sharply immediately after the September 11, 2001 terrorist attacks (see Appendix B for trends in non-Mexican foreign-born residents). Post-September 11 revisions of immigration law and procedures have slowed down the processing of immigrant petitions and visas. The United States' economic recession in 2001 and initially slow rebound, moreover, may have also slowed down migration.

Migration Trends: Countries of DR-CAFTA

When Congress considered the DR-CAFTA implementing legislation, migration trends from these nations arose as an issue.[43] There are several important differences between the migration patterns of the DR-CAFTA countries and Mexico that would bear on any predictions or models.

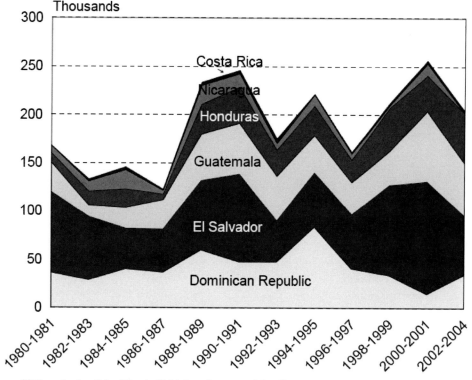

Source: CRS analysis of the March 2004 Supplement of the Current Population Survey.

Figure 5. Estimated Costa Rican, Nicaraguan, Honduran, Guatemalan, Salvadoran, and Dominican-Born Residents of the United States by Reported Year of Arrival, 1980-2004.

Foremost, even when viewed as the total of all six countries, as figure 5 depicts, migration from the DR-CAFTA countries is historically much smaller than that from Mexico. In 2004, the number of foreign-born U.S. residents from the DRCAFTA countries was 2.7

million compared to 10.7 million foreign-born U.S. residents from Mexico. Migration from Costa Rica has been so small that there was an estimate of only 53,000 Costa Rican-born residents in 2004.

Secondly, migration from the DR-CAFTA countries has fluctuated over the past several decades. These fluctuations are largely due to a variety of factors, including political instability, civil violence, and natural disasters that have affected several of these countries.

SELECTED POLICY QUESTIONS

The issues of trade and immigration generate a considerable number of policy questions and legislative issues, most of which have no direct bearing on the other,[44] yet there are policy questions that arise at the nexus of immigration and trade. This report concludes with three common policy questions and summaries of the competing answers.

Should FTAs Expressly Expand Immigration Avenues?

Some have expressed concern that FTAs, most recently the Chile and Singapore FTAs, included language that liberalized immigration law on temporary professional workers and bars the United States from future statutory changes to H-1B visas as well as other temporary business and worker nonimmigrant categories.[45] Some asserted that the Office of the U.S. Trade Representative (USTR) overstepped its authority by negotiating immigration provisions in FTAs and voiced opposition to trade agreements that purportedly prevent Congress from revising immigration law on temporary professional nonimmigrants. Some expressed concern that professional workers from Chile and Singapore are held to a less stringent standard than existing H-1B law as a result of the recent FTAs.[46]

Proponents of these trade agreements argue that they are merely reflecting current immigration law and policy, and that the movement of people is subsumed under the broader category of "provision of services" and thus an inherent part of any free trade agreement. Such agreements on the flow of business people and workers, they maintain, are essential to U.S. economic growth and business vitality. The USTR states that the labor attestations, education and training fees, and numerical limits provisions have been added to the FTAs in response to congressional concerns. The USTR further argues that the temporary business personnel provisions in the FTAs are not immigration policy because they only affect temporary entry.[47]

This question has become one of the most controversial issues at this stage of the negotiations in services that the World Trade Organization (WTO) are engaged in now in the "round" of negotiations called the Doha Development Agenda. Several developing countries have criticized the visa restrictions placed on temporary workers entering the United States, particularly workers not directly affiliated with companies located in the United States and have also called for greater transparency of U.S. immigration policy on the temporary entry of personnel. The U.S. business community maintains that the United States needs to be more flexible in its offers, arguing that not doing so prevents the United States from obtaining useful commitments from developing countries.[48] In a May 2005 letter to the new USTR

Rob Portman, the then-Chairman and Ranking Member of the House Judiciary Committee (Representative F. James Sensenbrenner, Jr. and Representative John Conyers, Jr., respectively) asked the USTR to pledge, "not to negotiate immigration .... provisions in bilateral or multilateral trade agreements that require changes in United States law."[49]

Should Immigration Control Be a Condition for FTAs?

Arising initially in the context of NAFTA and Mexico, some have advocated hinging FTAs on bilateral agreements on stronger immigration enforcement.[50] Some proponents of this view argue the immigrant-sending countries that are parties to the agreement should agree to measures that curb the flow of migrants to the United States, while others maintain that the agreements should include strict numerical limits on the numbers of migrants who can enter the United States. More recently, some opine that FTAs should include immigration enforcement measures aimed at human trafficking and smuggling as well as terrorist tracking.[51]

Others argue that negotiating bilateral and multilateral immigration enforcement measures is not the appropriate role of the USTR and is best done by other federal departments and agencies, such as the Departments of Homeland Security and State. Some refer to Congress' primary role in setting U.S. immigration policy and a longstanding preference to have country-neutral immigration policies as further grounds to oppose inclusion of immigration enforcement provisions in FTAs.[52]

Should FTAs Be Considered a Policy Response to Reduce Illegal Migration?

Some express the view that FTAs are an important policy option to reduce unauthorized migration. In the debate over DR-CAFTA, for example, some called the agreement "good immigration policy." Proponents argue that trade liberalization will improve the economies in the migrant-sending countries and reduce the "push" factors that foster unwanted migration. As the workers' employment opportunities improve at home, they maintain, the workers will be less motivated to migrate.[53]

Others maintain that, while this theory may prove true in the long run, FTAs are more likely to trigger new migration, some of it illegal, for at least a generation. They assert that this additional migration, whether temporary or permanent, will take root and stimulate the traditional flows of family-based immigration to the United States. Some argue that FTAs should be evaluated on the particular terms of the agreement and not on their potential effects on unauthorized migration.[54]

APPENDIX A.
SELECTED TRADE AND ADMISSIONS DATA FOR TOP U.S. TRADING PARTNERS, 2004
(millions of U.S. dollars, Customs Basis)

Country	Balance of Trade	Total Trade	Entries with E, H, L and TN Visas	Total Entries (Nonimmigrant)
Australia	6,727	21,815	23,434	645,234
Belgium	4,428	29,325	6,795	208,754
Brazil	-7,294	35,020	22,954	534,163
Canada	-65,765	446,091	126,295	238,897
China	-161,978	231,420	26,477	687,148
Colombia	-2,785	11,794	21,507	394,152
France	-10,574	53,054	46,817	1,241,511
Germany	-45,855	108,617	62,193	1,630,247
Hong Kong	6,496	25,123	2,588	81,237
India	-9,467	21,657	111,355	611,327
Indonesia	-8,142	13,480	1,621	72,859
Iraq	-7,658	9,371	68	2,041
Ireland	-19,276	35,608	11,821	428,209
Israel	-5,329	23,725	15,593	337,513
Italy	-17,378	38,800	19,636	759,895
Japan	-75,194	183,995	118,441	4,335,975
Korea (South)	-19,829	72,496	28,940	829,031
Malaysia	-17,288	39,082	4,039	68,712
Mexico	-45,068	266,618	133,427	4,454,061
Netherlands	11,682	36,891	16,059	607,110
Nigeria	-14,694	17,798	1,873	61,550
Philippines	-2,072	16,216	9,751	266,840
Russia	-8,889	14,806	8,369	121,774
Saudi Arabia	-15,678	26,169	256	16,091
Singapore	4,295	34,907	3,715	98,849
South Africa	-2,772	9,116	9,613	111,563
Spain	-835	14,116	15,124	542,733
Sweden	-9,421	15,952	10,067	307,827
Switzerland	-2,374	20,911	8,229	276,433
Taiwan	-12,886	56,348	(in China)	(in China)
Thailand	-11,214	23,940	104,642	82,205
United Kingdom	-10,442	82,362	117,303	4,996,211
Venezuela	-20,181	29,744	24,028	363,962
World totals	-651,521	2,289,573	1,181,799	30,781,330

Source: Table 6 in CRS Issue Brief IB96038, *U.S. International Trade: Data and Forecasts*, by Dick K. Nanto and Thomas Lum; and temporary admissions data from DHS Office of Immigration Statistics, Yearbook of Immigration Statistics: 2004.

APPENDIX B. YEAR OF ARRIVAL FOR NON-MEXICAN FOREIGN-BORN RESIDENTS

The March Supplement of the Current Population Survey offers limited data on migration by year of arrival. The CPS is a representative sample of all persons living in the United States and, thus, includes unauthorized aliens, long-term nonimmigrants, and legal permanent residents, as well as U.S. citizens. Specifically, the CPS asks foreign-born residents: "When did you come to the U.S. to stay?" The CPS data represent a sample of those foreign born who still remain in the United States as of March 2004. The data understate the earlier migration trend because of the emigration and death of earlier migrants. As a result, the slope of the trend line depicted in figure 6 is biased upward.

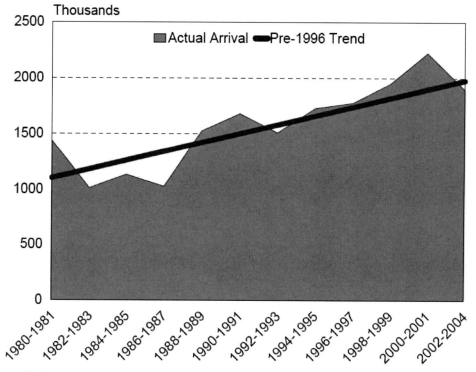

Source: CRS analysis of the March 2004 Supplement of the Current Population Survey.

Figure 6. Estimated Non-Mexican Foreign-Born Residents of the United States by Reported Year of Arrival, 1980-2004.

As figure 6 illustrates, the estimated number of non-Mexican foreign-born residents of the United States who report that they came after 1995 tracks fairly closely to the trend line based upon the numbers who came prior to 1996. Migration to the United States dropped sharply after the September 11, 2001 terrorist attacks. Post-September 11 revisions of immigration law and procedures have slowed down the processing of immigrant petitions and visas. The United States' economic recession in 2001 and initially slow recovery, moreover, may have also slowed down migration.

REFERENCES

[1]   The Immigration Act of 1924 was comprehensive for its day. Among other things, it authorized consular officers to issue visas to intending immigrants and nonimmigrants as well as required aliens entering the United States to have the appropriate immigration documents.

[2]   The specific legislative language of INA §101(a)(15)(E) is: "(i) solely to carry on substantial trade, including trade in services or trade in technology, principally between the United States and the foreign state of which he is a national; or (ii) solely to develop and direct the operations of an enterprise in which he has invested, or of an enterprise in which he is actively in the process of investing, a substantial amount of capital." 8 U.S.C.

[3]   For a more on these trade agreements, see CRS Issue Brief IB10123, *Trade Negotiations During the 109th Congress*, by Ian Fergusson and Lenore Sek.

[4]   The statutory authority and requirements for the enactment and implementation of recently completed or planned trade agreements are contained in the provisions of the Bipartisan Trade Promotion Authority Act of 2002 (TPA Act) (Title XXI of the Trade Act of 2002, as amended by Section 2004(a)(17) of the Miscellaneous Trade and Technical Corrections Act of 2004; P.L. 108-429). The legislative procedure for their implementation is set out in Section 151 of the Trade Act of 1974 (P.L. 93-618). For further information, see CRS Report RL31974, *Trade Agreements: Requirements for Presidential Consultation, Notices, and Reports to Congress Regarding Negotiations*; and CRS Report RL32011, *Trade Agreements: Procedure for Congressional Approval and Implementation*, both by Vladimir N. Pregelj.

[5]   This last point was made clear by House Committee on the Judiciary Chairman James Sensenbrenner during the 2003 debate over the Chile and Singapore FTAs. Chairman Sensenbrenner offered the following summation in his opening remarks: "Members of this Committee spoke with a united bipartisan voice that immigration provisions in future free trade agreements will not receive the support of this Committee." He went on later in the proceedings to state: "I am also concerned that there not be future changes in the basic immigration law contained in future trade agreements. Article I, Section 8 of the Constitution makes immigration and naturalization law an exclusive enumerated power of the Congress, and we intend to follow the Constitution and not to delegate this authority to the executive branch of Government." H.Rept. 108-224, Part 2, *United States-Chile Free Trade Agreement Implementation Act*, 2003.

[6]   Major exceptions to this tradition involve humanitarian migrants, refugees, and asylees who are admitted to the United States on the basis of country conditions and the likelihood that they would be persecuted if returned home. For more background, see CRS Report RL31269, *Refugee Admissions and Resettlement Policy*, by Andorra Bruno; CRS Report RL32621, *U.S. Immigration Policy on Asylum Seekers*, by Ruth Ellen Wasem; and CRS Report RS20468, *Cuban Migration Policy and Issues*, by Ruth Ellen Wasem.

[7]   For an explanation of immigration policy on permanent admissions, see CRS Report RL32235, *U.S. Immigration Policy on Permanent Admissions*, by Ruth Ellen Wasem.

[8] For a full discussion and analysis of nonimmigrant visas, see CRS Report RL31381, *U.S. Immigration Policy on Temporary Admissions*, by Ruth Ellen Wasem.

[9] Most of these nonimmigrant visa categories are defined in §101(a)(15) of the INA.

[10] The term "guest worker" is not defined in law or policy and typically refers to foreign workers employed in low-skilled or unskilled jobs that are seasonal.

[11] The investor provision was added by P.L. 82-414 in 1952 when the INA was codified into the body of law that exists today, amended.

[12] 8 CFR §214.2(e).

[13] See CRS Report RL32030, Immigration Policy for Intracompany Transfers (L Visa): Issues and Legislation, by Ruth Ellen Wasem.

[14] 8 CFR §214.2(l)(ii).

[15] See CRS Report RL30498, Immigration: Legislative Issues on Nonimmigrant Professional Specialty (H-1B) Workers, by Ruth Ellen Wasem; and CRS Report RL32044, Immigration: Policy Considerations Related to Guest Worker Programs, by Andorra Bruno.

[16] In addition, persons with extraordinary ability in the sciences, arts, education, business, or athletics are admitted on O visas, while internationally recognized athletes or members of an internationally recognized entertainment group come on P visas. Aliens working in religious vocations enter on R visas.

[17] See CRS Report RL32861, *Farm Labor: The Adverse Effect Wage Rate (AEWR)*, by William Whittaker.

[18] Intracompany transfers from Mexico or Canada may be denied in the case of certain labor disputes. 8 CFR §214.2(l)(18).

[19] The United States currently has FTAs with Israel, Jordan, Chile, Singapore, Australia, Morocco, and (via NAFTA) with Canada and Mexico.

[20] General Agreement on Trade in Services, Uruguay Round Trade Agreements, Schedule of Specific Commitments. For legal analysis, see CRS Congressional Distribution Memorandum, *U.S. Immigration-Related Obligations Under the WTO General Agreement on Trade in Services*, by Jeanne J. Grimmett, May 12, 1998; and CRS Report RS21554, *Free Trade Agreements and the WTO Exceptions*, by Jeanne J. Grimmett and Todd Tatelman.

[21] For example, the GATS Schedule of Specific Commitments defines the specialist type of intra-corporate transferees as "persons within an organization who possess knowledge at an advanced level of continued expertise and who possess proprietary knowledge of the organization's services, research equipment, techniques, or management. (Specialists may include, but are not limited to, members of licensed professions.)"

[22] 8 CFR §214.2(l)(1)(ii)).

[23] The "TC" professional category was added to the INA by legislation implementing the U.S.-Canada Free Trade Agreement and initially applied only to Canada. An amendment to Section 214(e) of the INA extended the TC professional provision to Mexico, making it "TN."

[24] Chapter 16, of the North American Free Trade Agreement, Annex 1603 Section C, signed Dec. 17, 1992.

[25] Chapter 11, §3 of the U.S.-Singapore Free Trade Agreement, Annex 11A, signed May 6, 2003.

[26] Chapter 14, §3 of the U.S.-Chile Free Trade Agreement, Annex 14.3, signed June 6, 2003.

[27] U.S. Congress, House, *Conference Report on H.R. 1268*, H.Rept. 109-72, May 3, 2005.

[28] Lawrence Assous, "Regional Integration and Migration Flows: A Critical Review of Recent Literature," *Globalisation, Migration and Development*, OECD, 2000.

[29] The author analyzed 2004 data on trade and nonimmigrant admissions for the 34 countries listed in table 1. The findings presented in this portion of the report are statistically significant (based on Pearson correlation coefficients ranging from 0.95 to 0.98).

[30] For more detailed data, see Appendix A at the end of this report.

[31] Steven Globerman, *Trade Liberalism and the Migration of Skilled Workers*, Perspectives on North American Free Trade Series No. 3, Industry Canada Research Publications, Apr. 1999. (Hereafter cited as Globerman, *Trade Liberalism and the Migration of Skilled Workers*).

[32] Ibid.

[33] Ibid.

[34] United States International Trade Commission, *The Likely Impact on the United States of a Free Trade Agreement with Mexico*, USITC Publication 2353, Feb. 1991, p. viii.

[35] Commission for the Study of International Migration and Cooperative Economic Development, *Unauthorized Migration: An Economic Development Response*, July 1990, p. xxxvi.

[36] Philip Martin, *Trade and Migration: NAFTA and Agriculture*, Institute for International Economics, 1993.

[37] Philip Martin, *Economic Integration and Migration: The Mexico-US Case*, prepared for the United Nations University World Institute for Development Economics Research Conference, Sept. 2002. (Hereafter cited as Martin, *Economic Integration and Migration*.)

[38] Section 202(a)(2) of the INA (8 U.S.C. 1151) establishes per-country levels at 7% of the worldwide level. In FY2003, the per-country ceiling was set at 27,827 and in FY2002 was 25,804.

[39] "Immediate relatives" are defined by the INA to include the spouses and unmarried minor children of U.S. citizens, and the parents of adult U.S. citizens.

[40] For analysis of immigration admissions categories and numerical limits, see CRS Report RL32235, *U.S. Immigration Policy on Permanent Admissions*, by Ruth Ellen Wasem.

[41] For a discussion on estimates of how many unauthorized aliens are currently in the U.S. workforce, see CRS Report RL32044, *Immigration: Policy Considerations Related to Guest Worker Programs*, by Andorra Bruno, pp. 6-7. For trends in apprehensions of unauthorized aliens, see CRS Report RL32562, *Border Security: The Role of the U.S. Border Patrol*, by Blas Nuñez-Neto.

[42] For trends in unauthorized alien migration, see CRS Report RS21938, *Unauthorized Aliens in the United States: Estimates Since 1986*, by Ruth Ellen Wasem. For analysis of the IIRIRA's effect on unauthorized alien residents, see Wayne Cornelius, "Death at the Border: Efficacy and Unintended Consequences of U.S. Immigration Control Policy," *Population and Development Review*, vol. 27, no. 4, Dec. 2001.

[43] For complete discussion and analysis of DR-CAFTA, see CRS Report RL31870, *The Dominican Republic-Central America-United States Free Trade Agreement (DR-CAFTA)*, by J. F. Hornbeck; and CRS Report RL32322, *Central America and the Dominican Republic in the Context of the Free Trade Agreement (DR-CAFTA) with the United States*, coordinated by K. Larry Storrs.

[44] For full discussions of the range of these issues, go to the CRS Current Legislative Issues web pages on the CRS website at [http://beta.crs.gov/cli/level_2. aspx?PRDS_CLI_ITEM_ ID=69] and [http://beta.crs.gov/cli/level_2. aspx?PRDS_CLI_ITEM_ ID =23].

[45] For example, if amendments to the INA altered the professional qualifications for an H-1B visa, they might be ruled in violation of trade agreements if the changes raised the standards.

[46] For examples of these perspectives, see H.Rept. 108-224, Part 2, *United States-Chile Free Trade Agreement Implementation Act*, 2003.

[47] For examples of these views, see U.S. Congress, Senate Judiciary, Proposed United States-Chile and United States-Singapore Free Trade Agreements with Chile and Singapore, July 14, 2003.

[48] For a full discussion of these talks, see CRS Report RL3308, *Trade in Services: The Doha Development Agenda Negotiations and U.S. Goal*, by William H. Cooper.

[49] Letter to USTR Robert Portman from Representative F. James Sensenbrenner, Jr. and Representative John Conyers, Jr, dated May 19, 2005. It is publically available in *Inside U.S. Trade*, May 27, 2005.

[50] The Federation for American Immigration Reform (FAIR), an organization which favors increased restrictions on immigration, criticized "the lack of any mention of illegal immigration" as the most significant omission in NAFTA. Quoting further, "NAFTA is about business and labor; illegal immigration is the focal point of our labor relationship with Mexico." FAIR argued that "explicit bilateral cooperation on immigration must be part of any trade agreement with Mexico," stating without further explanation that "the agreement will lure immigrants to the border, increasing the potential number of illegal immigrants to the U.S.," *Free Trade Agreement Ignores Key Immigration Link*, FAIR Immigration Report, Sept./Oct. 1992.

[51] For an additional example of these arguments, see Jessica Vaughan, "Trade Agreements and Immigration," *In the National Interest*, Apr. 13, 2004, available online at [http://www.cis.org/articles/2004/jessicaoped041304.html].

[52] For examples of the approach, see White House Office of the Press Secretary, *Fact Sheet: Security and Prosperity Partnership of North America*, Mar. 23, 2005.

[53] For examples of these views, see "Statement by President George W. Bush on the Central American and Dominican Republic Free Trade Agreement," Washington, June 23, 2005 available at [http://geneva.usmission.gov/Press2005/0623Bushon CAFTA. htm]; and U.S. Congress, House Committee on Ways and Means, *Exchange of Letters on Issues Concerning the Negotiation of a North American Free Trade Agreement*, committee print, 102d Cong., 1ˢᵗ sess., May 1, 1991, WMCP 102-10 (Washington: GPO, May 1, 1991).

[54] For examples of these perspectives, see Martin, *Economic Integration and Migration*; Jessica Vaughan, *Be Our Guest: Trade Agreements and Visas*, Center for Immigration

Studies, Dec. 2003; and Robert Manning, *Five Years After NAFTA: Rhetoric and Reality of Mexican Immigration in the 21st Century*, Mar. 2000.

In: Immigration Crisis: Issues, Policies and Consequences   ISBN: 978-1-60456-096-1
Editors: P. W. Hickman and T. P. Curtis, pp. 153-177 © 2008 Nova Science Publishers, Inc.

Chapter 6

U.S. Immigration Policy on Temporary Admissions[*]

Ruth Ellen Wasem and Chad C. Haddal

Abstract

U.S. law provides for the temporary admission of various categories of foreign nationals, who are known as nonimmigrants. Nonimmigrants are admitted for a designated period of time and a specific purpose. They include a wide range of visitors, including tourists, foreign students, diplomats, and temporary workers. There are 24 major nonimmigrant visa categories, and 72 specific types of nonimmigrant visas issued currently. These visa categories are commonly referred to by the letter and numeral that denotes their subsection in the Immigration and Nationality Act (INA), e.g., B-2 tourists, E-2 treaty investors, F-1 foreign students, H-1B temporary professional workers, J-1 cultural exchange participants, or S-4 terrorist informants.

Interest in nonimmigrant visas soared immediately following the September 11, 2001 terrorist attacks, which were conducted by foreign nationals apparently admitted to the United States on legal visas. Since that time, policy makers have raised a series of questions about aliens in the United States and the extent that the federal government monitors their admission and presence in this country. Some of the specific visa categories are the focus of legislative activity (e.g., guest workers).

The U.S. Department of State (DOS) consular officer, at the time of application for a visa, as well as the Department of Homeland Security (DHS) immigration inspectors, at the time of application for admission, must be satisfied that the alien is entitled to nonimmigrant status. The burden of proof is on the applicant to establish eligibility for nonimmigrant status and the type of nonimmigrant visa for which the application is made. Both DOS consular officers (when the alien is petitioning abroad) and DHS inspectors (when the alien is entering the United States) must confirm that the alien is not ineligible for a visa under the so-called "grounds for inadmissibility" of the INA, which include criminal, terrorist, and public health grounds for exclusion.

Nonimmigrant visas issued abroad dipped to 5.0 million in FY2004 after peaking at 7.6 million in FY2001. The FY2005 data inched back up to 5.4 million nonimmigrant visas issued. Over the past 12 years, DOS has typically issued around 6 million

---

[*] Excerpted from CRS Report RL31381, dated February 7, 2007.

nonimmigrant visas annually. The growth in the late 1990s has been largely attributable to the issuances of border crossing cards to residents of Canada and Mexico and the issuances of temporary worker visas. Combined, visitors for tourism and business comprised the largest group of nonimmigrants in FY2005, about 3.42 million, down from 5.7 million in FY2000. Other notable categories were students and exchange visitors (9.4%) and temporary workers (17.9%).

The law and regulations usually set strict terms for nonimmigrant lengths of stay in the United States, typically have foreign residency requirements, and often limit what aliens are permitted to do in the United States (e.g., gain employment or enroll in school), but many observers assert that the policies are not uniformly or rigorously enforced. Achieving an optimal balance among major policy priorities, such as ensuring national security, facilitating trade and commerce, protecting public health and safety, and fostering international cooperation, remains a challenge.

OVERVIEW

Introduction

U.S. law provides for the temporary admission of various categories of foreign nationals, who are known as nonimmigrants. Nonimmigrants are admitted for a designated period of time and a specific purpose. Nonimmigrants include a wide range of people, such as tourists, foreign students, diplomats, temporary agricultural workers, exchange visitors, internationally-known entertainers, foreign media representatives, intracompany business personnel, and crew members on foreign vessels.

Legislative activity usually focuses on specific visa categories, and legislative revisions to temporary visa categories have usually occurred incrementally. Interest in nonimmigrant visas as a group, however, soared immediately following the September 11, 2001 terrorist attacks, which were conducted by foreign nationals admitted to the United States on temporary visas. Since that time, policy makers have raised a series of questions about aliens in the United States and the extent that the federal government monitors their admission and presence in this country. The Enhanced Border Security and Visa Entry Reform Act (P.L. 107-173), provisions in the Homeland Security Act (P.L. 107-296), and the Intelligence Reform and Terrorism Prevention Act of 2004 (P.L. 108-458) are examples of broad reforms of immigration law to tighten procedures and oversight of aliens temporarily admitted to the United States.

Foreign nationals may be admitted to the United States temporarily or may come to live permanently.[1] Those admitted on a permanent basis are known as immigrants or legal permanent residents (LPRs), while those admitted on a temporary basis are known as nonimmigrants. Aliens who are in the United States without authorization (i.e., illegal aliens) are not discussed in this report.

U.S. immigration policy, embodied in the Immigration and Nationality Act (INA), presumes that all aliens seeking admission to the United States are coming to live permanently.[2] As a result, nonimmigrants must demonstrate that they are coming for a temporary period and for a specific purpose. The U.S. Department of State (DOS) consular officer, at the time of application for a visa, as well as the Department of Homeland Security (DHS) immigration inspectors, at the time of application for admission, must be satisfied that the alien is entitled to a nonimmigrant status.[3] The burden of proof is on the applicant to establish eligibility for nonimmigrant status and the type of nonimmigrant visa for which the application is made. The law exempts only the H-1 workers, L intracompany transfers, and V family members from the requirement that they prove that they are not coming to live permanently.[4]

This report begins with a synthesis of the nonimmigrant categories according to the purpose of the visa. It discusses the periods of admission and length of stay and then summarizes grounds for inadmissibility and removal as well as reasons for termination of status. It describes the circumstances under which nonimmigrants may work in the United States and follows with an analysis of nonimmigrant admissions. The narrative concludes with a discussion of concern issues, followed by two detailed tables analyzing key admissions requirements across all nonimmigrant visa types.

Broad Categories of Nonimmigrants

There are 24 major nonimmigrant visa categories, and 72 specific types of nonimmigrant visas issued currently.[5] Most of these nonimmigrant visa categories are defined in §101(a)(15) of INA. These visa categories are commonly referred to by the letter and numeral that denotes their subsection in §101(a)(15), e.g., B-2 tourists, E-2 treaty investors, F-1 foreign students, H-1B temporary professional workers, J-1 cultural exchange participants, or S-4 terrorist informants. These temporary visas may be grouped under the broad labels described below.

Diplomats and other International Representatives

Ambassadors, consuls, and other official representatives of foreign governments (and their immediate family and servants) enter the United States on A visas. Official representatives of international organizations (and their immediate family and servants) are admitted on G visas. Those nonimmigrants entering under the auspices of the North Atlantic Treaty Organization (NATO) have their own visa categories. Aliens who work for foreign media use the I visa.

Visitors as Business Travelers and Tourists

B-1 nonimmigrants are visitors for business and are required to be seeking admission for activities other than purely local employment or hire. The difference between a business visitor and a temporary worker depends also on the source of the alien's salary. To be classified as a visitor for business, an alien must receive his or her salary from abroad and must not receive any remuneration from a U.S. source other than an expense allowance and reimbursement for other expenses incidental to temporary stay.

The B-2 visa is granted for temporary visitors for "pleasure,"otherwise known as tourists. Tourists, who are encouraged to visit as a boon to the U.S. economy, have consistently been the largest nonimmigrant class of admission to the United States. A B-2 nonimmigrant may not engage in any employment in the United States.

Many visitors, however, enter the United States without nonimmigrant visas through the Visa Waiver Program. This provision of INA allows the Attorney General to waive the visa documentary requirements for aliens coming as visitors from 28 countries (e.g., Australia, France, Germany, Italy, Japan, New Zealand, Switzerland, and the United Kingdom).[6]

Multinational Corporate Executives and International Investors

Intracompany transferees who are executive, managerial, and have specialized knowledge and who are continuing employment with an international firm or corporation are admitted on the L visas. Aliens who are treaty traders enter as E-1 while those who are treaty investors use E-2 visas.

Temporary Workers

The major nonimmigrant category for temporary workers is the H visa. Professional specialty workers (H-1B), nurses (H-1C) agricultural workers (H-2A) and unskilled temporary workers (H-2B) are included.[7] Persons with extraordinary ability in the sciences, arts, education, business, or athletics are admitted on O visas, while internationally recognized athletes or members of an internationally recognized entertainment group come on P visas. Aliens working in religious vocations enter on R visas. Temporary professional workers from Canada and Mexico may enter according to terms set by the North American Free Trade Agreement (NAFTA) on TN visas.

Cultural Exchange

The broadest category for cultural exchange is the J visa. The J visa includes professors and research scholars, students, foreign medical graduates, teachers, camp counselors and au pairs who are participating in an approved exchange visitor program. Participants in special international cultural exchange programs from the former Soviet Union and Eastern bloc countries enter on Q-1 visas. Q-2 visas are for Irish young adults from the border counties who participate in approved cultural exchange programs.

Foreign Students

The most common visa for foreign students is the F-1 visa. It is tailored for international students pursuing a full-time academic education. Those students who wish to pursue a non-academic, e.g., vocational, course of study apply for an M visa. Foreign students are just one of many types of aliens who may enter the United States on a J-1 visa for cultural exchange.[8]

Family-Related

Fiances and fiancees of U.S. citizens come in on K visas. The 106th Congress added a transitional nonimmigrant visa — the V visa — for immediate relatives (spouse and children) of LPRs who have had petitions to also become LPRs pending for three years.

Law Enforcement-Related

The law enforcement-related visas are among the most recently created. The S visa is used by informants in criminal and terrorist investigations.[9] Victims of human trafficking who participate in the prosecution of those responsible may get a T visa. Victims of other criminal activities, notably domestic abuse, who cooperate with the prosecution are eligible for the U visa.

Aliens in Transit and Crew Members

Two miscellaneous nonimmigrant categories are some of the earliest nonimmigrant categories enacted. The C visa is for aliens traveling through the United States en route to another destination, and the D visa is for alien crew members on vessels or aircraft.

Exclusion and Removal

Inadmissibility

Both DOS consular officers (when the alien is petitioning abroad) and INS inspectors (when the alien is entering the United States) must confirm that the alien is not ineligible for a visa under the so-called "grounds for inadmissibility" of the INA.[10] These criteria categories are:

- health-related grounds;
- criminal history;
- security and terrorist concerns;
- public charge (e.g., indigence);
- seeking to work without proper labor certification;
- illegal entrants and immigration law violations;
- lacking proper documents;
- ineligible for citizenship; and
- aliens previously removed.[11]

The law provides waiver authority of these grounds (except for most of the security and terrorist-related grounds) for nonimmigrants on a case-by-case basis.[12]

Termination of Status

Consistent with the grounds of inadmissibility, the legal status of a nonimmigrant in the United States may be terminated based upon the nonimmigrant's behavior in the United States. Specifically, the regulations list national security, public safety and diplomatic reasons for termination. If a nonimmigrant who is not authorized to work does so, that employment constitutes a failure to maintain a lawful status. A crime of violence that has a sentence of more than one year also terminates nonimmigrant status.[13]

Periods of Admission

Length of Stay

Congress has enacted amendments and the executive branch has promulgated regulations governing areas such as the length and extensions of stay. For example, A-1 ambassadors are allowed to remain in the United States for the duration of their service, F-1 students to complete their studies, R-1 religious workers for up to three years, and D crew members for

29 days. Many categories of nonimmigrants are required to have a residence in their home country that they intend to return to as a stipulation of obtaining the visa. The law actually requires J-1 cultural exchange visa holders to go home for two years prior to returning to the United States (with some exceptions).

On April 12, 2002, the former INS proposed regulations on the length of stay for aliens on visitor visas (B-2) aimed at curbing abuses in that nonimmigrant visa category, such as working, enrolling in school, or overstaying. The rule would have eliminated the minimum six-month admission period and would have replaced it with "a period of time that is fair and reasonable for the completion of the purpose of the visit." The burden would have been on the alien to explain to the immigration inspector the nature and purpose of visit so the inspector can determine an appropriate time limit. In those cases where the inspector could not have determined the time needed to complete the visit, the visitors would have been limited to 30-day periods.[14] Ultimately the Administration announced that it was not promulgating this regulation.

DHS recently announced plans to revise the regulations to expand the time restriction on BCCs used by Mexicans to enter the United States for temporary visits. This decision reportedly was coordinated between U.S. Secretary for Homeland Security Tom Ridge and Mexican Secretary of Government Santiago Creel.

According to the DHS press release, the forthcoming rule would extend the time limit for BCC visitors from 72 hours to a period of 30 days. Laser visaholders planning to stay in the United States for more than 30 days are expected to be included in USVISIT.[15]

Duration of Visa

Separate from the length of stay authorized for the various nonimmigrant visas is the validity period of the visa issued by DOS consular officers. These time periods are negotiated country-by-country and category-by-category, generally reflecting reciprocal relationships for U.S. travelers to these countries. For example, a B-1 and B-2 visitor visa from Germany is valid for 10 years while B-1 and B-2 visas from Indonesia are valid for five years. The D crew member visa is valid for five years for Egyptians, but only one year for Hungarians.

Employment Authorization

Permission to Work

With the obvious exception of the nonimmigrants who are temporary workers or the executives of multinational corporations, most nonimmigrants are not allowed to work in the United States. Exceptions to this policy are noted in table 2, which follows at the end of this report. As stated above, working without authorization is a major violation of law and results in loss of nonimmigrant status.

Labor Market Tests

The H-2 visas require that employers conduct an affirmative search for available U.S. workers and that DOL determine that admitting alien workers will not adversely affect the wages and working conditions of similarly employed U.S. workers. Under this process — known as labor certification — employers must apply to the U.S. Department of Labor for certification that unemployed domestic workers are not available and that there will not be an adverse effect from the alien workers' entry.

The labor market test required for H-1 workers, known as labor attestation, is less stringent than labor certification. Any employer wishing to bring in an H-1B nonimmigrant must attest in an application to the DOL that the employer will pay the nonimmigrant the greater of the actual compensation paid other employees in the same job or the prevailing compensation for that occupation; the employer will provide working conditions for the nonimmigrant that do not cause the working conditions of the other employees to be adversely affected; and, there is no strike or lockout. Employers recruiting the H-1C nurses must attest that their employment will not adversely affect the wages and working conditions of similarly employed registered nurses; the H-1C nurses will be paid the wage rate paid by the facility to similarly employed U.S. registered nurses; the facility is taking significant steps to recruit and retain sufficient U.S. registered nurses; and the facility is abiding by specified anti-strike and layoff protections.

STATISTICAL TRENDS

When analyzing the issuances of nonimmigrant visas issued by DOS and the admissions data issued by DHS, many of the same distributions that were present in recent years once again appeared.[16] As figure 1 shows, there was a larger percentage of visas being distributed to Asia than to any other region, accounting for 38.3% of the roughly 5.4 million nonimmigrant visas the DOS issued in FY2005. North American nonimmigrants (which included nationals of countries in Central America) accounted for the next largest group of visa issuances at 24.9%, or approximately

1.34 million individuals. Europe and South America accounted for the third and fourth largest groups with 17.5% and 14.2% of the nonimmigrant visa issuances, respectively. Africa tallied 4.3% of the visas, while visa issuances for Oceania, The United Nations (UN) and individuals with no nationality combined for less than 1% of the total visa issuances in FY2005.

Further breaking down the visa issuance data for FY2005, figure 2 demonstrates that 63.3 % of the visas issued for entry into the United States was by individuals entering on visitor visas. Consequently, the volume of visitors visa was at a rate 3.5 times higher than the next largest category. The subsequent two largest categories of issuances in FY2005 were for employee visas, which accounted for 17.9% of visas issued, and students, which represented 9.4% of issuances. In absolute terms, employees and students accounted for approximately 967,000 and 507,000 visas, respectively, out of a total of approximately 5.4 million in FY2005. Additionally, the visas issued for crew members and others in transit accounted for 5.5% of the visa issuances for FY2005. The remaining visas issued constituted 4% of the total.

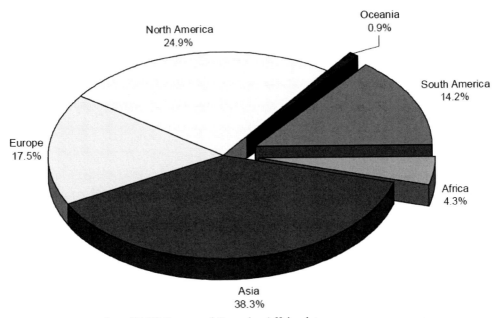

Source: CRS presentation of DOS Bureau of Consular Affairs data.

Figure 1. Nonimmigrant Visas *Issued* by Region, FY2005.

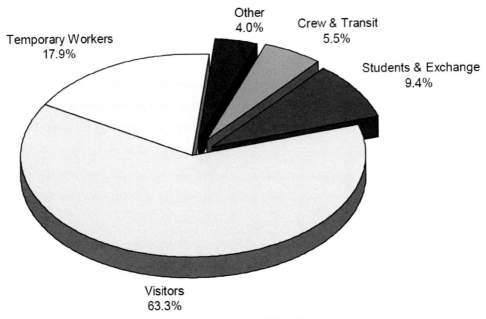

Source: CRS presentation of DOS Bureau of Consular Affairs data.

Figure 2. Nonimmigrant Visas *Issued* by Category, FY2005.

An alternative method of measuring temporary migrations to the United States is with the nonimmigrant admissions data collected by DHS. These data come with two important caveats. First, the admissions are of individuals required to fill out I-94 forms for entry into the United States, thus constituting a total of approximately 32 million admissions. Mexican nationals with Border Crossing Cards and Canadian nationals traveling for business or tourist purposes are not counted in these admission totals. These two groups accounted for the vast majority of admissions to the United States, with approximately 143 million admissions.[17] Thus, the total number of admissions to the United States in FY2005 was approximately 175 million. Second, these data are tallies of admissions and not of individuals. Since many individuals depart and re-enter the United States during the same year, individuals may have multiple admissions in the DHS admissions data.

The admissions data illustrated a different distributional pattern than the visa issuance data. Figure 3 shows the plurality of foreign nationals admitted into the United States in FY2005 were nationals of a European state, which represented 37.1% of admissions. The second largest category of admitted individuals were foreign nationals from other North American countries with 26.5% of the admissions total. Foreign nationals from Asian countries, which constituted the largest visa issuance category, were the third largest regional admission group and account for 23.7% of admissions into the United States. These Asian admissions constituted 7.58 million entries into the United States, while by comparison the European entries accounted for 11.88 million admissions. The fact that 24 of the 27 countries participating in the Visa Waiver Program were European,[18] in conjunction with the majority of all admissions being visitors, a plurality of European admissions was to be expected. South American entries accounted for 6.9% of FY2005 entries, or approximately 2.2 million persons, while the remaining categories of nationals from African and Oceanic regions (and individuals of "unknown" classification) constituted 1.87 million persons with 5.8% of the admissions total.

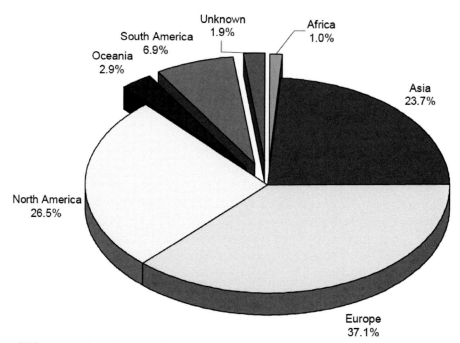

Source: CRS presentation of DHS Office of Immigration Statistics data.

Figure 3. Nonimmigrant *Admissions* by Region, FY2005.

Figure 4 below shows that for FY2005, 89.1% of the foreign nationals admitted into the United States were classified into the visitor categories of visas (including the "Visa Waiver Program" and "other business and travel"). This figure depicts roughly 32 million persons admitted at various ports of entry. The only other category of admissions which constituted more than 4% of the admissions total were those of temporary workers, which when combined accounted for 4.9% of admissions, or approximately 1.57 million temporary worker admissions. Students and exchange admissions was the third largest category with 1.04 million arrivals, and accounted for 3.3% of the total. The remaining categories of nonimmigrant admissions all constituted less than 3 percent of admissions individually, but when combined represented 2.7% of foreign nationals admitted. Thus, foreign nationals categorized into any remaining categories (including unknown category) accounted for 2.2 million admissions into the United States.

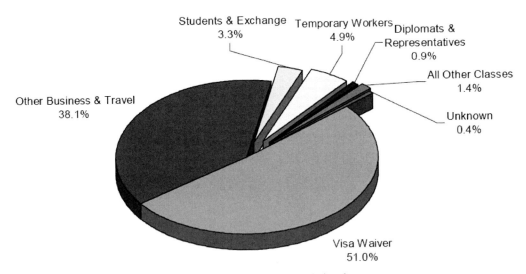

Source: CRS presentation of DHS Office of Immigration Statistics data.

Figure 4. Nonimmigrant *Admissions* by Category, FY2005.

When analyzing the longitudinal data for both the admissions and the visa issuances, certain patterns became apparent in the data. In terms of the visa issuances as depicted in figure 5 below, the number of visas issued by the DOS was lower than it was in the mid-1990s. However, this trend was reversed with the terrorist attacks of September 11, 2001, as security concerns resulted in more stringent criteria for visa issuances and a greater burden of qualification placed upon the nonimmigrant visa applicant. Consequently, the visa issuances declined from their FY2001 peak of approximately 7.6 million visas to theFY2005 level of 5.4 million visas issued.

The decline in these levels was largely due to the reduction of North American visas issued, which experienced its levels in FY2005 being reduced to half of its levels in FY2001. The growth in the late 1990s has been largely attributable to the issuances of border crossing cards (laser visas) to residents of Mexico and the issuances of temporary worker visas. Visa issuance levels for other regions remained approximately the same as they were in FY2001. The only other notable changes in the longitudinal data for the given time span were a slight decrease in visas for European nationals, a slight increase in visas for Asian nationals, and a decrease in the visas granted to nationals from countries in the Oceanic region.

Visas Issued

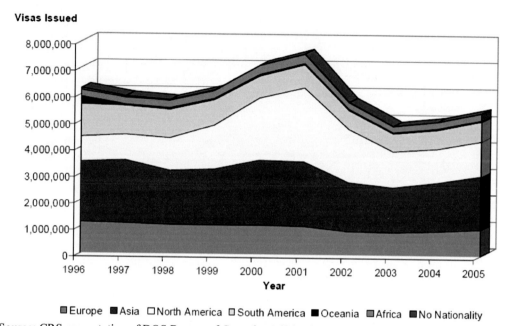

Source: CRS presentation of DOS Bureau of Consular Affairs data.

Figure 5. Nonimmigrant Visas *Issued* by Region, FY1996-FY2005.

The data for figure 6, which depicts the nonimmigrant admissions into the United States between FY1996-FY2005, offered a different picture of the temporary visitors to the United States. Unlike the data for figure 5, the admissions data provided two periods of upward movement that increased the number of admissions of nonimmigrants by approximately 29% over the course of a decade. In FY1996 the number of nonimmigrants admitted at United States Ports of Entry was just under 25 million, but by FY2005 this number had increased to 32 million admissions. The most significant sources of the trend were increasing numbers of nonimmigrants from the European and North American region. Whereas other regions witnessed lesser increases in their admission levels, the European-based admissions increased from

9.39 million in FY1996 to 11.88 million in FY2005, an increase of 2.49 million nonimmigrants. Furthermore, the North American-based nonimmigration admissions increased from a level of 3.56 million in FY1996 to 8.47 million in FY2005. This change constituted an increase of 4.91 million in annual admissions or an a percentage increase of 237.9% over the course of the decade.

Although this increase was partly attributable to the new rule structure under the North American Free Trade Agreement (NAFTA), it is worth noting that the more significant upward trends in North American-based admissions occurred in FY1998, several years after NAFTA's implementation.[19] Finally, in contrast to the visa issuances for North American-based nonimmigrants from figure 5, the admission levels of nationals from North American countries was largely unchanged following the September 11 attacks, as figure 6 shows. This finding not only contrasted the visa issuances, but the admissions levels of nationals based out of other regions. Every other region experienced some reduction of admissions of their nationals in FY2002, but recovered to near FY2001 levels in FY2005.

Admissions

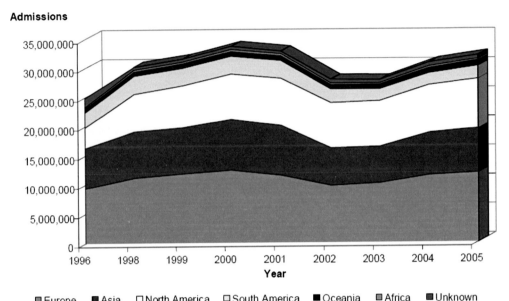

Source: CRS presentation of DHS Office of Immigration Statistics data. Note: DHS did not publish nonimmigrant data for FY1997.

Figure 6. Nonimmigrant *Admissions* by Region, FY1996-FY2005.

CURRENT ISSUES

Achieving an optimal balance among major policy priorities, such as ensuring national security, facilitating trade and commerce, protecting public health and safety, and fostering international cooperation, remains a challenge. Efforts to establish a comprehensive automated system that tracks the arrival and departure of nonimmigrants (US-VISIT) is well underway but remains incomplete.[20] Requirements for individuals entering into the United States (including U.S. citizens and visitors from Canada and other Western Hemisphere countries) to bear passports or other documents sufficient to denote citizenship and identity are now going into effect. All the while, legislative revisions to specific temporary visa categories continue to arise incrementally.

This section of the report highlights several of the specific temporary visa concerns that are of legislative interest to Congress: temporary workers, foreign medical graduates, foreign investors, and foreign students.

Temporary Workers

Temporary Skilled and Professional Workers[21]

Many business people have expressed concern that a scarcity of labor in certain sectors may curtail the pace of economic growth. A leading legislative response to skills mismatches and labor shortages has been to increase the supply of temporary foreign workers. Proponents of raising the H-1B levels assert that H-1B workers are essential if the United States is to remain globally competitive. Some proponents argue that employers should be free to hire the best people for the jobs, maintaining that market forces should regulate H-1B visas, not an arbitrary ceiling.

Those opposing any further increases or easing of admissions requirements assert that there is no compelling evidence of a labor shortage in these professional areas that cannot be met by newly graduating students and retraining the existing U.S. work force. They argue further that the education of U.S. students and training of U.S. workers should be prioritized instead of fostering a reliance on foreign workers.

Guest Workers[22]

There is ongoing pressure to increase unskilled temporary foreign workers, commonly referred to as guest workers. The admission of H-2B visas are numerically limited, and the ceiling has been exceeded the past few years as more sectors of the economy vie for the visas. The current discussion of guest worker programs takes place against a backdrop of historically high levels of unauthorized migration to the United States. Supporters of a large-scale temporary worker program argue that such a program would help reduce unauthorized immigration by providing a legal alternative for prospective foreign workers.

Critics reject this reasoning and instead maintain that a new guest worker program would likely exacerbate the problem of illegal migration. Some allege that employers prefer guest workers because they are less demanding in terms of wages and working conditions, and that expanding guest worker visas would have a deleterious effect on U.S. workers.

Foreign Medical Graduates[23]

The J cultural exchange visa has become a gateway for foreign medical graduates (FMGs) to gain admission to the United States as nonimmigrants for the purpose of graduate medical education and training. As exchange visitors, FMGs can remain in the United States on a J visa until the completion of their training, typically for a maximum of seven years. After that time, they are required to return home for at least two years before they can apply to change to another nonimmigrant status or LPR status.

The authority to issue a waiver of the foreign residence requirement to a FMG based on the request of a state public health department currently applies to J-visa holders through June 1, 2008. More specifically, these J-visa holders do not have to leave the United States at the conclusion of their residencies if they agree to practice medicine for three years in an area designated by the Secretary of Health and Human Services as having a shortage of health care professionals.

The original intent underlying the foreign residency requirement for FMG is to encourage American-trained foreign doctors to return home to improve health conditions and advance the medical profession in their native countries. Some now argue that the J-1 visa waiver for FMGs should be made permanent or extended for a number of years to allow an evaluation of the use of foreign physicians to meet healthcare shortages and their impact on American physicians.

Foreign Investors[24]

There are currently two categories of nonimmigrant investor visas: E-1 for treaty traders; and the E-2 for treaty investors. According to DHS statistics, there were 192,843 investor visa arrivals in the United States in FY2005.

The investor visas offered by the United States operate on the principal that foreign direct investment into the United States should spur economic growth in the United States. According to the classical theory, if these investments are properly targeted towards the U.S. labor force's skill sets, it should reduce the migration pressures on U.S. workers. To attract such investors, research indicates that temporary migrants are motivated most significantly by employment and wage prospects, while permanent migrants are motivated by professional and social mobility. Theoretically, it is unclear to what extent potential migration provides additional incentive for investment activity. Investors from developed countries may sometimes lack incentive to settle in the United States since they can achieve foreign direct investment (FDI) and similar standards of living from their home country. However, in cases where foreign investors have been attracted, the economic benefits have been positive and significant.

Foreign Students[25]

In the wake of post-September 11 security reforms, the security concerns over foreign student visas are being weighed against competitiveness concerns. Potential foreign students, as well as all aliens, must satisfy Department of State (DOS) consular officers abroad and immigration inspectors upon entry to the United States that they are not ineligible for visas under the so-called "grounds for inadmissibility" of the Immigration and Nationality Act, which include security and terrorist concerns. The consular officers who process visa applicants are required to check the consolidated Terrorist Screening Database (TSDB) before issuing any visa. In part because of these security measures, student visa debates have expanded to include both security and market-based discussions.

Higher education institutions in the United States are concerned over their ability to attract the numbers and quality of foreign students, and whether the post-September 11 security measures impede the entry of potential students into the U.S. education system. The fields of science, technology, engineering and mathematics (STEM) increasingly rely on foreign students, and these fields hold a top priority with most research institutions. Furthermore, the U.S. economy has a high demand for the skill-sets produced in these fields of study, and the STEM students often provide a major link between the academic community and the labor market. Consequently, many groups in higher education and the private sector are seeking to expand pathways for foreign students to emigrate.

ENFORCING CURRENT LAW

Currently the law and regulations usually set strict terms for nonimmigrant lengths of stay in the United States, typically have foreign residency requirements, and often limit what the aliens are permitted to do in the United States (e.g., gain employment or enroll in school). Many observers, however, assert that these policies are not uniformly or rigorously enforced. Some maintain that further legislation is not necessary if the laws currently in place are enforced.

The two tables that follow, among other things, illustrate the complexity and diversity of policy on temporary admissions, and the challenge for policy makers who may seek to revise it. Table 1 indicates whether the INA or regulations set any limits or requirements on how long nonimmigrants may stay in the United States and whether they must maintain a residence in their home country for each of the 72 visa classifications. Table 2 details whether there are any labor market tests or any limits on the numbers of aliens who can enter the United States according to each of the 72 visa classifications. Table 2 also presents DOS data on the number of nonimmigrant visas issued in FY2000. *When a cell in the table is blank, it means the law and regulations are silent on the subject.*

REFERENCES

[1] For background and analysis of visa issuance policy, see CRS Report RL31512, *Visa Issuances: Policy, Issues, and Legislation*, by Ruth Ellen Wasem.

[2] §214(b) of INA.

[3] 22 CFR §41.11(a).

[4] §214(b) of INA. Nonimmigrant visas are commonly referred to by the letter and numeral that denotes their subsection in §101(a)(15), hence "H-1" workers, "L" intracompany transfers, and "V" family members.

[5] Law on nonimmigrants dates back to the Immigration Act of 1819. An immigration law enacted in 1924 defined several classes of nonimmigrant admission. The disparate series of immigration and nationality laws were codified into INA in 1952. Major laws amending INA are the Immigration Amendments of 1965, the Refugee Act of 1980, the Immigration Reform and Control Act of 1986, the Immigration Act of 1990, and the Illegal Immigration Reform and Immigrant Responsibility Act of 1996. The newest nonimmigrant visa — known as the V visa — was folded into the District of Columbia FY2001 appropriations conference agreement (H.R. 4942, H.Rept. 106-1005), which became P.L. 106-553.

[6] See CRS Report RL32221, *Visa Waiver Program*, by Alison Siskin.

[7] See CRS Report RL30498, Immigration: Legislative Issues on Nonimmigrant Professional Specialty (H-1B) Workers; CRS Report RL30852, Immigration of Agricultural Guest Workers: Policy, Trends, and Legislative Issues, both by Ruth Ellen Wasem; CRS Report RL32044, Immigration: Policy Considerations Related to Guest Worker Programs, by Andorra Bruno, and CRS Report RS20164, Immigration: Temporary Admission of Nurses for Health Shortage Areas (P.L. 106-95), by Joyce Vialet.

[8]   For further discussion and analysis, see CRS Report RL31146, *Foreign Students in the United States: Policies and Legislation*, by Chad C. Haddal.

[9]   For more information, see CRS Report RS21043, *Immigration: S Visas for Criminal and Terrorist Informants*, by Karma Ester.

[10] §212(b) of INA.

[11] For a fuller analysis, see CRS Report RL32480, *Immigration Consequences of Criminal Activity*, by Michael John Garcia; and CRS Report RL32564, *Immigration: Terrorist Grounds for Exclusion of liens*, by Michael John Garcia and Ruth Ellen Wasem.

[12] §212(d)(3) and (4) of INA.

[13] §214.1 of 8 CFR.

[14] *Federal Register*, vol. 67, no. 71, Apr. 12, 2002, pp. 18065-18069.

[15] U.S. Department of Homeland Security, Office of the Press Secretary, *DHS Announces Expanded Border Control Plans*, Aug. 10, 2004; available at [http://www.dhs.gov/dhspublic/display?content=3930].

[16] Additional analysis of DHS data is provided in U.S Department of Homeland Security, Office of Immigration Statistics, *Temporary Admissions of Nonimmigrants to the United States: 2005*, July 2006.

[17] U.S. Department of Homeland Security, Office of Immigration Statistics, *Temporary Admissions of Nonimmigrants to the United States: 2005*, July 2006, pp. 1-2.

[18] The exceptions being Singapore, Japan, and Brunei.

[19] CRS Report RL32982, *Immigration Issues in Trade Agreements*, by Ruth Ellen Wasem.

[20] CRS Report RL32234, U.S. Visitor and Immigrant Status Indicator Technology (US-VISIT) Program, by Lisa M. Seghetti and Stephen R. Viña.

[21] CRS Report RL30498, Immigration: Legislative Issues on Nonimmigrant Professional Specialty (H-1B) Workers, by Ruth Ellen Wasem.

[22] CRS Report RL32044, Immigration: Policy Considerations Related to Guest Worker Programs, by Andorra Bruno.

[23] CRS Report RL31460, Immigration: Foreign Physicians and the J-1 Visa Waiver Program, by Karma Ester, and CRS Report RS22584, Foreign Medical Graduates: A Brief Overview of the J-1 Visa Waiver Program, by Karma Ester.

[24] CRS Report RL33844, Foreign Investor Visas: Policies and Issues, by Chad C. Haddal.

[25] CRS Report RL31146, Foreign Students in the United States: Policies and Legislation, by Chad C. Haddal.

Table 1. Periods of Stay and Foreign Residency Requirements for Nonimmigrant Visas

Visa	Class Description	Period of Stay	Renewal Option	Foreign Residence Required
A-1	Ambassador, public minister, career diplomat, consul, and immediate family	Duration of assignment		
A-2	Other foreign government official or employee, and immediate family	Duration of assignment		
A-3	Attendant, servant or personal employee of A-1/A-2, and immediate family	Up to three years	Up to two years intervals	
B-1	Visitor for business	Up to one year	Up to six months	Yes
B-2	Visitor for pleasure	Six months to one year	Up to six months	Yes
B-1/B-2	Business and pleasure	Six months to one year	Up to six months	Yes
BCC	Border Crossing Cards	72 hours [unless coupled with B-1 or B-2] proposed extension to 30 days		Yes
C-1	Alien in transit	Up to 29 days		
C-1/D	Transit/crew member	Up to 29 days		
C-2	Person in transit to United Nations Headquarters	Up to 29 days		
C-3	Foreign government official, immediate family, attendant, servant, or personal employee in transit	Up to 29 days		
D	Crew member	Up to 29 days		
E-1	Treaty trader, spouse and child, and employee	Up to two years	Up to two years	
E-2	Treaty investor, spouse and child, and employee	Same as E-1	Same as E-1	
F-1	Foreign student (academic or language training program)	Period of study (one year secondary students)		Yes
F-2	Spouse or child of F-1	Same as F-1		
G-1	Principal resident representative of recognized foreign member government to international organization, staff, and immediate family	Duration of assignment		
G-2	Other representative of recognized foreign member government to international organization, staff, and immediate family	Duration of assignment		
G-3	Representative of non-recognized or nonmember foreign member government to international organization, staff, and immediate family	Duration of assignment		
G-4	International organization officer or employee, and immediate family	Duration of assignment		
G-5	Attendant, servant or personal employee of G-1 through G-4, and immediate family	Up to two years	Up to two-year intervals	

Table 1. (Continued).

Visa	Class Description	Period of Stay	Renewal Option	Foreign Residence Required
H-1A	Temporary worker — nurse (statutory authority expired)	Up to three years	Up to two-year intervals; up to five years max	
H-1B	Temporary worker — professional specialty occupation	Up to three years	Up to three-year intervals; up to six years max	
H-1C	Temporary worker — nurse (new category)	Three years		
H-2A	Temporary worker — agricultural workers	Up to one year	Up to one year; three years total	Yes
H-2B	Temporary worker — non-agricultural workers	Up to one year	Up to one year; three years total	Yes
H-3	Temporary worker — trainee	Up to two years		
H-4	Spouse or child of H-1A/B/C, H-2A/B, or H-3	Same as Principal		
I	Representative of foreign information media, spouse and child	Duration of employment		
J-1	Cultural exchange visitor	Period of program		Yes
J-2	Spouse or child of J-1	Same as J-1		Yes
J-3	Au Pair	14 months		Yes
K-1	Fiancé(e) of U.S. citizen	Valid for 4 month; must marry within 90 days to adjust status		
K-2	Child of K-1	Same as K-1		
K-3	Spouse of U.S. citizen awaiting LPR visa			
K-4	Child of K-3			
L-1	Intracompany transferee (Executive, managerial, and specialized knowledge personnel continuing employment with international firm or corporation)	Up to three years	up to two-year extension: five years max; executives seven years	
L-2	Spouse or child of L-1	Same as L-1		
M-1	Vocational student	Duration of study		Yes
M-2	Spouse or child of M-1	Same as M-1		Yes

Table 1. (Continued).

Visa	Class Description	Period of Stay	Renewal Option	Foreign Residence Required
NATO-1	Principal permanent representative of member nations to NATO, high ranking NATO officials, and immediate family members	Tour of duty		
NATO-2	Other representatives of member states to NATO (including any of its subsidiary bodies), and immediate family members; dependents of member of a force entering in accordance with provisions of NATO agreements; members of such force if issued visas	Tour of duty		
NATO-3	Official clerical staff accompanying a representative of a member state to NATO, and immediate family	Tour of duty		
NATO-4	Officials of NATO (other than those classifiable as NATO-1), and immediate family	Tour of duty		
NATO-5	Experts, other than NATO-4 officials, employed in missions on behalf of NATO, and their dependents	Tour of duty		
NATO-6	Civilian employees of a force entering in accordance with the provisions of NATO agreements or attached to NATO headquarters, and immediate family	Tour of duty		
NATO-7	Attendants, servants, or personal employees of NATO-1 through NATO-6, and immediate family	Up to three years	Two-year intervals	
N-8	Parent of certain special immigrants (pertaining to international organizations)	Up to three years	Up to three-year intervals until child becomes an adult	
N-9	Child of N-8 or of certain special immigrants (pertaining to international organizations)	Up to three years	Up to three-year intervals until child becomes an adult	
O-1	Person with extraordinary ability in the sciences, arts, education, business or athletics	Up to three years	Up to one year	
O-2	Person accompanying and assisting in the artistic or athletic performance by O-1	Up to three years	Up to one year	Yes
O-3	Spouse or child of O-1 or O-2	Same as O-1 or O-2	Up to one year	
P-1	Internationally recognized athlete or member of an internationally recognized entertainment group and essential support	Up to five years individual artist; up to one year group or team		Yes

Table 1. (Continued).

Visa	Class Description	Period of Stay	Renewal Option	Foreign Residence Required
P-2	Artist or entertainer in a reciprocal exchange program and essential supports	Up to one year	One-year increments	Yes
P-3	Artist or entertainer in a culturally unique program and essential support	Up to one year	One-year increments	Yes
P-4	Spouse or child of P-1, P-2 or P-3	Same as P-1, P-2 or P-3	One year increments	Yes
Q-1	International cultural exchange program participant	Duration of program; up to 15 months		
Q-2	Irish Peace Process Program participant	Duration of program; up to three years		
Q-3	Spouse or child of Q-2			
R-1	Religious worker	up to three years	up to two-year intervals; up to five years max	
R-2	Spouse or child of R-1	same as R-1	same a R-1	
S-5	Criminal informant	up to three years		
S-6	Terrorist informant	up to three years		
S-7	Spouse or child of S-5 and S-6	same as S-5 and S-6		
T-1	Victim of human trafficking	If T-1 cooperates and is needed in prosecution of traffickers, may lead to adjustment to legal permanent residence		
T-2	Immediate family of T-1			
TN	NAFTA professional	one year	one year	
TD	Spouse or child of TN	one year	one year	
U-1	Victim or informant of criminal activity	May lead to adjustment to legal permanent residence if specified conditions are met.		
U-2	Spouse or child of U-1			
V-1	Spouse of Legal Permanent Resident (LPR) who has petition pending for three years or longer	Transitional nonimmigrant visa that leads to adjustment to legal permanent residence status when visa become available		

Table 1. (Continued).

Visa	Class Description	Period of Stay	Renewal Option	Foreign Residence Required
V-2	Child of LPR who has petition pending for three years or longer			
V-3	Child of V-1 or V-2			

Source: §101(a)(15), §212, and §214 of the Immigration and Nationality Act and §214 of 8 CFR.
Note: When a cell in the table is blank, it means the law and regulations are silent on the subject.

Table 2. Employment Authorization, Numerical Limits, and FY2005 Issuances for Nonimmigrant Visas

Visa	Class Description	Employment Authorization	Labor Market Test	Annual Numerical Limit	FY2005 Issuances
A-1	Ambassador, public minister, career diplomat, consul, and immediate family	Within scope of official duties			9,944
A-2	Other foreign government official or employee, and immediate family	Within scope of official duties			83,051
A-3	Attendant, servant or personal employee of A-1/A-2, and immediate family	Within scope of official duties			1,227
B-1	Visitor for business				52,649
B-2	Visitor for pleasure		No		245,816
B-1/B-2	Business and pleasure				2,709,468
BCC	Border Crossing Cards				732,566
C-1	Alien in transit				65,272
C-1/D	Transit/crew member				229,115
C-2	Person in transit to United Nations Headquarters				44
C-3	Foreign government official, immediate family, attendant, servant, or personal employee in transit				10,537
D	Crew member of vessel or aircraft	Only as employee of carrier			19,988
E-1	Treaty trader, spouse and child, and employee	Within the scope of treaty conditions			8,867
E-2	Treaty investor, spouse and child, and employee	Within the scope of treaty conditions			28,290

Table 2. (Continued).

Visa	Class Description	Employment Authorization	Labor Market Test	Annual Numerical Limit	FY2005 Issuances
E-3	Australian specialty occupation professional	Within the scope of treaty conditions		10,500	4
E-3D	Spouse or child of Australian specialty occupation professional				3
F-1	Foreign student (academic or language training program)	Off campus work is restricted, with limited exceptions			237,890
F-2	Spouse or child of F-1	No			18,016
F-3	Border commuter academic or language student				42
G-1	Principal resident representative of recognized foreign member government to international organization, staff, and immediate family	Within scope of official duties			4,995
G-2	Other representative of recognized foreign member government to international organization, and immediate family	Within scope of official duties			13,703
G-3	Representative of nonrecognized or nonmember foreign government to international organization, and immediate family	Within scope of official duties			309
G-4	International organization officer or employee, and immediate family	Within scope of official duties			20,930
G-5	Attendant, servant, or personal employee of G-1 through G-4, and immediate family	Within scope of official duties			998
H-1A	Temporary worker — nurse (statutory authority expired)		Yes		-
H-1B	Temporary worker — professional speciality occupation		Yes	65,000 (with certain exceptions)	124,100
H-1B-1	Free trade agreement professional		No	1,400 for Chile; 5,400 for Singapore	274
H-1C	Temporary worker — nurse		Yes	500	63
H-2A	Temporary worker — agricultural worker		Yes		31,892
H-2B	Temporary worker — non- agricultural worker		Yes	66,000	87,492
H-2R	Returning H2B worker				1,643

Table 2. (Continued).

Visa	Class Description	Employment Authorization	Labor Market Test	Annual Numerical Limit	FY2005 Issuances
H-3	Temporary worker — trainee	Yes, as part of the training program		Some restrictions on special education exchange programs	1,763
H-4	Spouse or child of H-1A/B/C, H-2A/B, or H-3	No			70,266
I	Representative of foreign information media, spouse and child	Only as employee of foreign media			16,975
J-1	Cultural exchange visitor	Yes, if program has work component			275,161
J-2	Spouse or child of J-1	Only as approved by DHS			28,661
J-3	Au Pair				NA
K-1	Fiancé(e) of U.S. citizen				33,910
K-2	Child of K-1				5,308
K-3	Spouse of U.S. citizen awaiting LPR visa				11,312
K-4	Child of K-3				3,438
L-1	Intracompany transferee (executive, managerial, and specialized knowledge personnel continuing employment with international firm or corporation)	Yes			65,458
L-2	Spouse or child of L-1	No			57,523
M-1	Vocational student	Only practical training related to degree			5,822
M-2	Spouse of child of M-1	No			153
NATO-1	Principal permanent representative of member nations to NATO, high ranking NATO officials, and immediate family	Within scope of official duties			28
NATO-2	Other representatives of member states to NATO (including any of its subsidiary bodies), and immediate family; dependents of member of a force entering in accordance with provisions of NATO agreements; members of such force if issued visas	Within scope of official duties			5,893
NATO-3	Official clerical staff accompanying a representative of member state to NATO, and immediate family	Within scope of official duties			1
NATO-4	Officials of NATO (other than those classifiable as NATO-1), and immediate family	Within scope of official duties			353

Table 2. (Continued).

Visa	Class Description	Employment Authorization	Labor Market Test	Annual Numerical Limit	FY2005 Issuances
NATO-5	Experts, other than NATO-4 officials, employed in missions on behalf of NATO, and their dependents	Within scope of official duties			69
NATO-6	Civilian employee of a force entering in accordance with the provisions of NATO agreements or attached to NATO headquarters, and their immediate family	Within scope of official duties			201
NATO-7	Attendants, servants, or personal employees of NATO-1 through NATO-6, and immediate family	Within scope of official duties			5
N-8	Parent of certain special immigrants (pertaining to international organizations)	Yes			10
N-9	Child of N-8 or of certain special immigrants (pertaining to international organizations)	Yes			4
O-1	Person with extraordinary ability in the sciences, arts, education, business, or athletics	Yes			6,712
O-2	Person accompanying and assisting in the artistic or athletic performance by O-1	Yes			3,387
O-3	Spouse or child of O-1 or O-2	Only as approved by DHS			1,861
P-1	Internationally recognized athlete or member of an internationally recognized entertainment group and essential support	Yes			23,907
P-2	Artist or entertainer in a reciprocal exchange program and essential support	Yes			125
P-3	Artist or entertainer in a culturally unique program and essential support	Yes			9,611
P-4	Spouse or child of P-1, P-2, or P-3	Only as approved by DHS			1,022
Q-1	International cultural exchange program participant	Yes, with employer approved by program			1,972
Q-2	Irish Peace Process Program participant	Yes, with employer approved by program			6
Q-3	Spouse or child of Q-2	No			0
R-1	Religious worker	Yes			8,538
R-2	Spouse or child of R-1	No			3,267

Table 2. (Continued).

Visa	Class Description	Employment Authorization	Labor Market Test	Annual Numerical Limit	FY2005 Issuances
S-5	Criminal informant	Yes		200	NA
S-6	Terrorist informant	Yes		50	NA
S-7	Spouse or child of S-5 or S-6				NA
T-1	Victim of human trafficking	Yes		5,000	NA
T-2	Immediate family of T-1	Yes			NA
TN	NAFTA professional	Yes			1,902
TD	Spouse or child of TN				1,941
U-1	Victim or informant of criminal activity	Yes		10,000	NA
U-2	Spouse or child of U-1	Yes			NA
V-1	Spouse of Legal Permanent Resident (LPR) who has petition pending for three years or longer	Yes			911
V-2	Child of LPR who has petition pending for three years or longer	Yes, assuming they meet age requirements			951
V-3	Child of V-1 or V-2	Yes, assuming they meet age requirements			1,165

Source: §101(a)(15), §212, and §214 of the Immigration and Nationality Act and §214 of 8 CFR.

Note: When a cell in the table is blank, it means the law and regulations are silent on the subject.

In: Immigration Crisis: Issues, Policies and Consequences   ISBN: 978-1-60456-096-1
Editors: P. W. Hickman and T. P. Curtis, pp. 179-196 © 2008 Nova Science Publishers, Inc.

Chapter 7

FARM LABOR SHORTAGES AND IMMIGRATION POLICY*

Linda Levine

ABSTRACT

The connection between farm labor and immigration policies is a longstanding one, particularly with regard to U.S. employers' use of workers from Mexico. The Congress is revisiting the issue as it continues debate over initiation of a broad-based guest worker program, increased border enforcement, and employer sanctions to curb the flow of unauthorized workers into the United States.

Two decades ago, the Congress passed the Immigration Reform and Control Act (IRCA, P.L. 99-603) to reduce illegal entry into the United States by imposing sanctions on employers who knowingly hire individuals who lack permission to work in the country. In addition to a general legalization program, IRCA included legalization programs specific to the agricultural industry that were intended to compensate for the act's expected impact on the farm labor supply and encourage the development of a legal crop workforce. These provisions of the act, however, have not operated in the offsetting manner that was intended, as substantial numbers of unauthorized aliens have continued to join legal farmworkers in performing seasonal agricultural services (SAS).

Currently, a little more than one-half of the SAS workforce is not authorized to hold U.S. jobs. Perishable crop growers contend that their sizable presence implies a shortage of native-born workers willing to undertake seasonal farm jobs. (An increasing share of IRCA-legalized farmworkers have entered the ages of diminished participation in the SAS workforce, as well.) Grower advocates argue that farmers would rather not employ unauthorized workers because doing so puts them at risk of incurring penalties. Farmworker advocates counter that crop growers prefer unauthorized workers because they are in a weak bargaining position with regard to wages and working conditions. If the supply of unauthorized workers were curtailed, it is claimed, farmers could adjust to a smaller workforce by introducing labor-efficient technologies and management practices, and by raising wages, which, in turn, would entice more U.S. workers to seek farm employment. Farmers respond that further mechanization would be difficult for some crops, and that substantially higher wages would make the U.S. industry uncompetitive in

---

* Excerpted from CRS Report RL30395, dated January 31, 2007.

the world marketplace — without expanding the legal farm labor force. These remain untested arguments because perishable crop growers have rarely, if ever, operated without unauthorized aliens in their workforces.

Trends in the agricultural labor market generally do not suggest the existence of a nationwide shortage of domestically available farmworkers, in part because the government's databases cover authorized *and* unauthorized employment. (This finding does not preclude the possibility of spot labor shortages, however.) Farm employment did not show the same upward trend of total U.S. employment during the 1990s expansion. The length of time hired farmworkers are employed has changed little or decreased over the years. Their unemployment rate has varied little and remains well above the U.S. average, and underemployment among farmworkers also remains substantial. These agricultural employees earn about 50 cents for every dollar paid to other employees in the private sector. This report will be updated as warranted.

INTRODUCTION

Questions often have arisen over the years about (1) whether sufficient workers are available domestically to meet the seasonal employment demand of perishable crop producers in the U.S. agricultural industry[1] and (2) how, if at all, the Congress should change immigration policy with respect to farmworkers. Immigration policy has long been intertwined with the labor needs of crop (e.g., fruit and vegetable) growers, who rely more than most farmers on hand labor (e.g., for harvesting) and consequently "are the largest users of hired and contract workers on a per-farm basis."[2] Since World War I, the Congress has allowed the use of temporary foreign workers to perform agricultural labor of a seasonal nature as a means of augmenting the supply of domestic farmworkers.[3] In addition, a sizeable fraction of immigrants historically have found employment on the nation's farms.[4]

The intersection between farm labor and immigration has again emerged as a policy issue. The terrorist attacks of September 11, 2001 effectively quashed the discussions on this subject between the Bush and Fox Administrations that took place shortly after President Bush first came into office, but the proposal of a broad-based temporary foreign worker program that President Bush sketched in December 2003 has revived interest in the labor-immigration nexus, which continues to this day. (For a discussion of bills and the President's proposal, see CRS Report RL32044, *Immigration: Policy Considerations Related to Guest Worker Programs*, by Andorra Bruno.)

This report first explains the connection made over the past several years between farm labor and immigration policies. It next examines the composition of the seasonal agricultural labor force and presents the arguments of grower and farmworker advocates concerning its adequacy relative to employer demand. The report closes with an analysis of the trends in employment, unemployment, time worked and wages of authorized and unauthorized farmworkers to determine whether they are consistent with the existence of a nationwide shortage of domestically available farmworkers.

FARMWORKERS AND ACTIVITIES OF SSA AND DHS

During the second half of the 1990s, attention began to focus on the growing share of the domestic supply of farmworkers that is composed of aliens who are not authorized to work in the United States. The U.S. Department of Labor (DOL) estimated that foreign-born persons in the country illegally accounted for 37% of the domestic crop workforce in FY1994-FY1995. Shortly thereafter (FY1997-FY1998), unauthorized aliens' share of the estimated 1.8 million workers employed on crop farms reached 52%.[5] By FY1999-FY2000, their proportion had increased to 55% before retreating somewhat — to 53% — in FY2001-FY2002.[6]

Although a number of studies found that no nationwide shortage of domestic farm labor existed in the past decade,[7] a case has been made that the considerable presence of unauthorized aliens in the seasonal agricultural labor force implies a lack of legal farmworkers relative to employer demand. Arguably, the purported imbalance between authorized-to-work farm labor and employer demand would become more apparent were the supply of unauthorized aliens curtailed sufficiently — a fear that has plagued growers for some time.

Crop producers and their advocates have testified at congressional hearings over the last several years that they believe the latest risk of losing much of their labor force comes from certain activities of the Bureau of Citizenship and Immigration Services and the Bureau of Immigration and Customs Enforcement within the Department of Homeland Security (DHS) and the Social Security Administration (SSA). Growers have asserted that these activities have disrupted their workforces by increasing employee turnover and therefore, decreasing the stability of their labor supply. The perception that government actions might negatively impact the agricultural workforce — allegedly to the extent that crops would not be harvested, farmers would go bankrupt or produce costs to U.S. consumers would rise — has prompted a legislative response in the past.

The SSA and DHS activities are briefly described below:

1. The SSA sends "no-match letters" to employers who submit a substantial number of W-2 forms for which the agency cannot find corresponding earnings records in its database.[8] The purpose of the letters is to make wage reports more accurate so that the agency can properly credit earnings to employees' records for future benefit payments. As part of this effort, the SSA has encouraged employers not to wait until the annual submission of W-2 forms and instead, to use its Enumeration Verification Service (EVS) to match the names/social security numbers of employees with those in the agency's database.[9]

Growers have told the SSA that their concern with using the EVS is that when they discuss any discrepancies with employees, the employees do not return to work. The National Council of Agricultural Employers testified in 2000 about the large and growing numbers of employers receiving no-match letters.[10] The American Farm Bureau Federation said at the time that growers are apprehensive about being liable for penalties (commonly referred to as employer sanctions[11]) due to "constructive knowledge" of illegal workers on their payrolls if they do not act on the SSA letters.[12] The agency's correspondence clearly states, however, that there are many reasons why discrepancies can occur and that the letter, by itself, should not form the basis for taking any adverse actions against employees.

SSA responded to the growers' concerns in a variety of ways in the past few years. For example, the agency translated into Spanish portions of the letter so that if growers show it to farmworkers they can see they have nothing to fear from it. In addition, based upon a change in selection criteria that went into effect in January 2003, SSA sends far fewer no-match letters to employers. In 2005, just 127,652 no-match letters were sent to employers.[13]

2. The Illegal Immigration Reform and Immigrant Responsibility Act of 1996 (IIRIRA, P.L. 104-288) provided for increased border enforcement efforts and for an employment verification pilot.[14] Employer participation in the program, which was set to last no more than four years, has been voluntary, and the program has involved a limited number of areas. Nonetheless, organizations of growers testified that inclusion of the pilot in P.L. 104-288 merely delayed the creation of a mandatory nationwide verification system.[15] Although Congress extended the program for five years through 2008 and expanded it through the Basic Pilot Program Extension and Expansion Act of 2003 (P.L. 108-156) to include all states, employer participation remains optional. The Basic Pilot continues to be little-used: as of early 2006, after the pilot was expanded nationwide, only about 5,500 employers (representing some 22,500 employer sites) had signed agreements with DHS and SSA.[16]

Currently, employers fulfill the legal requirement to not knowingly hire illegal workers by viewing documents that show the new-hire's identity and eligibility to work in the United States, and by completing an I-9 (employment eligibility verification) form. Under an initiative referred to as the Basic Pilot, employers can access the DHS system to validate a newly hired citizen's or non-citizen's eligibility to work.[17] If employers receive a final nonconfirmation of employment eligibility, they must either fire the new-hire or be subject to financial penalties.[18]

3. The Bureau of Immigration and Customs Enforcement (another former part of the Immigration and Naturalization Service, INS) reportedly increased its audits of I-9 forms even before September 11, 2001, but the incidence was and remains relatively low according to the agency. In the audits, the bureau checks the authenticity of employees' work authorization documents against government records. At the audits' completion, employers are given a list of employees whose documents were deemed to be invalid. According to a representative of the growers, "Frequently, INS audits of agricultural employers reveal that 60 to 70 percent of seasonal agricultural workers have provided fraudulent documents. The employer is then required to dismiss each employee on the list who cannot provide a valid employment authorization document, something few workers can do."[19] This estimate of hired farmworkers who have secured their jobs through presentation of fraudulent documents is at the high end of figures reported elsewhere, however.[20]

While a grower representative testified that "agriculture has historically not been a major target" of immigration enforcement activities, he pointed to some experiences involving

Vermont dairy farmers and Georgia onion growers in the last few years. The increased attention that has been paid to homeland security since September 11, 2001 and the better integration of agencies within DHS led the American Farm Bureau Federation to speculate during a 2004 hearing that more raids could be forthcoming.[21] A representative of the National Foundation for American Policy testified, however, that DHS "does not have the resources to enforce those [immigration] laws in a manner that would stop employers from using illegal workers."[22]

THE COMPOSITION OF THE SEASONAL FARM LABOR FORCE

Immigration legislation sometimes has been crafted to take into account the purported labor requirements of U.S. crop growers. In 1986, for example, Congress passed the Immigration Reform and Control Act (IRCA, P.L. 99-603) to curb the presence of unauthorized aliens in the United States by imposing sanctions on employers who knowingly hire individuals who lack permission to work in the country. In addition to a general legalization program, P.L. 99-603 included two industry-specific legalization programs — the Special Agricultural Worker (SAW) program and the Replenishment Agricultural Worker (RAW) program[23] — that were intended to compensate for the act's expected impact on the farm labor supply and encourage the development of a legal crop workforce. These provisions of the act have not operated in the offsetting manner that was intended, however, as substantial numbers of unauthorized aliens have continued to join legal farmworkers in performing seasonal agricultural services (SAS).[24]

On the basis of case studies that it sponsored, the Commission on Agricultural Workers concluded in its 1992 report that individuals legalized under the SAW program (i.e., SAWs) and other farmworkers planned to remain in the agricultural labor force "indefinitely, or for as long as they are physically able."[25] According to the DOL's National Agricultural Workers Survey, two-thirds of SAWs stated that they intended to engage in field work until the end of their working lives.[26]

For many SAWs, the end of their worklives — at least their worklives in farming — may now be near at hand. The diminished physical ability generally associated with aging in combination with the taxing nature of crop tasks could well be prompting greater numbers of SAWs to leave the fields. Relatively few farmworkers are involved in crop production beyond the age of 44 and even fewer beyond the age of 54 (19% and 7%, respectively, in FY2001-FY2002).[27] The Commission on Agricultural Workers noted that the typical SAW in 1990 was a 30 year-old male who "is likely to remain in farm work well into the 21st century."[28] As the average age of an authorized foreign-born cropworker in FY2001-FY2002 was 40,[29] he is now at the age of diminished participation in SAS labor. It thus appears that the 1986 legalization program has become less useful over time in fulfilling the labor requirements of crop producers.

A combination of factors likely has contributed to the decrease in SAWs' share of agricultural employment.[30] While the share of IRCA-legalized farmworkers has been falling over time due to aging and the availability of nonfarm jobs,[31] the leading factor probably is the substantially increased presence of illegal aliens.[32] In the first half of the 1990s, unauthorized workers rose from 7% to 37% of the SAS labor force.[33] Their share climbed to 52% by FY1997-FY1998;[34] then, rose further to 55% by FY1999-FY2000, before it dropped somewhat to 53% in FY2001-FY2002.[35] Moreover, the number of SAS workdays performed by unauthorized aliens more than tripled between FY1989 and FY2002.[36] In addition, of the many foreign-born newcomers to the sector in FY2000-FY2002, 99% were employed without authorization.

Unauthorized aliens, arguably, have been displacing legal workers from jobs in the agricultural industry. Farmworker advocates assert that crop producers prefer unauthorized employees because they have less bargaining power with regard to wages and working conditions than other employees. Growers counter that they would rather not employ unauthorized workers because doing so puts them at risk of incurring penalties. They argue that the considerable presence of unauthorized aliens in the U.S. farm labor force implies a shortage of legal workers.

Farmworker groups and some policy analysts contend that even if the previously described DHS and SSA activities were to deprive farmers of many of their unauthorized workers, the industry could adjust to a smaller supply of legal workers by (1) introducing labor-efficient technologies and management practices, and (2) raising wages which, in turn, would entice more authorized workers into the farm labor force. Grower advocates respond that further mechanization would be difficult to develop for many crops and that, even at higher wages, not many U.S. workers would want to perform physically demanding, seasonal farm labor under variable climactic conditions. Moreover, employer representatives and some policy analysts maintain that growers cannot raise wages substantially without making the U.S. industry uncompetitive in world markets which, in turn, would reduce farm employment. In response, farmworker supporters note that wages are a small part of the price consumers pay for fresh fruits and vegetables and accordingly, higher wages would result in only a slight rise in retail prices. These remain untested arguments as perishable crop growers have rarely, if ever, had to operate without unauthorized aliens in their workforces.

A FARM LABOR SHORTAGE?

Trends in the farm labor market generally do not suggest the existence of a nationwide shortage of domestically available farmworkers, in part because the government's statistical series cover authorized *and* unauthorized workers. This overall finding does not preclude the possibility of farm labor shortages in certain areas of the country at various times of the year (i.e., spot labor shortages).

Caution should be exercised when reviewing the statistics on farmworkers' employment, unemployment, time worked and wages that follow. The surveys from which the data are derived cover somewhat different groups within the farm labor force (e.g., all hired farmworkers as opposed to those engaged only in crop production or workers employed directly by growers as opposed to those supplied to growers by farm labor contractors), and they have different sample sizes. A household survey such as the Current Population Survey (CPS) could well understate the presence of farmworkers because they are more likely to live in less traditional quarters (e.g., labor camps) and of unauthorized workers generally because they may be reluctant to respond to government enumerators. And, some of the surveys have individuals as respondents (e.g., the CPS and DOL's National Agricultural Workers Survey) while others have employers as respondents (e.g., the U.S. Department of Agriculture's National Agricultural Statistics Service Farm Labor Survey). Surveys that query employers are more likely to pickup unauthorized employment than are surveys that query individuals.

Employment

The demand for and supply of labor typically cannot be measured directly. Instead, proxies are used such as the trend in employment. Decreases in an occupation's employment or small gains compared to those recorded for other occupations might signal that labor demand is not approaching a supply constraint.

Although the employment of hired workers engaged in crop or livestock production (including contract workers) has fluctuated erratically over time, the trend overall has been downward (see columns 3 and 7 in table 1). The employment pattern among crop workers hired directly by growers (i.e., excluding those supplied by farm labor contractors and crew leaders) has regularly risen and then fallen back, but to a higher level through 2000 (column 4). This ratcheting upward of employment produced a 12% gain over the 1990-2000 period. In contrast, other wage and salary workers have experienced steady and robust job growth over almost the entire period: from 1990 to 2000, wage and salary employment in nonfarm industries advanced by 18%. These divergent employment patterns suggest that hired farmworkers did not share equally in the nation's long economic expansion, and appear to be inconsistent with the presence of a nationwide farm labor shortage.

The labor market continued to contract in 2002, despite the 2001 recession's end in November 2001. Nonfarm wage and salary employment showed signs of revival in 2003 that have since continued. In contrast, employment of hired farmworkers has not followed a consistently upward trend. (See columns 3 and 7 of table 1).

Farm employment is subject to considerable seasonal variation during the course of a year, which annual average data masks. Demand for hired farm labor typically peaks in July when many crops are ready to be harvested. The July employment data from the NASS Farm Labor Survey has ranged from less than 1.1 million to less than 1.5 million between 1990 and 2005. In July 2005, employment was a little more than 1.3 million.

Table 1. Hired Farm Employment
(numbers in thousands)

Year	Total nonfarm wage and salary employment[a]	Economic Research Service (ERS) [b]		National Agricultural Statistics Service (NASS) [c]		
		Hired farm workers[d]	Hired crop workers[e]	Hired farm workers[f]	Agricultural service workers[g]	Total
1990	105,705	886	419	892	250	1,142
1991	104,520	884	449	910	259	1,169
1992	105,540	848	409	866	252	1,118
1993	107,011	803	436	857	256	1,113
1994	110,517	793	411	840	250	1,090
1995	112,448	849	433	869	251	1,120
1996	114,171	906	451	832	236	1,068
1997	116,983	889	432	876	240	1,116
1998	119,019	875	458	880	246	1,126
1999	121,323	840	440	929	233	1,162
2000	125,114	878	468	890	243	1,133
2001	125,407	745	392	881	244	1,125
2002	125,156	793	370	886	225	1,111
2003	126,015	777	372	836	236	1,072
2004	127,463	712	368	825	277	1,102
2005	129,931	730	393	780	282	1,062
2006	132,449	748	351	752	255	1,007

Source: Created by the Congressional Research Service (CRS) from sources cited below.

Note: n.a. = not available.

a. Data are from the monthly CPS, a survey of households, as reported by the DOL's Bureau of Labor Statistics (BLS) for individuals age 16 or older.

b. Data are from the monthly CPS as reported by the U.S. Department of Agriculture's ERS for individuals age 15 or older.

c. Data are from the Farm Labor Survey (FLS), a quarterly survey of farm operators, as reported by the U.S. Department of Agriculture's NASS. The statistics reflect individuals on employers' payrolls during the survey week in January, April, July, and October. Data for Alaska are not included. 1990-1994 annual averages for all hired farmworkers and all annual averages for agricultural service workers were calculated by CRS.

d. In the CPS, an individual's occupation is based on the activity in which he spent the most hours during the survey week. Hired farmworkers are those whose primary job is farmwork and for which they receive wages, as opposed to unpaid family workers or self-employed farmers. Hired farmworkers include individuals engaged in planting, cultivating, and harvesting crops or tending livestock whom growers employ directly or through agricultural service providers (e.g., farm labor contractors and crew leaders), as well as farm managers, supervisors of farmworkers, and nursery and other workers.

e. The ERS disaggregates hired farmworkers by the kind of establishment employing them (i.e., establishments primarily engaged in crop production, livestock production or other). As "other" includes agricultural service providers, the figures for crop workers are limited to farmworkers whom growers employ directly.

f. The FLS counts as hired farmworkers only those persons paid directly by farmers. Hired farmworkers include field workers (i.e., those who plant, cultivate and harvest crops), livestock workers (i.e., those who tend livestock, milk cows or care for poultry) and supervisory workers (e.g., managers or range foremen) as well as other workers on farmers' payrolls (e.g., bookkeepers, secretaries or pilots).

g. Includes contract, custom, or other workers supplied to farmers but paid by agricultural service firms (e.g., farm labor contractors or crew leaders).

Unemployment

Employment data paint an incomplete picture of the state of the labor market. At the same time that employment in a given occupation is decreasing or increasing relatively slowly, unemployment in the occupation might be falling. Employers would then be faced with a shrinking supply of untapped labor from which to draw. A falling unemployment rate or level would offer some basis for this possibility.

As shown in table 2, the unemployment rate of hired farmworkers engaged in crop or livestock production (including contract labor) is quite high. Even the economic boom that characterized most of the 1990s did not reduce the group's unemployment rate below double-digit levels, or about twice the average unemployment rate in the nation at a minimum. Discouragement over their employment prospects in agriculture or better opportunities elsewhere may have prompted some unemployed farmworkers to leave the sector as evidenced by their reduced number after 1998 (see column 4 of the table).

Other observers have examined the unemployment rates in counties that are heavily dependent on the crop farming industry. The GAO, for example, found that many of these agricultural areas chronically experienced double-digit unemployment rates that were well above those reported for much of the rest of the United States. Even when looking at monthly unemployment rates for these areas in order to take into account the seasonality of farm work, the agency found that the agricultural counties exhibited comparatively high rates of joblessness.[37] These kinds of findings imply a surplus rather than a shortage of farmworkers.[38]

Another perspective on the availability of untapped farm labor comes from the DOL's National Agricultural Worker Survey (NAWS).[39] During FY2001-FY2002, the typical crop worker spent 66% of the year performing farm jobs. The remainder of the year, these farmworkers either were engaged in nonfarm work (10% of the year) or not working (16%) while in the United States, or they were out of the country (7%).[40] This pattern also suggests an excess supply of labor, assuming that the workers wanted more farm employment. Grower advocates contend that the pattern is a manifestation of working in a seasonal industry. Even in a month of peak industry demand, however, only a small majority of farmworkers hold farm jobs.[41]

Table 2. The Rate and Level of Unemployment

Year	Unemployment rate		Number of unemployed hired farmworkers (in thousands)
	All occupations	Hired farmworkers	
1994	6.1	12.1	109
1995	5.6	12.5	121
1996	5.4	11.5	118
1997	4.9	10.6	106
1998	4.5	11.8	117
1999	4.2	10.6	100
2000	4.0	10.6	104
2001	4.7	12.1	103
2002	5.8	11.4	102
2003	6.0	12.9	100
2004	5.5	11.4	92
2005	5.1	9.0	72
2006	4.6	9.4	78

Source: CPS data tabulated by the BLS (column 2) and the ERS (columns 3 and 4).

Note: In the CPS, an individual's occupation is based on the activity in which he or she spent the most hours during the survey week. The ERS defines hired farmworkers as individuals aged 15 or older whose primary job is farmwork and for which they receive wages. Hired farmworkers include individuals engaged in crop or livestock production whom growers employ directly or through agricultural service providers (e.g., farm labor contractors), as well as farm managers, supervisors of farmworkers, and nursery and other workers.

n.a. = not available.

Time Worked

Another indicator of supply-demand conditions is the amount of time worked (e.g., hours or days). If employers are faced with a labor shortage, they might be expected to increase the amount of time worked by their employees.

The Seasonality of Demand: Hours Versus Employment

Recent data reveal no discernible year-to-year variation in the average number of weekly hours that hired farmworkers are employed in crop or livestock production. According to the NASS Farm Labor Survey (FLS), the average workweek of hired farmworkers has ranged narrowly around 40.0 hours since the mid-1990s. Thus, neither the trend in employment nor in work hours imply the existence of a farm labor shortage.

There also is not much variability in demand over the course of a year based on hours worked. In 2006, for example, the average week of hired farmworkers was 33.2 hours in mid-January, 40.8 hours in mid-April, 41.0 hours in mid-July and 41.6 hours in mid-October.

The instability of the demand for farm labor within a year (i.e., seasonality) is reflected in employment levels more than in work hours per week. The FLS data show that in 2006, for example, farmers had 614,000 workers on their payrolls in mid-January; 720,000 in mid-April; 876,000 in mid-July; and 797,000 in mid-October.

The Number of Days Worked

Another measure of time worked available from the FLS is "expected days of employment" (i.e., farm operators are asked the number of days they intend to utilize their hired farmworkers over the course of a year). As shown in table 3, they anticipated a low of 579,000 farmworkers on their payrolls for at least 150 days in 2006 and a high of 679,000 (un)authorized workers in 2002. These "year-round" workers typically have accounted for at least three-fourths of hired farmworkers in the current decade.[42]

According to the NAWS, the number of actual farm workdays varies by legal status.[43] Unauthorized workers averaged 197 days in crop production, compared to 185 days for authorized workers in FY2001-FY2002. More unauthorized than authorized workers were likely to spend at least 200 days in farm jobs (58% and 50%, respectively). Within the authorized population, citizens averaged 175 days and permanent residents, 195 days of employment in farming during the year.

These figures potentially are relevant to legislation that would link eligibility for legalization to time spent in farm work. While some might wish to use the above-described data to roughly estimate the number of unauthorized farmworkers who would be eligible to adjust status, they describe the *expectations* of farmers and they do not distinguish between legal and illegal workers. In addition, the data could produce an underestimate because they omit the more than 200,000 contract workers on the payrolls of agricultural service providers. Alternatively, the data could produce an overestimate because they include employees not normally thought of as farmworkers (e.g., bookkeepers, secretaries or pilots).

Table 3. Hired Farmworkers by Expected Days of Employment (numbers in thousands)

Year	150 Days or more of expected employment		149 Days or less of expected employment
	Number of hired workers	Percent of all hired farmworkers	
1994	597	71	243
1995	598	69	271
1996	593	71	239
1997	629	72	247
1998	639	73	241
1999	666	72	263
2000	640	72	251
2001	658	75	224
2002	679	77	207
2003	635	76	201
2004	611	74	246
2005	594	76	185
2006	579	77	173

Source: Annual averages calculated by CRS from quarterly releases of the FLS.

Note: The NASS FLS counts as hired farmworkers only those persons paid directly by farmers (i.e., contract, custom or other workers paid directly by agricultural service providers are excluded). Hired farmworkers include field workers (i.e., those who plant, cultivate and harvest crops), livestock workers (i.e., those who tend livestock, milk cows or care for poultry) and supervisory workers (e.g., crew leaders or range foremen) as well as other workers on farmers' payrolls (e.g., bookkeepers, secretaries or pilots).

Wages

Economic theory suggests that if the demand for labor is nearing or has outstripped the supply of labor, firms will in the short-run bid up wages to compete for workers. As a result, earnings in the short-supply field would be expected to increase more rapidly than earnings across all industries or occupations. The ratio of, in this instance, farm to nonfarm wages also would be expected to rise if the former's labor supply were especially constrained.

Table 4. Average Hourly Earnings of Field Workers and Other Workers in the Private Sector (in nominal dollars)

Year	Average hourly wages of field workers	Average hourly wages of production or nonsupervisory workers in the private nonfarm sector	Ratio of hourly field worker wages to private nonfarm worker wages
1990	$5.23	$10.19	0.51
1991	5.49	10.50	0.52
1992	5.69	10.76	0.53
1993	5.90	11.03	0.53
1994	6.02	11.32	0.53
1995	6.13	11.64	0.53
1996	6.34	12.03	0.53
1997	6.66	12.49	0.53
1998	6.97	13.00	0.54
1999	7.19	13.47	0.53
2000	7.50	14.00	0.54
2001	7.78	14.53	0.54
2002	8.12	14.95	0.54
2003	8.31	15.35	0.54
2004	8.45	15.67	0.54
2005	8.70	16.11	0.54
2006	9.06	16.73p	0.54
1990-2006 change	66.2%	58.1%	—

Source: Created by CRS from FLS (column 2) and BLS (column 3) employer survey data.

Note: Field workers are a subset of hired farmworkers who engage in planting, tending and harvesting crops. The data relate to all field workers regardless of method of payment (i.e., those paid an hourly rate, by the piece or a combination of the two). Contract, custom, or other workers paid directly by agricultural service providers are excluded.

As shown above in table 4, the average hourly earnings of field workers (excluding contract workers) rose to a greater extent than those of other employees in the private sector between 1990 and 2006, at 73.2% and 64.2%, respectively. Nonetheless, field workers' pay has hardly increased compared to other workers' pay: at $9.06 per hour in 2006, field workers still earn little more than 50 cents for every dollar earned by other private sector workers.

NAWS data reveal much slower growth in wages compared to the FLS, which cannot be explained by the different periods covered in table 4 and table 5. Between 1990 and 2002, the most recent year for which NAWS data are available, the average hourly earnings of crop workers rose to a lesser extent based on the NAWS (39.6%) than on the FLS (55.3%). The NAWS also produces lower wage estimates than those from the FLS. In 2002, the average hourly earnings of crop workers were $7.30, according to the NAWS, while they were $8.12 according, to the FLS. These disparities likely are related to differences between the two surveys.[44]

The wages of crop workers, as shown in table 5, rose to a lesser extent in the 1990-2002 period than those of other workers in the private sector (39.6% and 46.7%, respectively) — just the opposite of the relationship between the FLS and BLS data (55.3% and 46.7%, respectively). As a result of the relatively lower wage estimates and the relatively slower wage growth derived from the NAWS, the typical crop worker was estimated to have dropped below 50 cents for every dollar paid to other private sector workers since the mid-1990s.

Table 5. Average Hourly Earnings of Crop Workers and
Other Workers in the Private Sector
(in nominal dollars)

Year	Average hourly wages of crop workers	Average hourly wages of production or nonsupervisory workers in the private nonfarm sector	Ratio of hourly crop worker wages to private nonfarm worker wages
1990	$5.23	$10.19	0.51
1991	5.57	10.50	0.53
1992	5.33	10.76	0.50
1993	5.46	11.03	0.50
1994	5.54	11.32	0.50
1995	5.72	11.64	0.49
1996	5.69	12.03	0.47
1997	5.81	12.49	0.47
1998	6.40	13.00	0.48
1999	6.54	13.47	0.48
2000	7.00	14.00	0.48
2001	7.11	14.53	0.49
2002[a]	7.30	14.95	0.49
1990-2002 change	39.6%	46.7%	—

Source: Created by CRS from NAWS worker (column 2) and BLS employer survey data (column 3).

Note: Crop workers include field packers, supervisors and other field workers who engage in such activities as planting, tending and harvesting crops. Initially, the survey included only field workers on perishable crop farms to comply with IRCA: NAWS was developed to enable the DOL to calculate changes in the supply of SAS labor, which was then used in the shortage calculation conducted by the U.S. Departments of Labor and Agriculture for triggering the RAW program. In the mid-1990s, the survey was expanded to include field workers in non-perishable crops (e.g., silage or other crops intended solely for animal fodder). The data relate to the farm earnings of field workers age 14 or older, regardless of method of payment (i.e., those paid an hourly rate, by the piece or a combination of the two). The sample includes direct-hires and contract labor. The survey is conducted at different times over the course of a year to capture seasonal variations.

a. Calendar year data, except for 2002 which covers January to September.

CONCLUSION

In summary, indicators of supply-demand conditions generally are inconsistent with the existence of a nationwide shortage of domestically available farmworkers in part because the measures include both authorized and unauthorized employment. This finding does not preclude the possibility of farmworker shortages in certain parts of the country at various times during the year. The analysis does not address the adequacy of authorized workers in the seasonal farm labor supply relative to grower demand.

Whether there would be an adequate supply of authorized U.S. farmworkers if new technologies were developed or different labor-management practices were implemented continues to be an unanswered question. Whether more U.S. workers would be willing to become farmworkers if wages were raised and whether the size of the increase would make the industry uncompetitive in the world marketplace also remain open issues. These matters remain unresolved because perishable crop growers have rarely, if ever, had to operate without unauthorized aliens being present in the domestic farm workforce.[45]

REFERENCES

[1]   In this report, the terms "agriculture" and "farming" will be used interchangeably as will the terms "producer," "grower," and "farmer."

[2]   Victor J. Oliveira, Anne B. W. Effland, Jack L. Runyan and Shannon Hamm, *Hired Farm Labor on Fruit, Vegetable, and Horticultural Specialty Farms*, U.S. Department of Agriculture, Economic Research Service, Agricultural Economic Report 676, Dec. 1993, p. 2. (Hereafter cited as, Oliveira, Effland, Runyan and Hamm, *Hired Farm Labor on Fruit, Vegetable, and Horticultural Specialty Farms*.)

[3]   U.S. Congress, Senate Committee on the Judiciary, *Temporary Worker Programs: Background and Issues*, committee print, 96th Cong., 2nd sess. (Washington: GPO, 1980).

[4]   Philip L. Martin, "Good Intentions Gone Awry: IRCA and U.S. Agriculture," *Annals of the American Academy of Political and Social Science*, July 1994.

[5]   According to *U.S. Department of Labor Report to Congress: The Agricultural Labor Market — Status and Recommendations*, the 1.8 million figure was developed by dividing the hourly earnings of field and livestock workers into farm labor expenditures to estimate the number of work hours on crop and livestock farms. As it was calculated that 72% of the hours were being worked on crop farms, the percentage was then applied to the Commission on Agricultural Workers' estimate for 1992 of 2.5 million persons employed for wages on U.S. farms to yield a current estimate of the hired crop

workforce. The Commission had developed its earlier farm employment figure from a variety of data sources because there is no actual head count of farmworkers. For other current estimates of hired farm and crop workers see table 1.

[6] DOL, Findings from the National Agricultural Workers Survey (NAWS) 2001-2002, Research Report No. 9, Mar. 2005. (Hereafter cited as DOL, Findings from the NAWS 2001-2002.)

[7] Commission on Agricultural Workers (CAW), *Report of the Commission on Agricultural Workers*, (Washington: GPO, Nov. 1992). (Hereafter cited as CAW, *Report of the Commission on Agricultural Workers*.). U.S. General Accounting Office (GAO), *H-2A Agricultural Guestworker Program: Changes Could Improve Services to Employers and Better Protect Workers*, GAO/HEHES-98-20, Dec. 1997. (Hereafter cited as GAO, *H-2A Agricultural Guestworker Program*). DOL, *A Profile of U.S. Farmworkers: Demographics, Household Composition, Income and Use of Services*, Research Report No. 6, Apr. 1997. (Hereafter cited as DOL, *A Profile of U.S. Farmworkers*.) And, annual calculations in the early 1990s by the U.S. Departments of Labor and Agriculture.

[8] For additional information on no-match letters, see CRS Report RL32004, *Social Security Benefits for Noncitizens: Current Policy and Legislation*, by Dawn Nuschler and Alison Siskin.

[9] Conversations with SSA staff.

[10] Testimony of James S. Holt on behalf of the National Council of Agricultural Employers before the Senate Judiciary Subcommittee on Immigration, May 4, 2000.

[11] For additional information on employer sanctions, see CRS Report RS22180, *Unauthorized Employment of Aliens: Basics of Employer Sanctions*, by Alison M. Smith.

[12] Testimony of Josh Wunsch on behalf of the American Farm Bureau Federation before the Senate Judiciary Subcommittee on Immigration, May 4, 2000; and Alexander T. Aleinikoff, "The Green Card Solution," *The American Prospect*, December 1999.

[13] Testimony of James B. Lockhart III, Deputy Commissioner of Social Security, before the Subcommittee on Oversight of the House Committee on Ways and Means, Feb. 16, 2006.

[14] Work eligibility verification demonstrations in addition to the IIRIRA pilots are authorized under Section 274A(d)(4) of the Immigration and Nationality Act and Presidential Executive Order 12781 of Nov. 20, 1991. For more information see Karen I. Miksch, *INS Pilot Programs for Employment Eligibility Confirmation*, Carnegie Endowment for International Peace, International Migration Policy Program, Nov. 1998.

[15] Testimony of Bob L. Vice on behalf of the National Council of Agricultural Employers and the American Farm Bureau Federation before the House Judiciary Subcommittee on Immigration and Claims, Sept. 24, 1997.

[16] Testimony of James B. Lockhart III, Deputy Commissioner of Social Security, and Barbara D. Bovbjerg, Government Accountability Office, before the Subcommittee on Oversight of the House Committee on Ways and Means, Feb. 16, 2006.

[17] Under the Basic Pilot, employers electronically send worker information to DHS, which forwards it to SSA. SSA compares the information provided against its database, and in the case of non-citizens, additionally refers the employer request to DHS. If DHS is

unable to verify the employee's work authorization against its automated records, the request is forwarded to a DHS field office where further research is conducted. If SSA is unable to confirm the worker's SSN, name, and date of birth or the DHS records search cannot verify worth authorization, the employer is sent a tentative nonconfirmation response. The employer then is to check the accuracy of the information with the worker, inform him or her of the government's finding, and refer the worker to either SSA or DHS to clear up the matter. If the worker does not contest the finding, a final nonconfirmation is issued to the employer.

[18] In addition to potential fines under immigration law, the Internal Revenue Service (IRS) may charge employers $50 for each W-2 form that omits or includes an incorrect Social Security number, up to $250,000 per employer in a calendar year. The IRS is unaware of any employer having to pay a penalty for submitting an erroneous wage report, according to testimony of Mark W. Everson, IRS Commissioner, before the Subcommittee on Oversight of the House Committee on Ways and Means, Feb. 16, 2006.

[19] Testimony of James S. Holt on behalf of the National Council of Agricultural Employers before the Senate Judiciary Subcommittee on Immigration, May 12, 1999.

[20] Perhaps one-fourth to three-fourths of the hired farm labor force may have relied on fraudulent documents to gain employment, according to U.S. Department of Agriculture, "Status Report: Hired Farm Labor in U.S. Agriculture," *Agricultural Outlook*, Oct. 1998.

[21] Testimony of Larry Wooten on behalf of the American Farm Bureau Federation before the House Committee on Agriculture, Jan. 28, 2004.

[22] Fawn H. Johnson, "Immigration: Goodlatte Calls for Prevailing Wage in H-2A Program, Condemns Amnesty," *Daily Labor Report*, Jan. 29, 2004, p. A-3.

[23] The INS approved more than 1 million of the applications that individuals filed under the SAW program to become legal permanent residents. Anticipating that SAWs would leave farming because IRCA did not require them to remain in order to adjust their status, P.L. 99603 included the RAW program as a back-up measure to ensure growers of an adequate labor supply. The RAW program was never used because the annual calculations of farm labor supply and demand that were made by the U.S. Departments of Labor and Agriculture during the FY1990-FY1993 period found no national shortages of farmworkers.

[24] Seasonal agricultural services (SAS) were defined broadly in IRCA as field work related to planting, cultivating, growing and harvesting of fruits and vegetables of every kind and other perishable commodities. The terms "SAS," "seasonal farm work," "field work" and "crop work" are used interchangeably in this report.

[25] CAW, Report of the Commission on Agricultural Workers, p. 75.

[26] DOL, U.S. Farmworkers in the Post-IRCA Period, Research Report No. 4, Mar. 1993. (Hereafter cited as DOL, U.S. Farmworkers in the Post-IRCA Period.)

[27] DOL, Findings from the NAWS 2001-2002.

[28] CAW, Report of the Commission on Agricultural Workers, p. 80.

[29] DOL, Findings from the NAWS 2001-2002.

[30] Alternatively, there are a number of reasons why SAWs would remain in farm employment (e.g., limited English-language fluency and little formal education). In light of these competing factors, the Commission on Agricultural Workers concluded

that it would be difficult to estimate the attrition rate of SAWs from the fields. The existence of fraud in the SAW program further complicates such a calculation because the stock of SAWs who genuinely were farmworkers is unknown: when Congress was debating immigration proposals in the mid-1980s, the U.S. Department of Agriculture estimated that there were 300,000 to 500,000 unauthorized farmworkers, but more than twice the upper-end estimate were legalized under the SAW program; this large discrepancy, as well as additional research, led to the widely held conclusion that fraud was extensive.

[31] DOL, Findings from the National Agricultural Workers Survey: 1997-1998, Research Report No. 8, Mar. 2000. (Hereafter cited as DOL, Findings from the National Agricultural Workers Survey: 1997-1998.). Note: In addition to the more than 1 million workers legalized through the SAW program, about 7% (119,000) of the 1.7 million aliens granted legal permanent resident status under IRCA's general amnesty program were employed in agriculture when they filed their applications. Oliveira, Effland, Runyan and Hamm, Hired Farm Labor in Fruit, Vegetable, and Horticultural Specialty Farms.

[32] The Commission on Agricultural Workers determined that the design of the SAW program was, at least in part, responsible for the increase in unauthorized immigration because if dependents of SAWs did not similarly have their status adjusted, they might have illegally entered the United States to join family members. In addition, the network or kinship recruitment process for SAS work continued to flourish and to facilitate not only job placement, but also migration by assisting in border-crossing and in acquiring fraudulent work authorization documents. These findings led the Commission to conclude that "the concept of a worker-specific and industry-specific legalization program was fundamentally flawed. It invited fraud, posed difficult definitional problems regarding who should or should not be eligible, and ignored the longstanding priority of U.S. immigration policy favoring the unification of families." CAW, *Report of the Commission on Agricultural Workers*, p. 67.

[33] DOL, A Profile of U.S. Farmworkers.

[34] DOL, Findings from the National Agricultural Workers Survey: 1997-1998.

[35] DOL, Findings from the NAWS 2001-2002.

[36] DOL, Farmworkers in the Post-IRCA Period and Findings from the NAWS 2001-2002.

[37] GAO, H-2A Agricultural Guestworker Program.

[38] See also testimony of Cecilia Munoz, on behalf of the National Council of La Raza before the Senate Judiciary Subcommittee on Immigration, May 12, 1999.

[39] See "Note" in table 5 for information about the survey.

[40] DOL, Findings from the NAWS 2001-2002.

[41] DOL, Findings from the National Agricultural Workers Survey: 1997-1998.

[42] These figures potentially are relevant to legislation that would link eligibility for legalization to time spent in farm work. While some might wish to use the above-described data to roughly estimate the number of unauthorized farmworkers who would be eligible to adjust status, they describe the *expectations* of farmers and they do not distinguish between legal and illegal workers. In addition, the data could produce an underestimate because they omit the more than 200,000 contract workers on the payrolls of agricultural service providers. Alternatively, the data could produce an

overestimate because they include employees not normally thought of as farmworkers (e.g., bookkeepers, secretaries or pilots).

[43] DOL, Findings from the NAWS 2001-2002.

[44] Although the populations covered by the NAWS and the FLS are similar, the NAWS's wage figures include contract labor while those from the FLS do not. As workers supplied to growers by farm labor contractors generally are paid less than direct-hires, this difference could have contributed to the lower hourly earnings of the NAWS. In addition, the NAWS questions workers; the FLS, employers. Figures supplied by employers usually are thought to be more accurate than those recalled by workers. And, while both surveys are designed to reflect seasonal variations during the course of a year, they do not cover identical reference periods.

[45] In the conference report for the DOL's FY2000 appropriation (H.Rept. 106-479), the Congress charged the DOL with reporting on ways to promote a legal domestic workforce in the farm sector and on options for such things as improving farmworker compensation, developing a more stable workforce, and enhancing living conditions. The report (*U.S. Department of Labor Report to Congress: The Agricultural Labor Market — Status and Recommendations*), issued in December 2000, recommended that the federal minimum wage be raised, agency funding for labor law enforcement increased, appropriations for AgWork (i.e., an internet-based, on-line job matching system specifically for agricultural employees and employers) continued, growers' greater use of automated employee verification systems encouraged, H-2A program streamlining further pursued while maintaining protections for U.S. and foreign farmworkers, and discussions held with countries from which farmworkers come to "explore ways in which their legal rights can be better protected." The DOL concluded that IRCA's farm legalization program failed to turn an unauthorized into an authorized workforce. It asserted that congressional proposals to ease growers' access to temporary farmworkers outside the existing H-2A program "would not create a legal domestic agricultural workforce" and instead "would lower wages and working and living conditions in agricultural jobs resulting in fewer domestic workers continuing employment in agriculture and perpetuating the industry's dependence on a foreign labor force." The DOL pointed out that another approach to creating an authorized supply of crop workers has never been tried — increasing wages and improving working conditions "by normalizing legal protections for farm workers and increasing mechanization," which has the potential to attract more U.S. workers to agriculture and raise the productivity of a possibly smaller farm labor force. In recognition that there might be short-run increases in growers' labor costs were its recommendations implemented, the DOL urged the Congress to consider ways to temporarily assist them.

In: Immigration Crisis: Issues, Policies and Consequences ISBN: 978-1-60456-096-1
Editors: P. W. Hickman and T. P. Curtis, pp. 197-202 © 2008 Nova Science Publishers, Inc.

Chapter 8

ALIEN LEGALIZATION AND ADJUSTMENT OF STATUS: A PRIMER*

Ruth Ellen Wasem

ABSTRACT

Immigration patterns have changed substantially since 1952, when policy makers codifying the Immigration and Nationality Act assumed that most aliens becoming legal permanent residents (LPRs) of the United States would be arriving from abroad. In 1975, more than 80% of all LPRs arrived from abroad. By 2005, however, only 34% of all aliens who became LPRs had arrived from abroad; most LPRs adjust status within the United States. This report summarizes the main avenues for foreign nationals currently in the United States — legally or illegally — to become LPRs. Alien legalization or "amnesty," as well as adjustment of status and cancellation of removal options, are briefly discussed. Designed as a primer on the issues, the report provides references to other CRS products that track pertinent legislation and analyze these issues more fully. This report will be updated as needed.

BACKGROUND

Alien legalization or "amnesty," as well as special provisions to allow certain aliens to adjust to legal permanent resident (LPR) status, are among the most controversial issues of U.S. immigration policy. President George W. Bush has proposed comprehensive immigration reform that includes an expanded guest worker program and an increase in permanent legal immigration as key components.[1] Among the thorny questions raised by such proposals are: would unauthorized aliens (i.e., illegal aliens) currently in the United States be eligible for the visa? and would the proposal include a mechanism for guest workers to obtain LPR status?[2]

---

* Excerpted from CRS Report RS22111, dated January 23, 2007.

During the 109th Congress, the Senate passed the Comprehensive Immigration Reform Act of 2006 (S. 2611), which would have enabled certain groups of unauthorized aliens in the United States to obtain legal permanent residence and certain guest workers to adjust to LPR status.[3] This report summarizes the main options for foreign nationals currently in the United States — legally or illegally — to become LPRs. As discussed more fully below, most of these options would hinge on Congress enacting special legislation.

Immigrant admissions, as well as adjustments to LPR status, are subject to a complex set of numerical limits and preference categories that give priority for admission on the basis of family relationships, needed skills, humanitarian concerns, and geographic diversity.[4] When Congress first codified the assortment of immigration laws into the Immigration and Nationality Act (INA) in 1952, the assumption was that most aliens who would receive LPR status would be coming to the United States from abroad. Indeed, 30 years ago, more than 80% of the 386,194 aliens who became LPRs of the United States had arrived from abroad. In FY2005, 65.8% of all LPRs were adjusting status within the United States.[5] That the number of LPRs arriving from abroad has generally remained around 400,000 for the past 30 years while the total number of LPRs now hovers around one million annually, highlights the contribution that aliens adjusting to LPR status after being in the United States is making to the growth of permanent legal immigration.

In addition to LPRs, each year millions of foreign nationals come temporarily on nonimmigrant visas (e.g., tourists, foreign students and intra-company business transfers). It is estimated that annually hundreds of thousands of foreign nationals either overstay their nonimmigrant visas or enter the country illegally and thus may become unauthorized aliens.[6] Recent analyses estimate the average growth in unauthorized alien residents at 700,000 to 800,000 annually. As of March 2005, there were an estimated 11.1 million aliens living here without legal authorization to do so.[7] Almost 40%, an estimated 4.4 million, have arrived in the past five years.[8]

OVERVIEW OF AVENUES TO LPR STATUS

There are several main options for aliens in the United States to become LPRs without leaving the country, and as figure 1 illustrates, most involving unauthorized aliens would require Congress to enact a law. To adjust status under current law, aliens must be in the United States legally on a temporary visa and eligible for a LPR visa;[9] aliens fleeing persecution may be granted asylum;[10] or — in very limited circumstances — unauthorized aliens may become LPRs through cancellation of removal by an immigration judge. Even aliens in the United States legally on a temporary visa can only adjust to LPR status if they qualify under the statutory set of numerical limits and preference categories that give priority for admission on the basis of family relationships, needed skills, and geographic diversity.

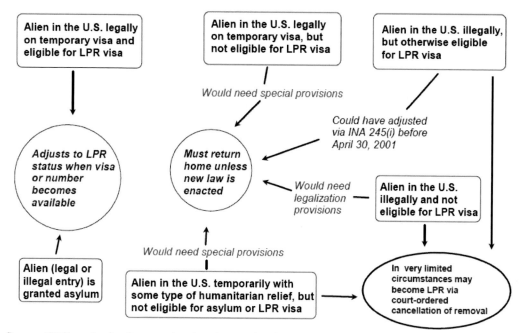

Source: CRS synthesis of current legal options under the Immigration and Nationality Act.

Figure 1. Principal Avenues for Legal Permanent Residence.

INA §245 permits an alien who is legally but temporarily in the United States to adjust to LPR status if the alien becomes eligible on the basis of a family relationship or job skills, without having to go abroad to obtain an immigrant visa. INA §245 was limited to aliens who were here legally until 1994, when Congress enacted a three-year trial provision (commonly referred to as §245(i)) that allowed aliens here illegally to adjust status once they became eligible for an LPR visa, provided they paid a large penalty fee. In 2000, Congress temporarily reinstated §245(i) through April 30, 2001(P.L. 106-554).[11]

SPECIAL PROVISIONS FOR ADJUSTMENT OF STATUS

Over the years, Congress has enacted statutes that enable certain aliens in the United States on a recognized — but non-permanent — basis to adjust their status to legal permanent residence when they are not otherwise eligible for an immigrant visa. Since the codification of the INA in 1952, there have been at least 16 Acts of Congress that have enabled certain aliens in the United States in some type of temporary legal status to adjust to LPR status. Most of these adjustment of status laws focused on humanitarian cases, e.g., aliens paroled into the United States by the Attorney General or aliens from specific countries who were given blanket relief from removal such as temporary protected status (TPS), deferred enforced departure (DED), or extended voluntary departure (EVD).[12]

The other major group of aliens adjusting status through special provisions involved nonimmigrants and typically were employment-based.[13] Beneficiaries of these special provisions included nonimmigrant alien physicians who had graduated from a medical school or qualified to practice medicine in a foreign state and were fully and permanently licensed and practicing medicine in a U.S. state on January 9, 1978; nonimmigrant retired employees of international organizations and/or their immediate families who have lived in the United States for specified periods of time, totaling at least 15 years for eligible adults and 7 years for children; and nonimmigrant nurses here as of September 1, 1989 who had been employed in the United States as registered nurses for at least three years before application for adjustment and whose continued employment met specified certification standards.

LEGALIZATION

The issue of whether aliens residing in the United States without legal authorization may be permitted to become LPRs has been debated periodically, and at various times Congress has enacted legalization programs. In 1929, for example, Congress enacted a law that some consider a precursor to legalization because it permitted certain aliens arriving prior to 1921 "in whose case there is no record of admission for permanent residence" to register with INS's predecessor agency so that they could become LPRs. In 1952, Congress included a registry provision (aimed at aliens who had been admitted but whose files were lost) when it codified the INA, and this provision ultimately evolved into an avenue for unauthorized aliens to legalize their status.[14]

When Congress passed the Immigration Reform and Control Act (IRCA) of 1986, it included provisions that enabled several million aliens illegally residing in the United States to become LPRs. Generally, legislation such as IRCA is referred to as an "amnesty" or a legalization program because it provides LPR status to aliens who are otherwise residing illegally in the United States.[15] Although legalization is considered distinct from adjustment of status, most legalization provisions are codified under the adjustment or change of status chapter of INA.

There were two temporary legalization programs created by IRCA.[16] The "pre-1982" program provided legal status for otherwise eligible aliens who had resided continuously in the United States in an unlawful status since before January 1, 1982. They were required to apply during a 12-month period beginning May 5, 1987. The "special agricultural worker" (SAW) program provided legal status for otherwise eligible aliens who had worked at least 90 days in seasonal agriculture in the United States during the year ending May 1, 1986. They were required to apply during an 18-month period beginning June 1, 1987 and ending November 30, 1988. Approximately 2.7 million aliens qualified for legal status under the pre-1982 and SAW programs. Of this total, 1.6 million or 59% qualified under the pre-1982 program, and 1.1 million or 41% qualified under the SAW program.[17]

CANCELLATION OF REMOVAL

The Attorney General has the discretionary authority under the INA to grant relief from deportation and adjustment of status to otherwise illegal aliens who meet certain criteria. Generally, aliens seeking this type of relief are those who have established "deep roots" in the United States and who can demonstrate good moral character as well as hardship to their family here if they are returned to their native country. Decisions to grant relief are made on a case-by-case basis. This avenue, formerly known as suspension of deportation, is now called cancellation of removal as a result of the Illegal Immigrant Reform and Immigrant Responsibility Act (IIRIRA) of 1996 (P.L. 104-208, Division C).

In addition to changing the terminology, IIRIRA established tighter standards for obtaining this relief. The hardship threshold previously was "extreme" hardship to the alien, the alien's citizen or permanent resident alien spouse, children, or parent. Now the language states "exceptional and extremely unusual hardship." The length of time the alien had to be physically residing in the United States was increased from 7 to 10 years. Moreover, the time span used to calculate the 10-year physical presence requirement now terminates when the alien receives a notice to appear (the document that initiates removal proceedings) or when the alien commits a serious crime. IIRIRA also established for the first-time limits on the number of people who could receive cancellation of removal — 4,000 each fiscal year.[18]

REFERENCES

[1]   The White House, Fact Sheet: Fair and Secure Immigration Reform, Jan. 7, 2004.

[2]   For a full analysis of these issues, see CRS Report RL32044, Immigration: Policy Considerations Related to Guest Worker Programs, by Andorra Bruno; and CRS Report RL32235, U.S. Immigration Policy on Permanent Admissions, by Ruth Ellen Wasem.

[3]   CRS Report RL33125, Immigration Legislation and Issues in the 109th Congress, coordinated by Andorra Bruno.

[4]   For analysis of immigration admissions, numerical limits, and visa priority dates, see CRS Report RL32235, U.S. Immigration Policy on Permanent Admissions, by Ruth Ellen Wasem.

[5]   CRS analysis of data published by the U.S. Department of Justice in the 1975 Statistical Yearbook of the Immigration and Naturalization Service (1977), and U.S. Department of Homeland Security in the 2005 Statistical Yearbook of Immigration (2006).

[6]   CRS Report RS22446, Nonimmigrant Overstays: Brief Synthesis of the Issue, by Ruth Ellen Wasem.

[7]   CRS Report RS21938, Unauthorized Aliens in the United States: Estimates Since 1986, by Ruth Ellen Wasem.

[8]   "The Size and Characteristics of the Unauthorized Migrant Population in the U.S.: Estimates Based on the March 2005 Current Population Survey," by Jeffrey S. Passel, Pew Hispanic Center.

[9]   Business travelers and tourists who come through the Visa Waiver Program are not eligible for adjustment of status. CRS Report RL32221, Visa Waiver Program, by Alison Siskin.

[10] CRS Report RL32621, U.S. Immigration Policy on Asylum Seekers, by Ruth Ellen Wasem.

[11] For background and analysis, see CRS Report RL31373, Immigration: Adjustment to Permanent Resident Status Under Section 245(i), by Andorra Bruno.

[12] For background on blanket forms of relief and the nationals who have received them, see CRS Report RS20844, Temporary Protected Status: Current Immigration Policy and Issues, by Ruth Ellen Wasem and Karma Ester.

[13] CRS Congressional Distribution Memorandum, Special Adjustment of Status Legislation, 1957-1996, by Joyce Vialet, Mar. 28, 1998. (Available from author of this report.)

[14] For background and analysis, see CRS Report RL30578, Immigration: Registry as Means of Obtaining Lawful Permanent Residence, by Andorra Bruno.

[15] Some consider the Nicaraguan Adjustment and Central American Relief Act (NACARA) of 1997 a legalization program because the primary beneficiaries were Nicaraguans and Cubans who had come to the United States by December 1, 1995, but who had not been given any recognized legal status typically afforded to humanitarian migrants such as Temporary Protected Status, or Deferred Enforced Departure. Others view the Nicaraguans as having a special status because the Nicaraguan Review Program of then-Attorney General Edwin Meese gave special attention to the Nicaraguans who had been denied asylum.

[16] Act of Nov. 6, 1986, P.L. 99-603; 100 Stat. 3359. The legalization provisions under discussion here were amendments to INA. The pre-1982 program was authorized by §245A of the INA and the special agricultural worker (SAW) program by §210 of the INA.

[17] CRS Congressional Distribution Memorandum, Alien Legalization Provisions of IRCA, by Joyce Vialet, Feb. 26, 1999. (Available from author of this report.)

[18] CRS Report 97-606, Suspension of Deportation: Tighter Standards for Canceling Removal, by Larry M. Eig; and CRS Report 97-702, Suspension of Deportation: Effect of §309(c)(5) of IIRIRA on Pending Deportation Cases, by Larry M. Eig and Andre O. Mander.

INDEX

G

H

T

U